SAM HOLLAND'S KITCHEN KICKSTART

/ Simple, Budget-Friendly Recipes for Beginner Cooks

Photography by **David Loftus**

Dedicated to my original
cookery teacher, Granny Tess.

Hello and Welcome!
PAGE. 5-7

Kitchen Basics
PAGE. 8-39

HOW TO COOK ON A BUDGET / 10
GET YOURSELF KITTED OUT / 12-13
STORE CUPBOARD ESSENTIALS / 15
READY, STEADY, COOK! / 16
LEARN THE LINGO! / 17
BASIC RULES FOR FOOD HYGIENE AND SAFETY / 18-19
HOW TO ORGANIZE A FRIDGE / 20
BASIC TECHNIQUES / 22-31
SUNDAY LUNCH CRIB SHEET / 32-35
KITCHEN HACKS / 36
KNIFE SKILLS / 38-39

HANGOVER HELPERS
PAGE. 40-63

FOOD IN A FLASH
PAGE. 64-105

FAKEAWAY FAVORITES
PAGE. 106-31

WHEN DID I LAST EAT A VEGETABLE?
PAGE. 132-61

MONDAY MEAL PREP
PAGE. 162-95

THE SWEET SPOT
PAGE. 196-217

THANKS
PAGE. 218

INDEX
PAGE. 219-223

HELLO AND WELCOME!

I'm so excited for you to be here and to share some of my food with you. Pulling these recipes together has been such a fun and rewarding process, and it blows my mind that you're holding it in your hands right now. I really hope you like it!

A BIT ABOUT ME

Food brings people together. I grew up, one of four brothers, in a busy, noisy house where everyone was running in different directions and going about their days at full throttle. That was, until mealtimes.

Mealtimes were family time. Every night almost without fail we would sit around the table, sharing stories, laughing at my dad's jokes, eating good food and reconnecting after our days apart. Dad always sat at the one end of the table, mum at the other and us brothers would jostle for position in between, bickering and bashing elbows to gain more space. It was rarely peaceful, and whenever any of us got our moment, we'd had better deliver a story that landed or else a damning and sarcastic, "great story" would ring out to everyone else's hilarity. It was brutal but great fun and made even worse for having a dad who is a comedian. These moments were really special and brought us closer together as a family, and when Team Holland gets together today nothing has really changed. Now that we've all grown up and left home, and my brother Tom often spends long periods of time abroad, the moments that we are all together sat around that table are even more precious. To me, food means home and that's the reason that I love it.

It's also one of the reasons that I no longer work in professional kitchens. I'd always loved cooking and eating delicious food, but initially saw it more as a

hobby than a career choice. Like so many other young people, I thought university was the natural progression from school and dutifully moved into uni halls in London to study for a degree. But it quickly became apparent that it wasn't the right path for me. I wasn't enjoying my course and crucially, the food in my catered halls was terrible! I was anxious I was on the wrong track. My mum encouraged me to consider other options and in particular, things which excited me. Food was an obvious route. My Granny Tess who features in this book has had a profound impact on my family life. A brilliant self-taught home cook, any dinner at her house was legendary and inspiring. And I had already enjoyed an earlier foray into food entrepreneurialism when selling brownies door-to-door with my twin brother Harry as a kid (see page 198 for the recipe!). And so, with a renewed sense of purpose, I spent the most amazing year training at Leith's Cookery School, making amazing friends and learning so, so much.

Once I graduated, I was hungry (pun intended!) to learn more and got knee-deep and dirty in some amazing professional kitchens. First at the world-famous Gleneagles Hotel in Scotland and then at Chez Bruce, one of London's top restaurants. Both extraordinary kitchens and steep learning curves!

But though I loved cooking, I missed the connection that comes from making food for your friends and family brings. A restaurant kitchen is remote, and you don't get to see the faces of the people (hopefully!) enjoying your food. For me, there was an emotional connection that was missing, which is why I knew that I wanted to be cooking and sharing recipes and techniques online with real people. People I could connect with. People like you.

WHO iS THiS BOOK FOR?

I am aware of just how lucky I am to have my own cookbook. If cookbooks are notoriously unread, then I wanted mine to be different by making it genuinely useful and indispensable for young people leaving home and fending for themselves. A book that I could see my friends turning to time and again to create easy, tasty meals at home. As someone who is relatively young (25 at the time of writing) and who has not long left my own family home, I know what a shock it can be to suddenly be responsible for cooking all of your own meals, and I'm a trained chef! With that in mind, I wanted to create a book that gives people the tools to really take ownership of their kitchen, allowing them to cook quick,

easy, tasty food that didn't use loads of faddy equipment or expensive ingredients. A book for anyone moving out or moving on at any stage of their life.

So, yes, this is a book for students heading off to university and young professionals moving into hectic shared houses or their own space, but it's also for anyone who has never quite found their feet in the kitchen or just wants to widen their cooking skill-set. It's also for those people who find the pull of the takeaway menu too tempting and then despair at their depleted bank balance, and it's for parents who want to serve healthy, easy meals to their families at the end of the day. It's for anyone who, for whatever reason, suddenly finds themselves suddenly responsible for cooking for themselves and their loved ones at whatever stage of life. And, if you recognize yourself in any of the people mentioned above, this book is for you.

What You'll Find in These Pages

I'm a firm believer in not trying to run before you can walk, so the book starts with a really comprehensive section of kitchen basics. Advice on everything from working to a budget and basic kitchen hygiene to guidance on organizing your fridge and the basic kit you will need to start cooking. You'll also find some key techniques and basic recipes for everything from how to hold your knife to making a white sauce, boiling eggs or attempting your first roast dinner.

With the basics covered, we move on to the recipes. The eighty recipes are divided into chapters on Hangover Helpers (breakfasts), Food in a Flash (speedy, easy meals), Fakeaway Favorites (healthier and less expensive - win, win!), When did I Last Eat a Vegetable? (veggie and veg-heavy meals to hit those five-a-day goals), Monday Meal Prep (fridge-filling meals to get you through the week) and The Sweet Spot (treats and desserts), so basically, I've got you covered. I've tried to steer clear of hard-to-find or expensive ingredients and use as many pantry staples as possible.

These are everyday recipes, but they are also delicious, full of flavor and sure to make you smile. I hope that you enjoy cooking and eating them as much as I do and sharing great times with your friends and family.

SAM HOLLAND X

Kitchen Basics

The tips, tricks and basic recipes found in this chapter will form the foundation of your kitchen prowess. From mastering the art of chopping, casually knocking out a basic tomato or white sauce, or even impressing with a risotto, this is your one-stop-shop for kitchen skills that will have you cooking like a pro in no time. You'll also find info on what kit you actually need, how to stick to a budget and some basic hygiene tips for keeping your kitchen spick-and-span. Skip this chapter at your peril! (Or, you know, just skip it and come back later!)

HOW TO COOK ON A BUDGET

Cooking on a budget doesn't have to limit what you cook or how much flavor you put into your meals! I've got some helpful tips to make the most of your money so you can have a bit more freedom in the kitchen.

- Plan your meals ahead. Make a note of what days and evenings you're busy and when you're free. This way you'll know how many breakfasts, lunches and dinners you'll need for that week and if there are any blocks of time available to cook more than you need, so you'll have food ready to go when you need it. When you plan your meals ahead, you'll stay focussed in the supermarket on just the ingredients you need so you'll be less likely to impulse buy or double up on ingredients you might already have.

- Do a weekly shop. If you do a weekly shop instead of buying ingredients on a meal-by-meal basis, you'll naturally plan your week and your meals better. You can overlap ingredients for multiple meals and buy only the things you need, saving money and waste.

- I like to choose a mixture of veggie and meat meals throughout the week. In general, vegetables are a bit cheaper to buy than meat so I tend to pick out a balance of both to make my money go further. Sometimes I eat meat twice a week and the rest veggie – it's super effective as a budget saver.

- Once you've chosen the meals you'll be cooking that week, you're ready to write a shopping list. I do a quick check of everything I've got in the cupboard and fridge before I head to the supermarket, so I know exactly what I've got and what I'll need to buy. Writing a list will save you doubling up on any ingredients, it'll make it easier to utilize what you already have at home, and you can identify any ingredients that can be used across more than one meal. E.g. one butternut squash can be used for two meals: half for a curry and the other half for a risotto.

- Have your shopping list saved on your phone or stuck to the fridge. It's good practice to keep it updated with the basics, when you can see you've run out. E.g. pasta, rice, butter, milk etc.

- When it comes to choosing your ingredients, head for the supermarket own brand and basics/essentials ranges. A lot of the time they are just as good as the more expensive or branded ingredients and going for the cheaper option will save you a lot of money at the checkout. I tend to make the trip to a larger supermarket too as bigger shops are, on the whole, cheaper than the smaller convenience shops which are stocked with fewer products.

- Cook for your housemates and have them return the favor. As well as making mealtimes a bit more special, cooking for the people you live with saves everyone involved time and money!

GET YOURSELF KITTED OUT

When moving into your first kitchen, there are some bits and pieces that you'll need to get hold of before you can start cooking. If you're moving into a shared house, chances are that your new housemates will already have some of this stuff so it's a good idea to wait until you've moved in before deciding where the gaps are. I've broken the list down into essentials and nice-to-haves so that you can easily prioritize your purchases. If you're moving out of a family home, your parents may have extras that they'll be more than happy to pass on, so beg, borrow or (ideally not) steal, before spending any of that hard-earned cash. Charity shops, eBay and Facebook Marketplace are all goldmines for secondhand kitchen equipment.

ESSENTIALS

- **BAKING SHEETS**
- **BOTTLE OPENER** (vital!)
- **BOX GRATER**
- **CHEF'S KNIFE** (one good, sharp knife is all you really need)
- **CHOPPING BOARD** (preferably a heavy wooden one)
- **CUTLERY**
- **DINNER PLATE, BOWL, SIDE PLATE** (you might want to get a few of these, depending on how good you are at washing up!)
- **DRINKING GLASS, WINE GLASS, PINT GLASS** (again, you might want a few!)
- **FOIL, PLASTIC WRAP, BAKING PAPER**
- **FRYING PAN WITH LID** (a deeper sauté pan is really useful for one-pot meals too)
- **KITCHEN SCALES** (electric ones are far easier and more accurate, so get these if you can)
- **LADLE/BIG SERVING SPOON**
- **MEASURING SPOONS**
- **MIXING BOWLS**
- **OVEN DISHES** (for lasagnes, pies, etc)
- **ROASTING PAN**
- **SAUCEPANS** (good to have a couple of these, and ideally with lids. If you don't have lids you can always put a baking tray or another pan on top)
- **SIEVE/COLANDER**
- **SPATULA**
- **TEA TOWELS AND OVEN GLOVES**
- **CAN OPENER**
- **TONGS**
- **TUPPERWARE** (a good range for meal prep and storing leftovers)
- **VEG PEELER**
- **WHISK**
- **WOODEN SPOON**

NICE-TO-HAVES

- **BLENDER** (I like Nutribullet types but others are great too)
- **CAKE PAN**
- **FISH SLICE**
- **GARLIC PRESS**
- **LOAF PAN**
- **MEASURING CUP** (can always use a weighing scale. Grams and milliliters are the same measurement. For example, 100g of water is the same amount as 100ml of water)

- **MICROPLANE GRATER**
- **MUFFIN PAN**
- **PASTRY BRUSH**
- **POTATO MASHER**
- **ROLLING PIN** (or you can use plastic wrap or an empty wine bottle)
- **HAND BLENDER**

STORE CUPBOARD ESSENTIALS

Planning your meals before doing your weekly shop is a really useful, practical way that you can keep your shopping focused and not buy expensive ingredients that you don't need. Another way of stretching the cost of your shopping is by keeping a stockpile of often-used ingredients that are more cost effective to buy in large or multipacks. A handful of spices is also a great thing to have on hand to bring punch and flavor to any dish - I've tried to limit the number I've used in the book, so with those listed below you should be able to make any of the recipes.

- BASMATI RICE
- CAJUN SPICE MIX
- COARSELY GROUND BLACK PEPPER
- DRIED MIXED HERBS
- DRIED PASTA (penne, fusilli, spaghetti)
- FINE SEA SALT
- GARAM MASALA
- GROUND CINNAMON
- GROUND CORIANDER
- GROUND CUMIN
- GROUND TURMERIC
- HARISSA PASTE (can be used to up the spice levels of any dish)
- JERK SEASONING
- LIGHT SOY SAUCE
- MILD CHILLI POWDER
- MILD CURRY POWDER
- PLAIN FLOUR
- RED OR GREEN THAI CURRY PASTE (keep in the fridge once opened)
- SELF-RISING FLOUR
- SESAME OIL
- SMOKED PAPRIKA
- STOCK CUBES (veg and chicken)
- CANNED BEANS (butter beans, cannellini beans, black beans)
- CANNED CHOPPED TOMATOES
- TOMATO PASTE
- VEGETABLE OIL (the most common oil I use in this book)
- GRANULATED SUGAR

READY, STEADY, COOK!

Feel free to roll your eyes and skip past this if you like, but following these few simple steps before you start cooking will help the process go a whole lot smoother and help avoid kitchen chaos! I wish someone had taken me aside and told me the below before the first time I started cooking!

- Start with a clean kitchen, it will make the clean-up so much easier!

- Set all your ingredients and equipment on the side and weigh out any ingredients if necessary.

- Place a damp cloth underneath your chopping board to prevent it from slipping.

- Fill a mug with warm water and place some teaspoons in it so you can taste your food and season as you go.

- Place a large container next to your chopping board to act as a bin. Throw away any packaging or vegetable trimmings in there as you go.

- Fill the sink up with hot soapy water so you can easily wash up as we go.

- Read the whole recipe once through.

- Ingredients are in the order you'll use them.

- Prep according to the ingredients list before you get going.

- Preheat the oven and boil the kettle (for pasta and/or stocks), if necessary. All temperatures in this book are for a fan oven.

- You're all set. Let's get cracking!

LEARN THE LINGO!

I've tried not to use any cheffy terminology when writing the recipes, but if you are unclear on any of the wording used in the book then hopefully you'll find an explanation in the list below.

SWEAT To cook a vegetable in fat (e.g. oil or butter) until soft without any color.

BROWN Similar to sweat, but cooking for longer so that the vegetables (or meat) take on color and start to caramelize in the pan.

FRY To cook something over high heat in fat (usually in a frying pan).

AL DENTE To cook pasta till it's just cooked and has a little bit of bite.

FOLD Using a spatula to mix a cake batter gently to maintain the air in the mixture.

SIFT Passing flour through a sieve to remove any lumps and add air to the mixture.

BOIL Heating a liquid over high heat until bubbling rapidly.

SIMMER Similar to a boil, but over a gentler heat and smaller bubbles (like Champagne bubbles).

ZEST To grate the outside rind of a citrus fruit (orange, lemon, lime, etc.) with the fine side of a grater. You only want the outer, colored layer, not the white pith that sits underneath.

CROSS-CONTAMINATE The spread of dangerous bacteria from one food onto another. For example, raw chicken breast being stored next to raw vegetables (see page 18).

BLITZ Using a stick food processor to blend something till smooth.

MINCE Very finely chopped (almost like a purée).

POACH To cook something by submerging it in simmering water/liquid.

REDUCE To boil a liquid until slightly evaporated to thicken the texture and intensify the flavor.

STEAM DRY To let cooked and drained ingredients sit in the pan, allowing any remaining moisture to steam off in the residual heat.

Basic Rules for Food Hygiene and Safety

I find that if I get the basics right, the rest will follow. Once you've got the essential knowledge in your back pocket, cooking delicious food that you know is safe to eat will be easy to achieve. It might sound basic but that's the beauty of it, food hygiene and safety is straightforward and quick to learn – some you'll probably already know – and once you know it, you always will.

- Wash your hands with soap and warm water thoroughly before handling ingredients. Doing this takes less than a minute and it means you're not spreading any unwanted bacteria and you're prepped to cook.

- Wipe down your surfaces with a cloth or sponge and washing-up liquid. Even better than washing-up liquid is anti-bacterial spray – there are lots of reasonably priced options at your local supermarket. Once clean make sure you dry with a clean tea towel.

- Cross-contamination can lead to food poisoning, and it usually happens when raw food, e.g. raw meat, fish or poultry comes into contact with or drips onto food that is ready to eat, equipment or surfaces. Make sure that any raw meat is covered and kept separate from any foods that are ready to eat. Always wash your hands well after touching raw meat, fish and poultry.

- Make sure that you use different chopping boards and utensils for:
  - raw meat, fish and poultry
  - ready-to-eat food, like cheese
  - fruits and vegetables

  For example, when you cut raw fish on a chopping board, bacteria from the fish will be on the chopping board and the knife. If you used the same chopping board and knife (unwashed) to slice a tomato, then the bacteria would spread to the tomato. Always clean as you go as a foolproof way to stop yourself causing any food poisoning.

- In general, you can avoid the risk of food poisoning by preparing food hygienically, by washing fruit and vegetables and by storing food properly.

- Make sure that you cook meat, fish and poultry all the way through. I will guide you in the recipes with cooking times and oven temperatures. Always make sure anything you cook is piping hot all the way through. Here are a few examples:

- o **FISH** is cooked when the flesh flakes nicely and is opaque in color.
- o **CHICKEN** is cooked when the meat is opaque and white throughout with no pink or red left. The juices will run clear.
- o **SAUSAGES** are cooked when they are no longer pink in the middle and when the juices run clear.

- Storing your food correctly is very important. Any leftovers are great to make use of so have a few food storage containers at the ready. Turn to page 20 to read about which foods go on what shelf. As a rule, leftovers that are stored in the fridge should be reheated all the way through and eaten within 2–3 days. Remember to never refreeze or refrigerate again after warming.

- If you are keeping rice, cool it thoroughly, put in the fridge in a sealed container and eat within 24 hours. When you reheat make sure it is piping hot.

- Always make sure that leftovers or batch-cooked meals are cooled properly before putting them in the fridge. This is to make sure that you don't increase the temperature inside the fridge and create somewhere that bacteria can multiply.

- However tempting it may be, if you wake up to find last night's kebab, don't reheat it!

- Store any pantry ingredients: pasta, rice, grains, bread, potatoes, cans, unopened jars in a cool dry cupboard.

- On food packaging a **USE BY DATE** is basically a safety deadline by which you can enjoy your food. After that date the food is considered not safe to eat. They are usually found on meat, fish and poultry, or ready-to-eat salads.

- The **BEST BEFORE DATE** means the quality of the food is best before the date on the packaging. Generally, you can enjoy the food shortly after that date too, provided it looks, smells and tastes good. They are usually found on dried, frozen and canned foods as well as cheese.

SOME HARD AND FAST RULES

- **Don't put any metal in the microwave, including foil, as it will create sparks and possibly set alight.**

- **Never put baking paper under the broiler as it will catch alight.**

- **Do not put metal cutlery in the toaster ... it's a conductor!**

- **Don't put pans with plastic handles into the oven, grill or microwave.**

- **If your milk smells sour, pour it away. If there is mold on anything don't risk eating it. Avoid using green potatoes and do not eat strong smelling meat, poultry or fish.**

HOW TO ORGANIZE A FRIDGE

Getting your fridge in good order will not only help you know where everything is but also helps food stay fresher for longer and prevents cross-contamination between ingredients. Use this guide to make sure everything is in the right place, and check your use-by dates regularly to avoid any unnecessary wastage of precious food.

(37°F [3°C]) the warmest shelf in the fridge

1 TOP SHELF

PREPPED LUNCHES

(35–37°F [2–3°C]) maintains the most constant temperature

2 MIDDLE SHELF

DAIRY PRODUCTS, EGGS & READY-TO-EAT FOODS

(34°F [1°C]) the coldest part of the fridge

3 BOTTOM SHELF

MEAT & FISH

(35°F [2°C]) the most humid part of the fridge

4 BOTTOM DRAWERS

FRUIT & VEG

(37–39°F [3–4°C]) frequent door opening causes fluctuation in temperature

5 DOORS

BOOZE, MILK & JARS

KITCHEN BASICS

Basic Techniques

On the following pages, you'll find tips, tricks and basic recipes covering everything from cooking rice and pasta to how to chop like a pro or even make a basic tomato sauce or risotto.

HOW TO COOK RICE AND PASTA

HOW TO COOK RICE

The golden rule with cooking all types of rice is that you need twice the volume of liquid as you do to rice. **1 cup rice = 2 cups water.** A portion of rice for one person is around half a standard kitchen mug.

Different types of rice cook at different times, so do check the packet and taste before draining to ensure the grains are tender. As a general rule, rinse the rice until the water runs clear, then add to a pan with the water and a pinch of salt, bring to a simmer and cook for:

- **BASMATI/LONG-GRAIN RICE:** 15–20 minutes
- **BROWN RICE:** 30–40 minutes
- **SHORT-GRAIN RICE:** (read on for how to make a risotto)

HOW TO MAKE A RISOTTO

SERVES. 4–6

Finely dice a large onion and cook with 2 tablespoons of vegetable oil in a large saucepan over medium heat until soft and translucent. Add in 2 cloves of crushed garlic and cook, stirring, for 1 minute. Add 2 cups (about 4 generous handfuls) of risotto rice (arborio or carnaroli) and cook, stirring, for 1 minute. Optionally, add ¾ cup of white wine and stir continuously until the liquid has evaporated. Make up 3½ cups of hot vegetable or meat stock and set next to your risotto pan. Add ¾ cup of the stock (1½ cups if you're not using wine) and cook until there is no liquid left, remembering to keep stirring. Continue adding in stock until the rice is cooked, usually around 12–15 minutes, adding more liquid if necessary. Top with a knob of butter and a handful of grated Parmesan, then cover with a lid and remove from the heat. Let the risotto relax for 5 minutes before serving.

KITCHEN BASICS

HOW TO COOK SMALL DRIED-PASTA SHAPES + PENNE, FUSILLI, FARFALLE, ETC.

Bring a pan of water up to the boil and season generously with salt. Add the pasta and cook for 9–10 minutes, until just tender. Drain (optionally reserving your pasta water, see below), and serve. A portion of pasta for one person is 3–3½ oz (85–100 g).

HOW TO COOK LONG DRIED PASTA + SPAGHETTI, LINGUINI, ETC.

Bring a large pan of salted water to a boil. Stand the spaghetti upright in the middle of the pan, give it a twist and let go so that it falls in a fan shape around the edge of the pan. The top parts of the spaghetti will not be submerged in the water but as the bottom half starts to cook it will soften and submerge in the water (or can be coaxed with tongs). Cook for 8 minutes until just tender.

Tip

Pasta water is the starchy, salty water that is left in the pan after you have cooked your pasta. Add a ladleful to simple sauces to season and bind (emulsify) the sauce, leaving you with a luxurious sauce that really coats your pasta.

HOW TO COOK EGGS

HOW TO CRACK AN EGG

Tap the egg onto a flat work surface. Place both thumbs into the indentation and open the egg into a bowl. If some shell creeps in with the egg, use the shell to scoop it out.

FRIED EGGS

Heat 1 tablespoon of vegetable oil in a frying pan over medium heat. Crack in the egg and cook for 3 minutes, then either spoon the hot oil over the yolk or place a lid on top for the final minute of cooking to cook the top part of the egg.

BOILED EGGS

Bring a large pan of water to a gentle simmer (anything more will be too rigorous and result in cracked shells), then add your eggs. Cook for 5 minutes for soft-boiled eggs, 6–7 minutes for slightly firmer 'jammy' yolks and 9–10 minutes for hard-boiled. (See image opposite for more info).

SCRAMBLED EGGS

SERVES. 1

Whisk 2–3 eggs together until smooth, then add to a saucepan with a large knob of butter. Place over a medium heat and whisk continuously until the eggs are almost set to your preferred consistency (take them off the heat when they are about 80% done). Season with salt and pepper and let the residual heat from the pan finish the cooking. Serve over toast.

POACHED EGGS

Add 1 tablespoon of white wine vinegar to a pan of barely simmering water. Crack your egg into a small bowl and place next to the pan, then whisk the water in the pan to create a vortex. Quickly tip the egg into the center of the vortex (this prevents the white from spreading and helps ensure a nice, neat poached egg). Poach for 3–4 minutes, until the white is set but the yolk is still runny.

> **Tip**
>
> *For the best poached eggs, try and use very fresh eggs. Older eggs tend to have thin, slightly watery whites and easier-to-break yolks, making them much harder to handle.*

BASIC OMELETTE

Place a frying pan containing a knob of butter over medium heat. Crack 2–3 eggs into a bowl, season with salt and pepper and whisk till smooth. Once the butter has melted and the pan is hot, tip the eggs into the pan and cook gently, agitating the eggs from the outside of the pan to the center. Now add any topping of your choosing, ensuring it's already cooked if necessary. Once the eggs are 80% cooked, use a spatula to fold each side of the omelette into the center, then flip out of the pan and onto the plate.

KITCHEN BASICS

HOW TO MAKE A BÉCHAMEL/ CHEESE SAUCE

This makes enough to fill a lasagna, make a cauliflower cheese or form the basis of a mac and cheese.

❶ Put **1½ TBSP OF BUTTER** into a saucepan and melt over low heat. Once melted, add **2½ TBSP OF PLAIN FLOUR** and mix until combined and thickened, then continue to cook, stirring for one minute before removing from the heat.

❷ Slowly add in **1 CUP OF MILK**, whisking until fully smooth between each addition to avoid any lumps. Once all the milk is added, return the pan back to the heat, stirring occasionally, and simmer for 2 minutes until thick and glossy.

❸ If making a cheese sauce, add **1¼ CUP OF GRATED CHEESE** of your choice, season with **SALT AND PEPPER** and stir again until the cheese has melted.

❹ The sauce is now ready to use, but a **PINCH OF GRATED NUTMEG** and/or a **TEASPOON OF MUSTARD** also make a nice addition.

HOW TO MAKE A TOMATO SAUCE

❶ Place a saucepan on a medium heat with **2 TABLESPOONS OF OLIVE OIL**.

❷ Add in a **FINELY CHOPPED WHITE ONION**, season with salt and sweat down for 8-10 minutes.

❸ Add in **2 CLOVES OF MINCED GARLIC** and **1 TABLESPOON OF TOMATO PASTE** and cook for 1 minute.

❹ Add in **1 15.5 OZ (439 G) CAN OF CHOPPED TOMATOES** and **1 TABLESPOON OF MIXED HERBS**. Top it up with **¾ CUP OF WATER** and a **BUNCH OF BASIL** and simmer for 10 minutes.

❺ Remove the basil and season with **SALT, PEPPER**, a **PINCH OF SUGAR** and a **DASH OF BALSAMIC VINEGAR**.

HOW TO COOK POTATOES

MASHED

Peel and chop your potatoes (I like red potatoes for mash) into equal sizes and place in a saucepan. Cover with cold water, season generously with salt and bring up to a boil, then simmer for 15–20 minutes. Once the potatoes are soft (i.e. a cutlery knife can go through them easily) drain through a colander and leave to steam dry for 5 minutes. Return the potatoes to the saucepan, add a knob of butter and a splash of warm milk then mash with a potato masher until smooth. Taste and season with salt and pepper and enjoy.

ROAST POTATOES

Preheat the oven to 350°F (180°C). Peel and chop your potatoes (I like Maris Pipers for roasties) into equal sizes, place in a saucepan and cover with cold water. Season generously with salt, bring to the boil and then leave to simmer for 12–15 minutes. Drain through a colander and leave to steam dry for 5 minutes. Shake them in the colander to fluff them up and add them into a roasting pan with ½ cup of vegetable oil. Season with salt and pepper and roast them in the oven for 45 minutes to an hour, stirring occasionally. Finish with more salt and chopped rosemary, if you're feeling fancy.

BOILED NEW POTATOES

Bring a pan of salted water up to the boil and add the potatoes. Reduce to a simmer and cook for 10–12 minutes or until a cutlery knife can be inserted into them easily. Drain them and finish with a knob of butter and chopped parsley or mint.

BAKED POTATOES

Oven

Cooking jacket potatoes in the oven takes much longer than the microwave method, below, but if you're after a golden, crunchy skin and a super fluffy interior then this is the best way to achieve it. Preheat your oven to 350°F (180°C). Prick your potato all over with a fork and lay on a baking sheet, drizzle with a teaspoon of vegetable oil and season with a generous grinding of salt and pepper. Transfer to the oven and cook for 1 hour and 15 minutes. Serve.

Microwave

For a speedy lunch, the convenience of a microwave jacket potato is hard to beat. Just don't expect that glorious crunchy skin that you get in the oven. Prick your potato all over with a fork and place on a microwavable plate in the microwave. Cook on full power for 4 minutes, then turn the potato over and cook for another 4 minutes. Test to see if potato is cooked all the way through and return to the microwave for another 2 minutes, if not. Continue until the potato is tender all of the way through.

OVEN CHIPS

Preheat the oven to 350°F (180°C). Peel and slice your potatoes (I like Maris Pipers for chips) into thick batons (we're going for chip-shop chips, not French fries). Place in a saucepan and cover with cold water, then season generously with salt, bring up to the boil and simmer for 6–8 minutes. Drain in a colander and leave to steam dry for 5 minutes. Put the chips into a roasting tin with ½ cup of vegetable oil and toss to coat. Season with salt and pepper and roast them in the oven for 45 minutes to an hour, turning occasionally. Finish with more salt and chopped rosemary, if you're feeling fancy.

Tip

To give your microwaved potato a bit of a glow-up, rub the cooked potato with a teaspoon of vegetable oil, season with salt and pepper and cook in an 350°F 180°C oven for 15 minutes to crisp up the skin slightly.

KITCHEN BASICS

HOW TO MAKE SALAD DRESSINGS

For basic salad dressings, use a ratio of three parts oil to one part vinegar or acid. Add your choice of add-ins and whisk to combine.

Oil (3 parts)	Acid (1 part)	Add-ins
Olive Oil	Red/White Wine Vinegar	Dijon/Wholegrain Mustard
Sesame Oil	Lemon/Lime Juice	Honey
	Soy Sauce	Crushed Garlic
		Chilli Flakes
		Chopped Fresh Herbs

HOW TO MAKE FANCY(ISH) CHEESE ON TOAST

In a bowl, mix 2½ cups of grated cheese with 1 small clove of crushed garlic and 3 tablespoons of ketchup. Turn your broiler on. Lay 4 slices of bread onto a baking sheet and place under the broiler until nicely toasted. Flip the toast and spread on the cheese mixture and place back under the broiler for it to get nice and melted. Garnish with a few basil leaves and enjoy.

SUNDAY LUNCH CRIB SHEET

Hosting your first Sunday lunch is a rite of passage, though none of the elements are particularly complicated, getting it all to come together at the same time can be a headache. I've given you some tips on recipes and timings below. Feel free to add any extra elements that you want to include to make your perfect Sunday lunch. Oven space is key here, so I haven't included bulky extras like homemade Yorkshire puddings or stuffing, but you can buy really good versions of these that can be reheated in the oven once your meat is out and resting.

ROAST DINNER

MEAT COOKING TIMES

Whether you're cooking chicken, turkey, pork, beef or lamb, if you get your timings right, you'll have the perfect roast dinner. Here are simple cooking times, temperatures and cooking methods for each.

Beef Top Round, 1–2 lbs (600 g–1 kg), 1 lb (600 g) serves 2–3, 2 lbs (1 kg) serves 4–6

1. First, brown the beef. On a baking tray drizzle with oil, cover with salt and pepper and place the beef in the oven for 20 minutes at 400°F (200°C).

2. Reduce the temperature to 350°F (180°C) and cook the beef through for 40 minutes. If your joint is around 1 lb (600 g), reduce the cooking time to 24 minutes at the same temperature.

3. Finally, take out of the oven and leave to rest for 30 minutes.

Half a leg of lamb, 2 lbs (1 kg), serves 4–6,
Whole leg of Lamb, 5 lbs (2.3 kg) serves 8–10

1. First, brown the lamb. Place the lamb on a baking tray, drizzle with oil and cover with salt and pepper. Put the lamb in the oven at 400°F (200°C) for 20 minutes.

2. Reduce the temperature to 325°F (160°C) and cook the lamb through for 40 minutes. For a whole leg of lamb, increase the cooking time to 1 hour 32 minutes.

3. Finally, take the lamb out of the oven and leave to rest for 30 minutes.

Chicken, 2½–3 lbs (1.2 k–1.5 kg), serves 4–6

1. First, brown the chicken. Place the chicken on a baking tray, drizzle with oil and cover with salt. Put the chicken in the oven at 350°F (180°C) for 20 minutes.

2. Reduce the temperature to 325°F (160°C) for 48 minutes, 1 hour for 3 lbs (1.5 kg).

3. Insert a knife into the thickest part of the leg and if the juices do not run clear, return to the oven for 10–15 minutes and check again.

4. Finally, take the chicken out of the oven and rest for 15 minutes.

Pork Loin, 2 lbs–3 lbs (1 kg–1.5 kg), serves 4–6

1. First, score the top of the pork, one way and then the other.

2. Then, brown the pork. Place the pork on a tray, drizzle with oil and cover with salt and pepper. Put the pork in the oven at 400°F (200°C) for 30 minutes.

3. Reduce the temperature to 325°F (160°C) and cook the pork through for 1 hour for 2 lbs (1 kg), 1 hour 12 minutes for 1.2kg and 1 hour 30 minutes for 3 lbs (1.5 kg).

4. If after the cooking time you don't have much crackling, crank up the temperature to 400°F (200°C) until the crackling is crisp.

5. Finally, take the pork out of the oven and leave to rest for 30 minutes.

Turkey, 2–4½ lbs (1 kg–2 kg), serves 4–6

1. In a baking tray, drizzle the turkey in oil and cover with salt and pepper. Place in the oven at 350°F (180°C) for 1 hour 30 minutes for 2 lbs (1 kg), 1 hour 40 minutes for 3 lbs (1.5 kg) and 1 hour 50 minutes for 4½ lbs (2 kg).

2. Insert a knife into the thickest part of the leg. If the juices do not run clear put it back in the oven for 10–15 minutes and check again.

3. Finally, take the turkey out of the oven and rest for 20–40 minutes.

Roast Dinner
SIDE DISHES

Pan-Fried Carrots and/or Parsnips

Peel and halve 3 carrots and 3 parsnips lengthways. Season them with salt and pepper and add them to a hot frying pan with 2 tablespoons of vegetable oil. Once they are nice and golden brown, flip them over and add ¼ cup of butter, 2 tablespoons of honey and 3 sprigs of rosemary. Add in a splash of water, top with a lid and simmer for 15 minutes until they are soft.

Cauliflower Cheese

Preheat the oven to 400°F (200°C). Cut a cauliflower into florets and put them in a roasting pan. Drizzle over 2 tablespoons of vegetable oil and season with salt and pepper. Roast in the oven for 10–15 minutes, then transfer into an ovenproof dish. Make a batch of Cheese Sauce (see page 26) and pour it over the roasted cauliflower. Top with another ¼ cup of grated cheese and return to the oven at 400°F (200°C) for 20 minutes, until golden and bubbling.

Gravy

Remove the cooked meat from the roasting pan and allow it to rest, covered, while you make the gravy. Place the roasting pan on the stove over low heat and add 2 tablespoons of flour. Cook for one minute, stirring the flour through the meat juices to thicken. Add ½ cup of wine (white for white meat, red for red meat) and 2 cups of hot chicken/beef/lamb stock and mix till smooth. Bring to a boil, then reduce to a simmer and cook, stirring occasionally, until reduced and thickened. Season with salt and pepper and enjoy.

Peas

Peas make the perfect low-effort addition to any Sunday lunch. Bring a pan of salted boiling water to a boil and add the peas. Boil for 2-3 minutes, then drain through a sieve. Add a tiny knob of butter and a pinch of salt and pepper to the peas to finish.

Broccoli

Cut the broccoli into florets. Bring a pan of salted boiling water to a boil and add the florets. Boil for 3–4 minutes, then drain through a sieve and serve.

Tip

You can make the cauliflower cheese (unbaked) the day before and keep it in the fridge and then bake it when you need it.

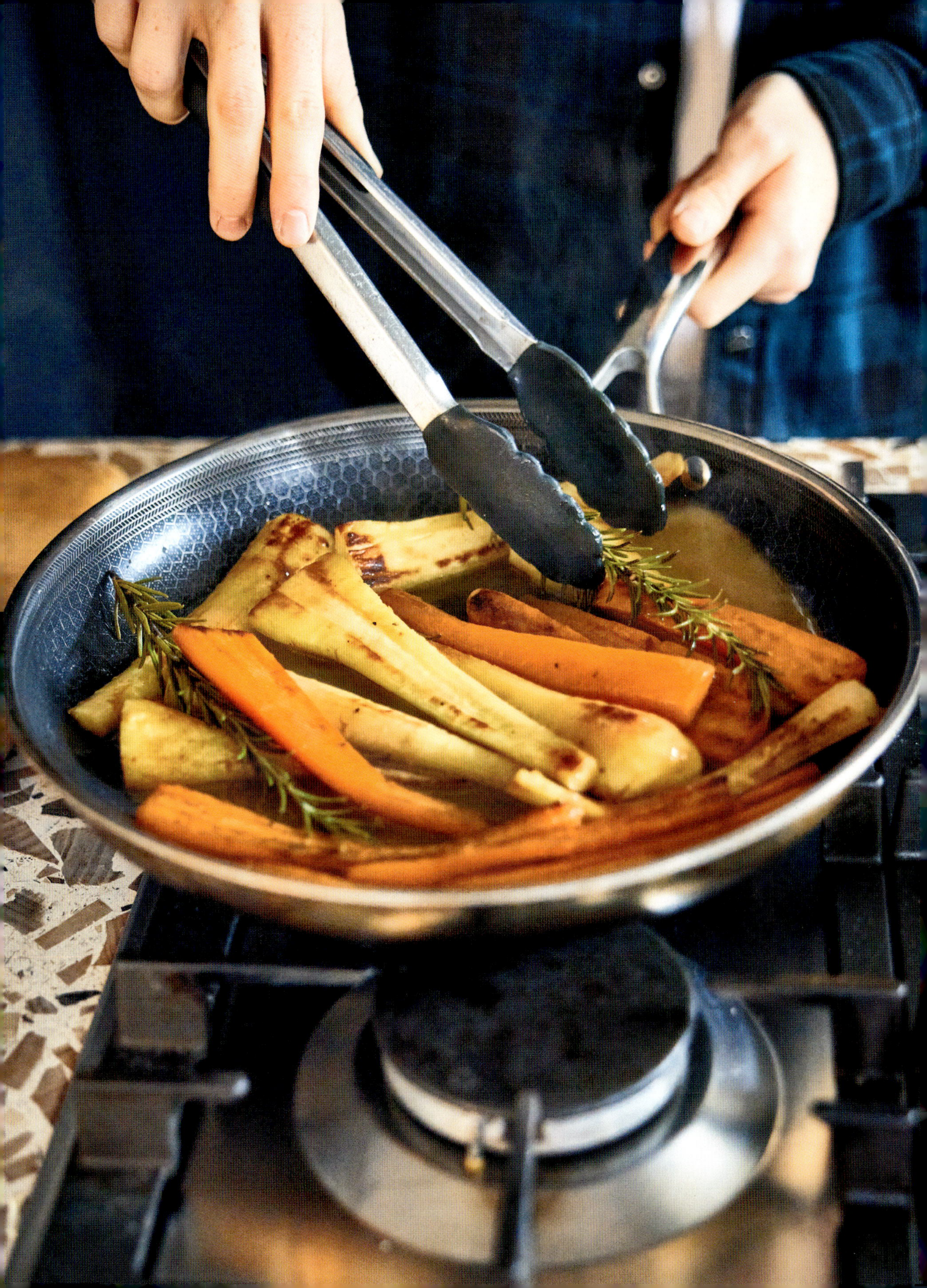

KITCHEN BASICS

Kitchen Hacks

Here are a few of my favorite tips and tricks that help make my life easier in the kitchen and will hopefully do the same for you!

HOW TO COOL DOWN BEERS IN A FLASH

Not strictly cooking, but vital nonetheless! Rip off a piece of paper towel and soak it in cold water. Wrap a bottle of beer in the cold damp cloth and place it in the freezer for 20 minutes. Voila! Icy cold beer!

HOW TO STORE FRESH HERBS

Fresh herbs are expensive and can turn from fresh to fusty in a flash if you don't store them correctly. Put a jar of water in your fridge door and submerge the stems of your herbs in the water to prolong their life.

HOW TO REFRESH PAST-ITS-BEST BREAD

If your bread is a little on the stale side, splash a slice or two with a little water and microwave for 5 seconds or so to bring back its bounce.

HOW TO PEEL GINGER

Peeling knobbly, fiddly ginger with a knife can lead to lots of waste. Instead, try removing the skin with the side of a teaspoon. The curved edge will allow you to work around all of the nooks and crannies and means that you don't waste nearly as much.

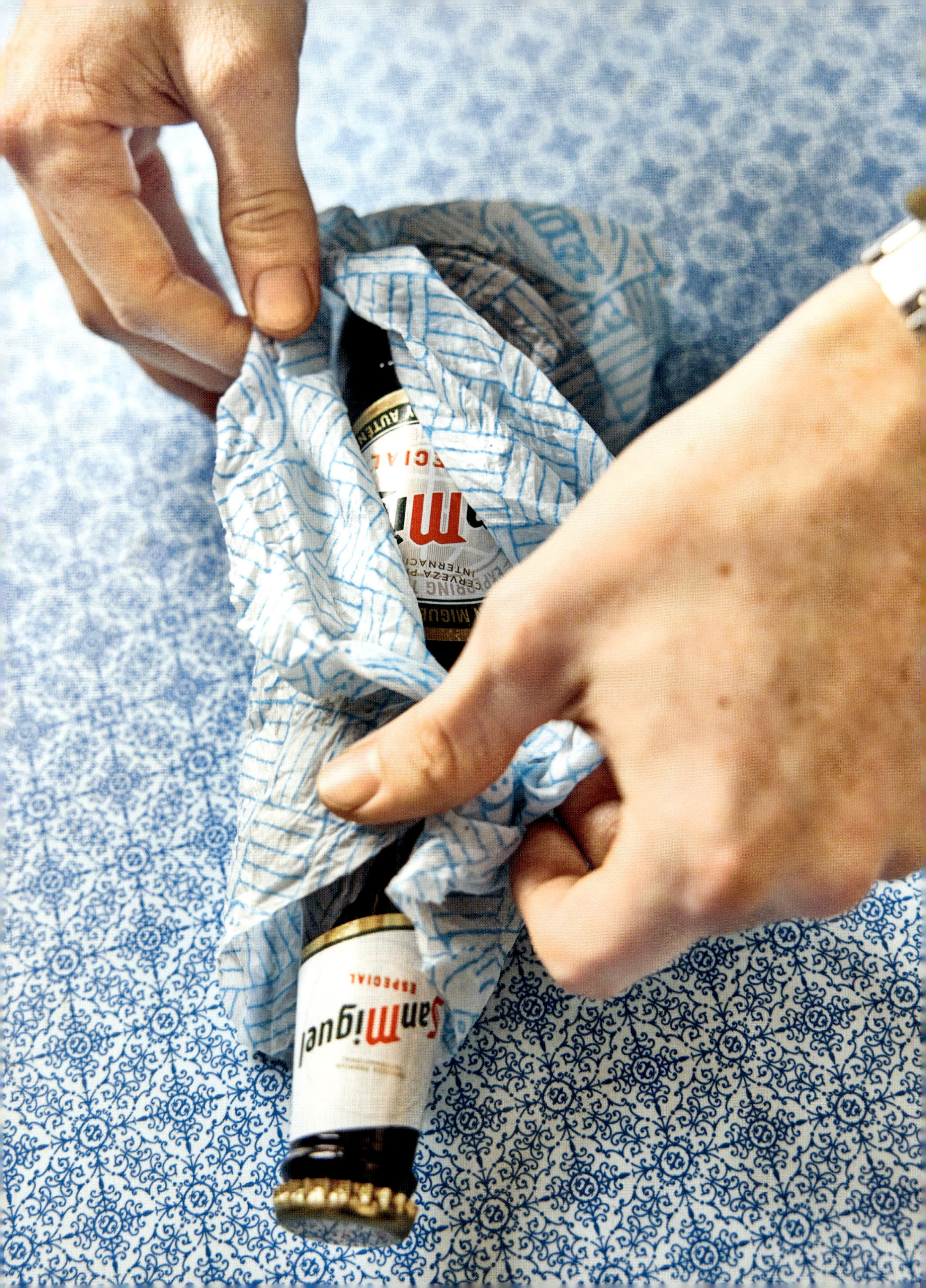
SanMiguel
ESPECIAL

KITCHEN BASICS

KNIFE SKILLS

A good knife is your kitchen best friend. You only really need one good-quality chef's knife and it's important that you keep it sharp. It might sound counterintuitive, but a dull knife is far more dangerous than a sharp one as it is far more likely to slip off whatever you are cutting and catch your fingers instead! If you're new to chopping, start off slow and be really careful. Once you've mastered the basics, you'll gain confidence in no time.

GRIP

Using your dominant hand, firmly grip your knife by the handle. Make a claw shape with your other hand, curling your fingertips underneath the first knuckle on your fingers and use this hand to secure whatever you are chopping on a stable chopping board, pressing your fingertips down just behind where you are looking to cut. Using the knuckles of your non-dominant (claw) hand as a guide, push the knife through what you are cutting, repeating the action and moving your non-dominant hand back as you work your way through.

ROUGHLY CHOP

Roughly chopped ingredients are for dishes where you are looking for a rustic, chunky texture in the end result, or perhaps where the final dish might be blitzed in a food processor. For a roughly chopped onion, simply peel and cut the onion in half through the root. Lay the 2 halves flat on your chopping board and make 3 or 4 cuts almost all of the way through the onion from the tip to the root (you don't want to cut all the way through as you need the basic shape to be still intact at this point). Turn the onion 90° and cut across its width leaving you with coarse chunks.

Finely Chop/Dice

To achieve a finer chop, simply place your cuts closer together. For an onion, peel and cut the onion in half through the root. Lay the 2 halves flat on your chopping board making several horizontal cuts (working top to bottom) almost all of the way through the onion. Now cut at regular intervals from tip to root (again not cutting all of the way through), then finally, turn the onion 90° and cut at regular intervals across its width leaving you with a fine dice.

Slice

Slicing can mean different things for different ingredients. For onions, it is usually half-moon shapes (cut the onion in half through the root as above, then simply slice across the width of the onion). For tomatoes, you may want full slices, in which case, make sure to slice across the stem as this will make for neater slices. For bell peppers, you are generally looking for long, slim strips, but there are no strict rules!

Hangover

HELPERS

If you're nursing a bad hangover or even if you're feeling under the weather in general, this chapter is for you. These are my soul-saving meals to start the day that are quick and simple to put together and will be ready in less time than your take-out order. They're your collection of immediate pick-me-ups, from a mouthwatering Breakfast Burrito to easy, chocolatey Nutella Twists and the ultimate Sausage and Egg Muffin.

HANGOVER HELPERS

MAKES. 4 / PREP TIME. 10 MINUTES / COOK TIME. 30 MINUTES

Burritos are the ultimate portable feast and this one, packed with scrambled eggs, sausage, guac, cheese and sour cream, is a powerhouse breakfast that will load you up for anything the day can throw at you. Hot sauce brings the spice here and you can use as much or as little as you like.

Breakfast Burritos

① Preheat the oven to 400°F (200°C).

② Bake the sausages for 25 minutes.

③ When the sausages are nearly cooked, crack the eggs into a small saucepan, add in the butter and season with salt and pepper. Place it over medium heat and stir continuously for around 4 minutes or until the eggs have firmed up and scrambled. Transfer from the pan to a plate and set aside.

④ Once the sausages are cooked, take them out of the oven and slice into thirds lengthways.

⑤ Lay out your flour tortillas, one at a time if you don't have surface space for all four, onto your work surface. Spread a heaped teaspoon of sour cream and one of guacamole onto the center of each tortilla. Add a few spoonfuls of scrambled egg, top with the sausages, cover with cheese and finally, top with a ½ tablespoon of the sriracha.

⑥ Now for the hard bit. With the filling laying horizontally, place your hands on either side of the filling and fold each side of the tortilla into the middle. Start to roll the burrito by folding the bottom side of the tortilla over the filling. Pull it back over the filling and fold in the sides to ensure it is nice and tight before rolling it up into a burrito shape.

⑦ In a hot frying pan with the vegetable oil, fry the burritos (sealed side down) for 1 minute on each side or until they are golden brown. Chop in half and serve up.

4 pork sausages
4-6 large eggs
2 tbsp butter
4 flour tortillas
4 heaped tsp sour cream
4 heaped tsp Guacamole (see page 128)
3 oz (85 g) Cheddar cheese, grated
1-2 tbsp sriracha
1 tbsp vegetable oil
Sea salt and black pepper

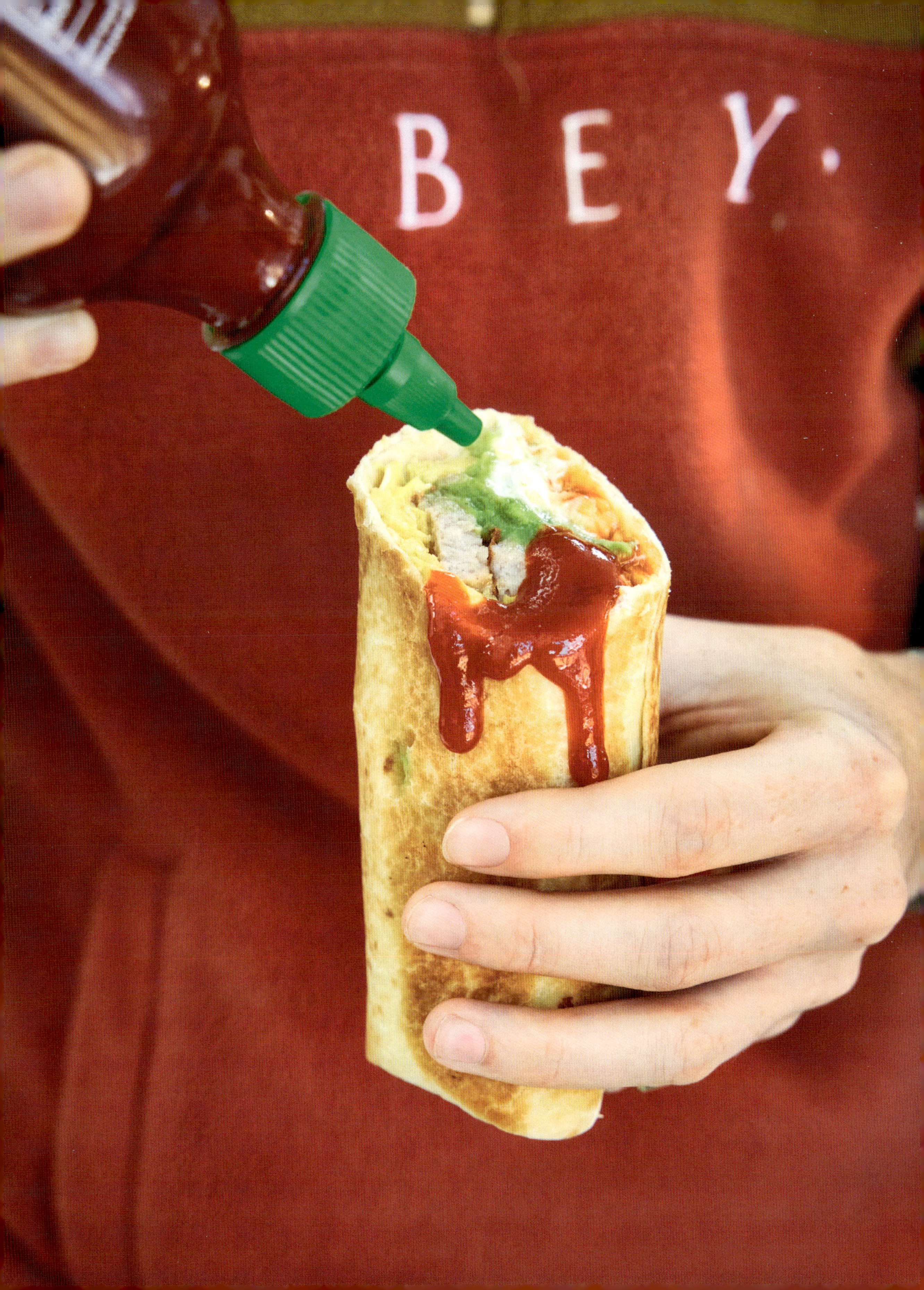
B E Y.

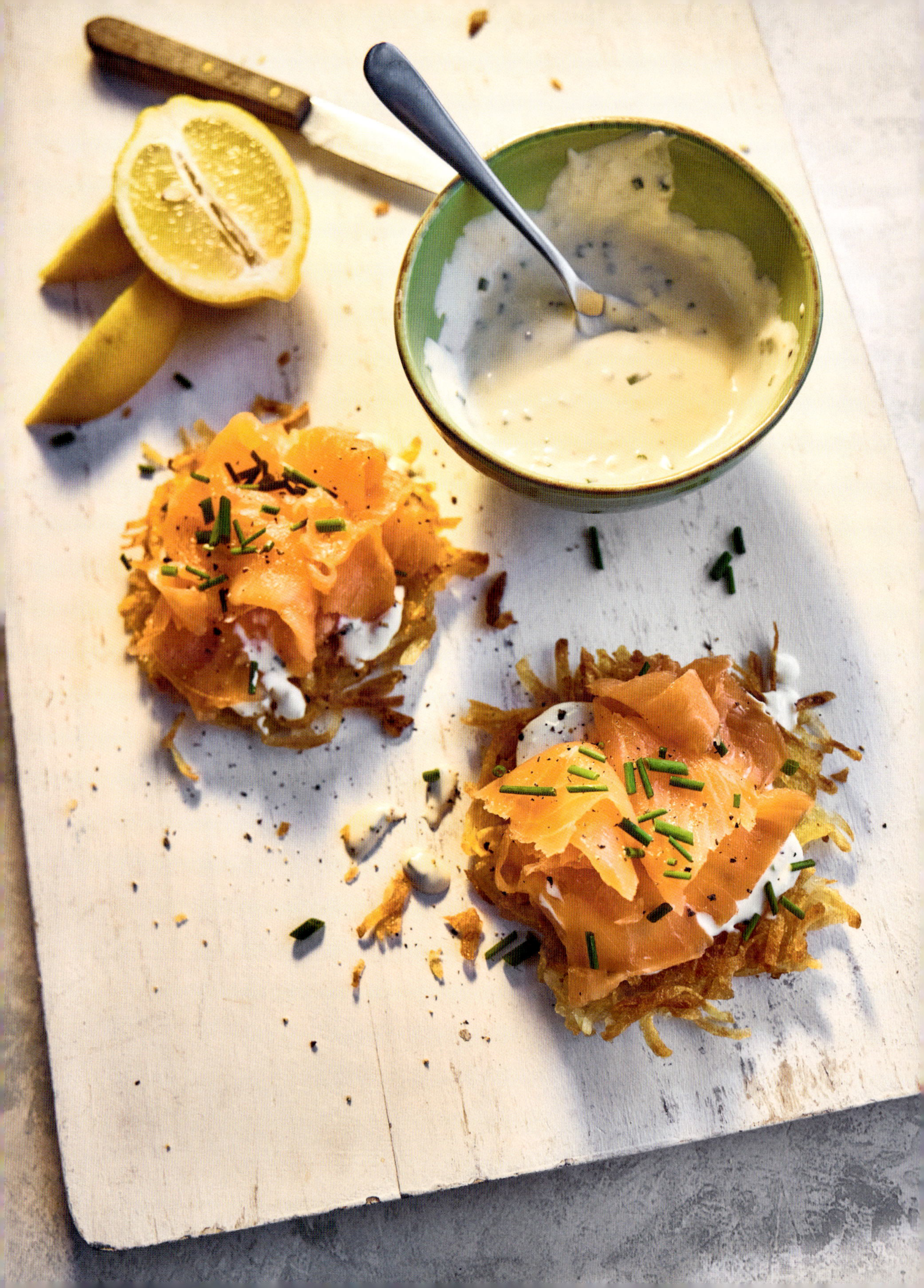

PREP TIME. 10 MINUTES / **COOK TIME.** 15 MINUTES / **SERVES.** 2

HANGOVER HELPERS

This comes together really quickly and is sure to impress. Smoked salmon may sound fancy but can actually be picked up relatively inexpensively and elevates this dish into something special-occasion-worthy. Perfect for a celebration breakfast or on the rare occasion you might need to get into someone's good books. Double tasty.

POTATO LATKES + SMOKED SALMON & HORSERADISH CREAM

① Peel and grate your potatoes. Season generously with salt and pepper, place into a clean tea towel and ring out any liquid from the potato. Don't be worried about squashing it – the drier it is, the crispier the latkes will be. Once dry, separate the potato into four portions.

② Pour the vegetable oil into a frying pan set over medium to high heat and spoon the portions of potato into the pan. Fry the latkes for 4–5 minutes until the underside is golden, then carefully flip each one and fry for another 4–5 minutes, or until they are golden brown all over. As the potato cooks, the starch will release and bind the potato together. Don't be tempted to try and flip them too early as the starch won't have had time to bind it all together.

③ Combine the crème fraîche, horseradish, lemon juice and chopped chives and season with salt and pepper.

④ Finally, once the latkes are cooked, drain them on some kitchen paper. Top with the horseradish cream and smoked salmon, garnish with some more chives and serve with extra lemon.

Ingredients
3 medium Maris Piper or Russet potatoes (around 1 lb/454 g)
4 tbsp vegetable oil
3½ oz (147 ml) crème fraîche
1 tsp horseradish sauce
Squeeze of lemon juice
1 tbsp chopped chives, plus extra to garnish
1 package of smoked salmon (around 3½ oz/100 g)
2 lemon wedges
Sea salt and black pepper

HANGOVER HELPERS

MAKES. 8–9   **PREP TIME.** 15 MINUTES / **COOK TIME.** 20 MINUTES

Crepes might sound intimidating, but let me tell you a secret, they're just pancakes with a French accent! I'm talking the large, flat variety that your mum or dad probably got wrong every pancake day, not the fluffy American kind. This recipe is my go-to and never lets me down. Literally, flipping brilliant.

CREPES

1. Put the flour in a large bowl with the salt and sugar and make a well in the middle of the flour. Crack in the eggs and whisk until smooth, slowly incorporating the flour from around the edge as you go.

2. Once the flour and eggs are nicely combined, slowly pour the milk and 3–4 tablespoons of water into the well while whisking. Keep gradually mixing in the flour from around the edge to avoid any lumps.

3. Once it is well mixed and smooth, pour the mixture into a jug and preheat your frying pan over medium heat.

4. Once your pan is hot, rub your butter onto the base of the pan to give yourself a thin butter layer. Pour in some of the pancake batter and swirl it quickly around to make one even layer.

5. Cook for about 60–90 seconds, or until it is nice and golden brown. Give it a flip and cook for a further 15 seconds before sliding it off onto a plate or tray, adding more butter to the pan and starting the next one.

6. As you cook you might need to adjust the heat. If the pan gets too hot the butter will burn. If this happens, just turn the heat down and remove the pan from the heat to cool down for a few seconds before starting your next pancake.

7. Enjoy these crepes with any topping of your choosing.

1 cup all-purpose flour
Pinch of salt
1 tbsp sugar
3 eggs
¾ cup milk
2 tbsp butter
FOR THE TOPPINGS
Classic lemon juice and sugar
Maple syrup and butter
Cinnamon sugar (4 tbsp superfine sugar mixed with ½ tsp ground cinnamon)
Easy chocolate sauce (2 heaped tbsp Nutella melted in a pan with a splash of milk over a low heat) – great with bananas, chopped nuts, strawberries and warmed peanut butter
Biscoff spread melted in a pan with a splash of milk
Easy raspberry coulis (put 4 oz (125 g) of raspberries in a sieve and use the back of a spoon to mash them and push through the sieve into a bowl)

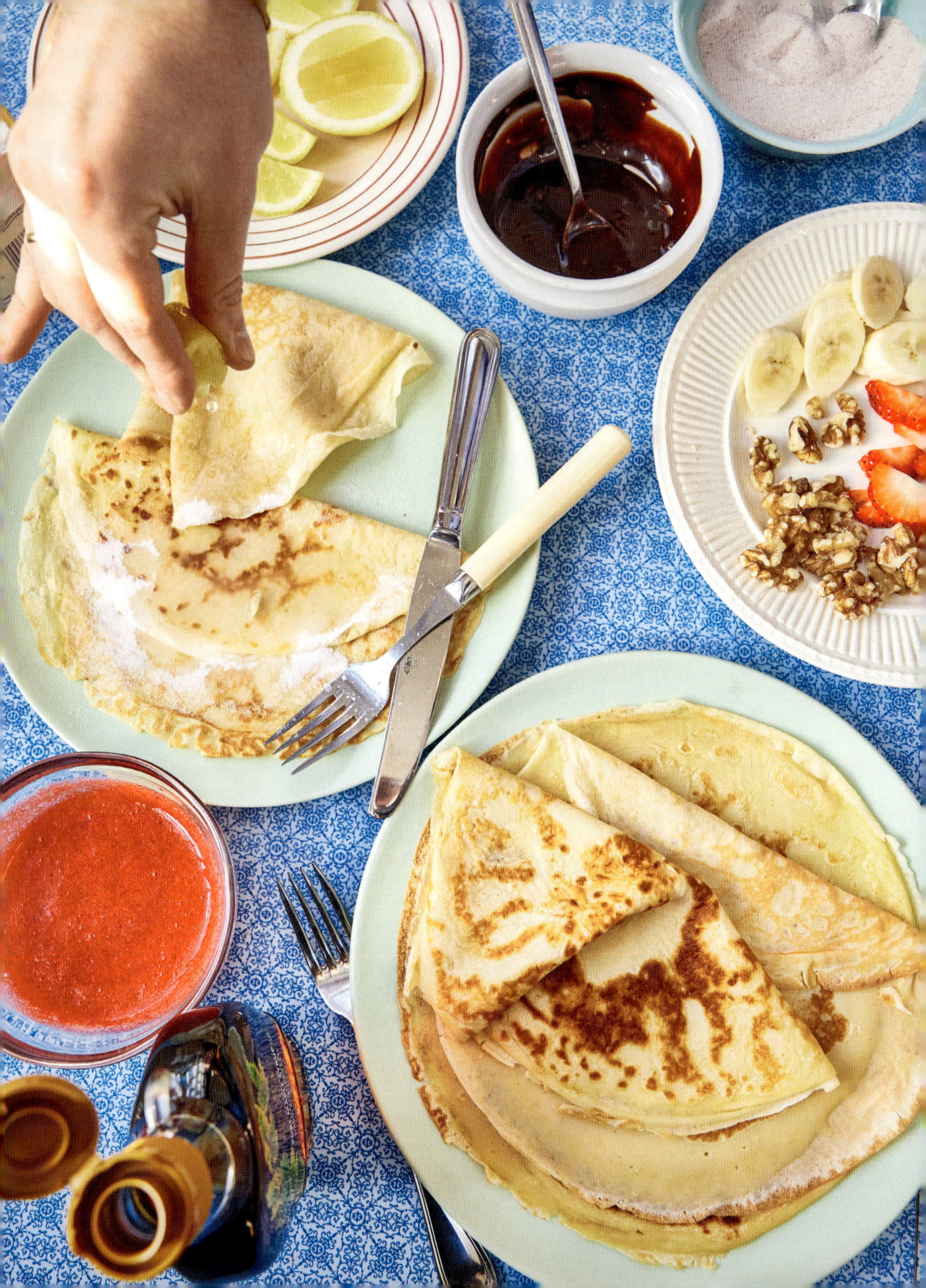

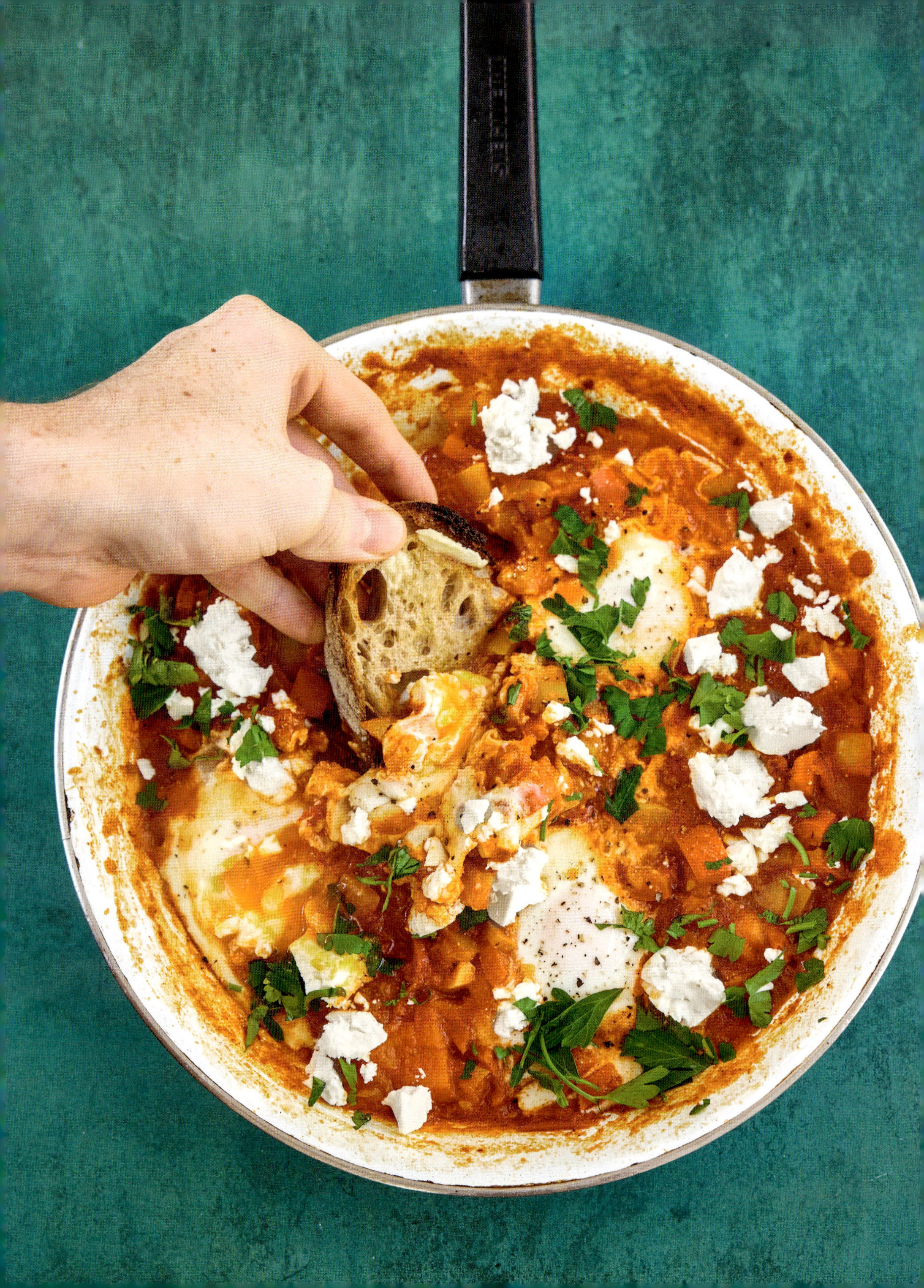

PREP TIME. 10 MINUTES / **COOK TIME.** 20 MINUTES / **SERVES.** 2

Hangover Helpers

This warm and comforting Middle Eastern breakfast is a staple on brunch menus around the world. The heat from the harissa paired with the rich tomato stew makes for a special breakfast. My favorite accompaniment is sourdough, but feel free to use whatever you have to hand. Despite sounding exotic, there are no expensive ingredients involved so splashing out on some posh bread seems like a master plan to me.

SHAKSHUKA

① Start by dicing your bell peppers and tomatoes into rough pieces and thinly slice your garlic.

② Pour the vegetable oil into a large frying pan over medium heat and fry the bell peppers for a couple of minutes until they start to soften.

③ Add the garlic into the pan with the cumin and paprika and cook for a minute. Add in the tomatoes, harissa and passata and stew them for 5–6 minutes or until the tomatoes have just started to break down.

④ Once the liquid has thickened, quickly taste and season the stew, then use a spoon to make four wells and crack your eggs into them.

⑤ Reduce the heat to a simmer. Place a lid on and cook the eggs slowly for 5–8 minutes, or until the whites of the egg are set but the yolks are still runny.

⑥ In the meantime, you can toast your bread.

⑦ Finally, season the eggs with a touch of salt and pepper, garnish with the crumbled feta and chopped parsley and serve alongside the toasted sourdough.

1 red bell pepper
1 yellow bell pepper
3 beefsteak tomatoes
2 cloves of garlic
1 tbsp vegetable oil
½ tsp ground cumin
1 tsp smoked paprika
2 tsp harissa paste
½ cup tomato passata
4 large eggs
2 large or 4 medium slices of sourdough bread
3½ oz (100 g) feta, crumbled
Handful of chopped parsley
Sea salt and black pepper

SERVES. 4 **PREP TIME.** 15 MINUTES / **COOK TIME.** 25 MINUTES

HANGOVER HELPERS

This takes the British staple of beans on toast and dresses it up with the addition of sausages, a little kick of spice and smoky paprika. It's great on toast (obviously), but can also be used to fill fajitas with a mix of sour cream and guacamole, as a pasta sauce or to top a jacket potato. Whichever way you use it, coming your way are some quick and delicious meals.

Spicy Sausage Beans on Toast

1. Start by roughly dicing the bell peppers and onion and setting aside in a bowl.
2. Make an incision down the length of the chorizo and peel away the casing. Roughly chop the chorizo and pinch the sausages to turn each one into four meatballs.
3. Pour 1 tablespoon vegetable oil into a large saucepan set over medium heat and add the chorizo and the sausages. Cook these for around 4–5 minutes, giving them a mix every so often, until the sausages are nicely browned.
4. Scoop the chorizo and the sausages out of the pan and set aside. Add the bell peppers and onion and cook for 5 minutes, seasoning with salt.
5. Once your veggies have softened, add in the minced garlic, tomato paste, smoked paprika and chilli flakes and cook for 1 minute.
6. Add the chorizo and the sausages back into the pan along with the drained beans. Add the chopped tomatoes and ¾ cup water.
7. Bring to a boil and simmer for 10 minutes or until the sauce has thickened up.
8. Taste and season with more salt and pepper as needed, then add in the chopped parsley and serve with some toasted sourdough bread.

1 red bell pepper
1 yellow bell pepper
1 red onion
1 ring of chorizo
6 sausages of choice
1 tbsp vegetable oil
3 garlic cloves
1 tbsp tomato paste
1 tsp smoked paprika
½ tsp chilli flakes
1 x 15.5 oz (439 g) can of cannellini beans, drained
1 x 15.5 oz (439 g) can of chopped tomatoes
Handful of chopped parsley
4 large or 8 medium slices of sourdough bread, toasted, to serve
Sea salt and black pepper

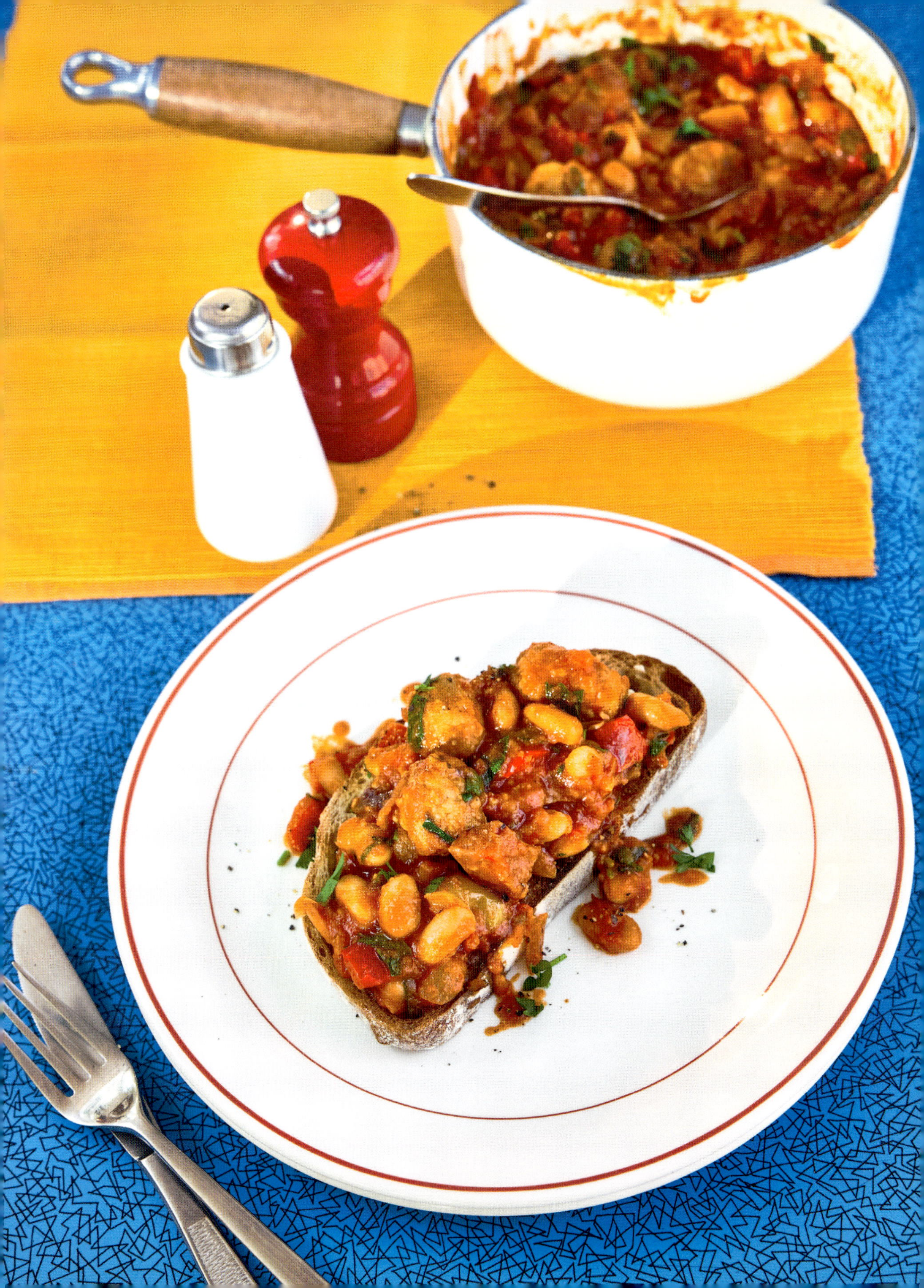

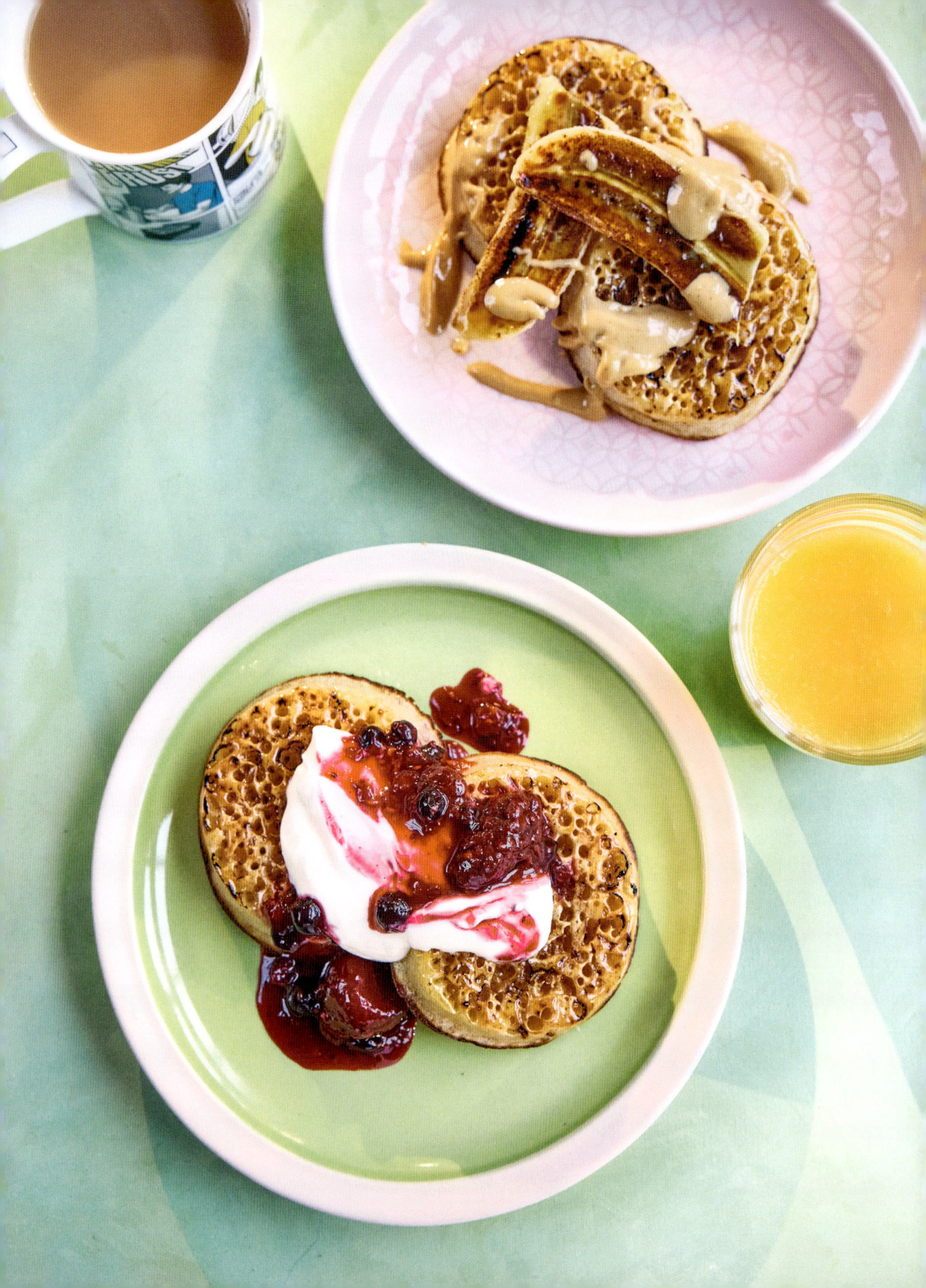

PREP TIME. 5 MINUTES / COOK TIME. 10 MINUTES / SERVES. 2

HANGOVER HELPERS

You might think it's hard to improve on a crumpet topped with lashings of butter, but try caramelizing them in honey, slathering in peanut butter and crowning with sliced banana and then we'll talk. Admittedly, not one for every day, but we all deserve the occasional treat, and this is hard to beat!

Caramelized Crumpets

4 crumpets
4 tbsp honey
Knob of butter

FOR THE YOGURT AND COMPOTE TOPPING

½ cup frozen berries
1 tbsp superfine sugar
Greek yogurt, to serve

FOR THE BANANA AND PEANUT BUTTER DRIZZLE

2 small bananas
3 tbsp peanut butter

① Place your frozen berries in a saucepan and add the sugar. Add 1 tablespoon of water and simmer for 5 minutes or until the berries have softened.

② Toast the crumpets in the toaster. Meanwhile, place a frying pan over medium heat. Add the honey and let it cook for 3–4 minutes or until it is bubbling and just starting to turn a light golden color.

③ Lower the heat and add the crumpets, holey side down. Continue to cook for a minute or two or until the holey side is a deep golden color and coated in the caramelized honey.

④ Carefully remove from the pan and slide the crumpets, holey side up, onto the plates. Smear the butter on top and serve with the berry compote and some yogurt.

Banana and peanut butter drizzle:

① For an alternative topping, place a frying pan over medium heat until hot. Slice 2 small bananas either in half lengthways and then across to make four pieces or into rounds. Place cut side down into the hot pan and cook for 1–2 minutes until golden and caramelized. Remove from the pan and leave caramelized side up while you cook your crumpets in the cleaned and dried pan.

② Put the peanut butter into a microwave-safe bowl and heat for 20–23 seconds, or until it is a runny sauce consistency. Smear the butter on the crumpets, then top with the banana and drizzle over the peanut butter.

HANGOVER HELPERS

SERVES. 4 / **PREP TIME.** 10 MINUTES / **COOK TIME.** 25 MINUTES

A fry-up is a wonderful thing. The cleanup? Not so much. This bite-sized brekky is super simple, all comes together in one muffin pan and is great for feeding a crowd. Perfect for when you have a houseful of sore heads and empty bellies!

BREAKFAST BASKETS

① Preheat your oven to 400°F (200°C).

② Cut the crusts off the bread slices and use a rolling pin (or an empty bottle of wine) to flatten them out. Grease your muffin tin with the butter and push your bread slices into four of the muffin cups.

③ Slice your sausage into eight pieces and thinly slice your bacon. Divide the meat into the bread baskets and bake for 10 minutes.

④ Crack your eggs into a jug, beat with a fork and season with salt and pepper. Finally, quarter your tomatoes and grate your cheese.

⑤ Take the breakfast baskets out of the oven. Pour in the egg mixture and top with the tomatoes, cheese and chives, if you are using them.

⑥ Bake for a further 10–13 minutes. Remove from the oven and then, using a teaspoon, gently remove each breakfast basket from the tin and serve immediately.

4 slices of white bread
Knob of butter
1 sausage of choice
2 strips of bacon
2 eggs
4 cherry tomatoes
1 oz (28 g) Cheddar cheese
1 tbsp chopped chives (optional)
Sea salt and black pepper

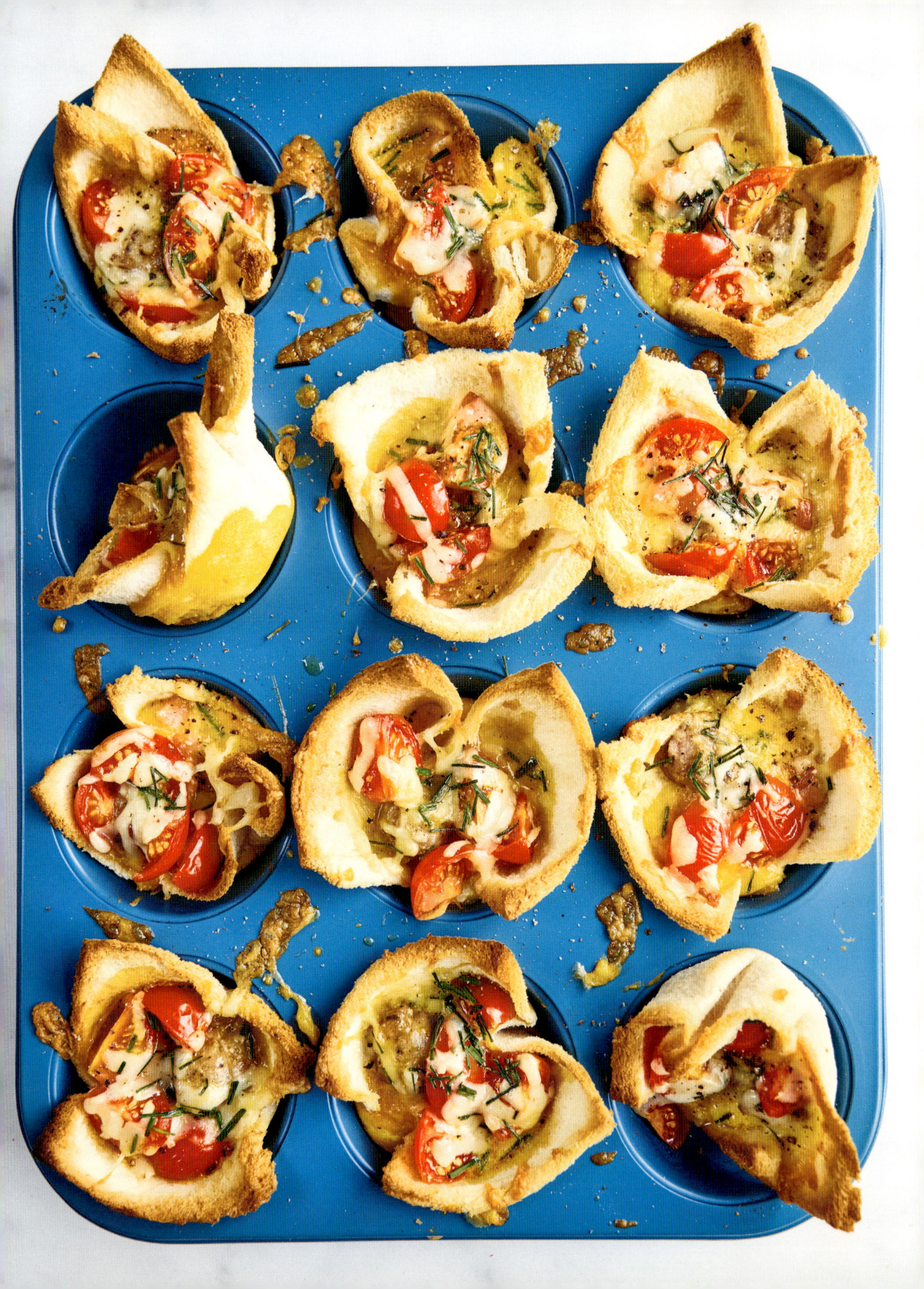

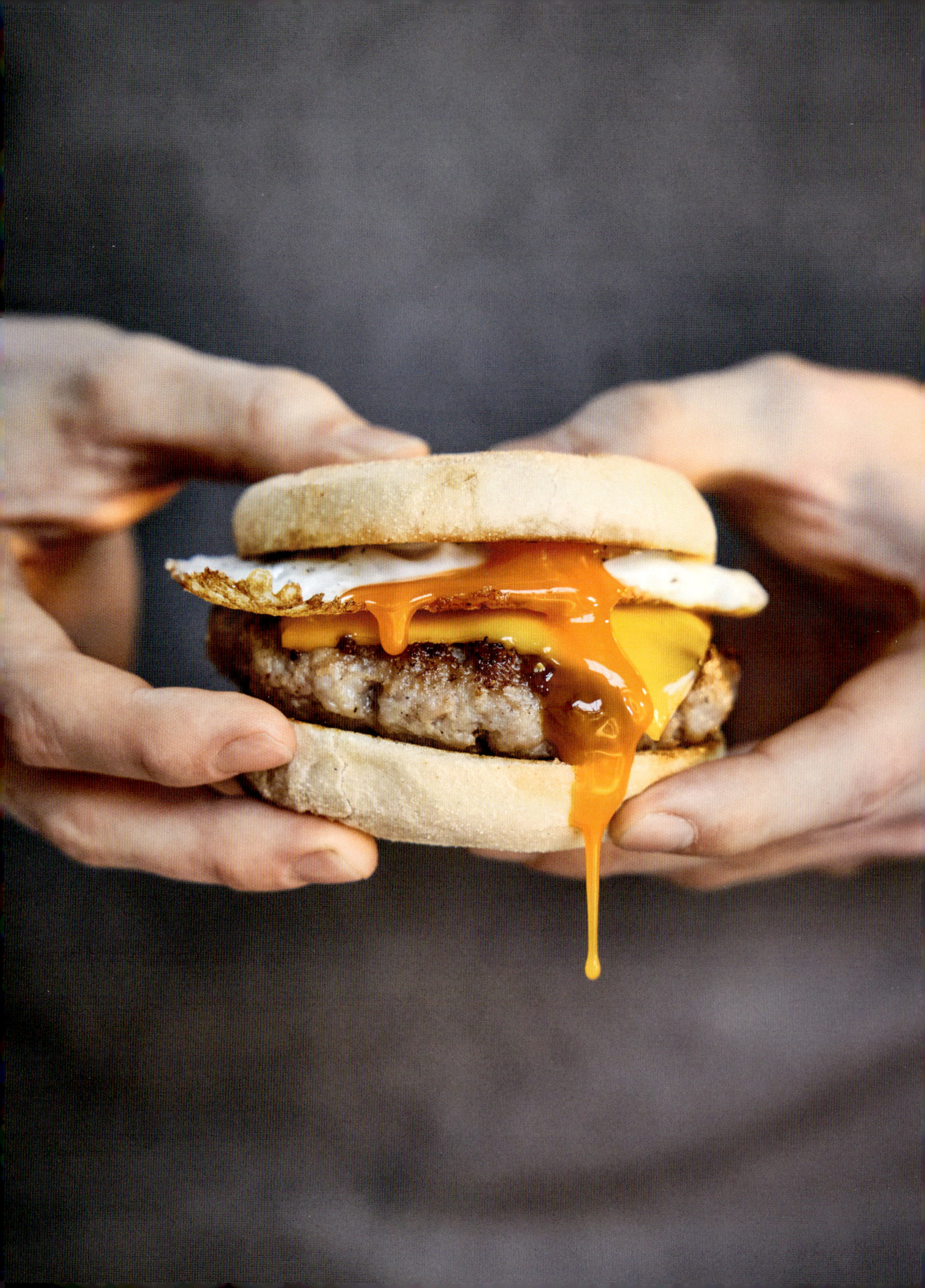

PREP TIME. 10 MINUTES / **COOK TIME.** 15 MINUTES / **SERVES.** 2 OR 1 VERY HUNGOVER PERSON

HANGOVER HELPERS

No hangover chapter is complete without a sausage and egg muffin. It is always my go-to and it never fails me. Having it delivered might seem like the easiest route, but it's hard to beat when it's hot and fresh from the pan. Get a batch on the go after a big night out and enjoy being very popular!

Sausage & Egg Muffins

3 pork sausages

2 tbsp vegetable oil

2 slices of American cheese

2 English muffins

2 eggs

Glass of orange juice (this isn't for the recipe, it's for your hangover)

① Preheat your oven to 400°F (200°C).

② Run a knife down the length of the sausages and remove the skins. Bring together the sausage meat and shape into two patties. Try to make the patties bigger than the muffins as the meat will shrink while cooking.

③ Pour 1 tablespoon of vegetable oil into a hot frying pan set over medium heat and cook the sausage patties for about 3 minutes on one side until golden brown and caramelized.

④ Flip the sausage patties, add the cheese on top and place them onto a baking sheet. Bake in the oven along with the halved muffins on a separate tray for 5 minutes.

⑤ Place the frying pan back over medium heat and crack the eggs into the pan. Add the additional tablespoon of vegetable oil at this time, if needed. Cook for around 1–2 minutes or until the egg whites are just set, then take off the heat and place a lid on top to finish cooking.

⑥ Once the eggs are cooked (but the yolks are still runny), the muffins are toasted and the cheese has melted, we are ready to build your sausage and egg muffins.

⑦ Fill the muffins with the sausage and egg, pour yourself a big glass of orange juice and enjoy. I'm sure they'll be all you need to recover from your hangover ... hopefully.

HANGOVER HELPERS

SERVES. 4 / **PREP TIME.** 10 MINUTES / **COOK TIME.** 15 MINUTES

One word, decadent. And another two words, *merci beaucoup*. A fresh croissant spread with béchamel, sliced cheese and ham. Baked and served under a fresh fried egg. *Ooh la la*.

CROQUE MADAME CROISSANTS

① Preheat your oven to 400°F (200°C)

② Cut your croissants in half and spread the béchamel onto the bottom half. Season with salt and pepper and scatter over the Parmesan.

③ Top with the ham and tear over the mozzarella. Place the croissant lids on top and place onto a baking sheet. Bake for 10–12 minutes.

④ Heat a large frying pan over medium heat. Pour in the vegetable oil and crack in the eggs. Cook for 3 minutes until the eggs are cooked but the yolks are still runny. Season with salt and pepper.

⑤ Once the croissants are crispy and the cheese has melted, transfer to plates and top with the fried eggs.

4 croissants
6 tbsp white sauce from a jar or Sam's Béchamel Sauce (see page 26)
1 oz (28 g) Parmesan cheese, grated
8 slices of ham
1 ball of mozzarella
1 tbsp vegetable oil
4 eggs
Sea salt and black pepper

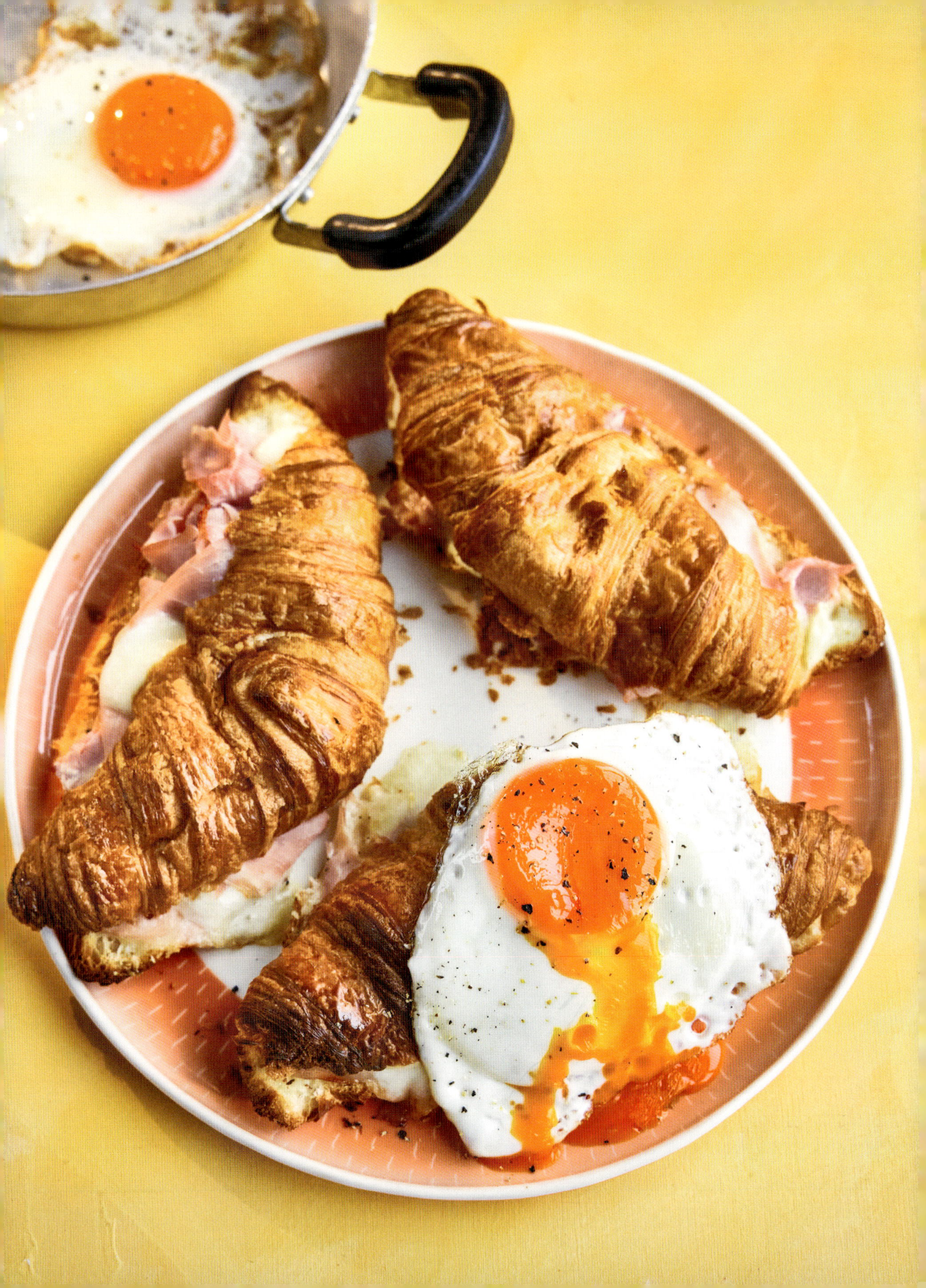

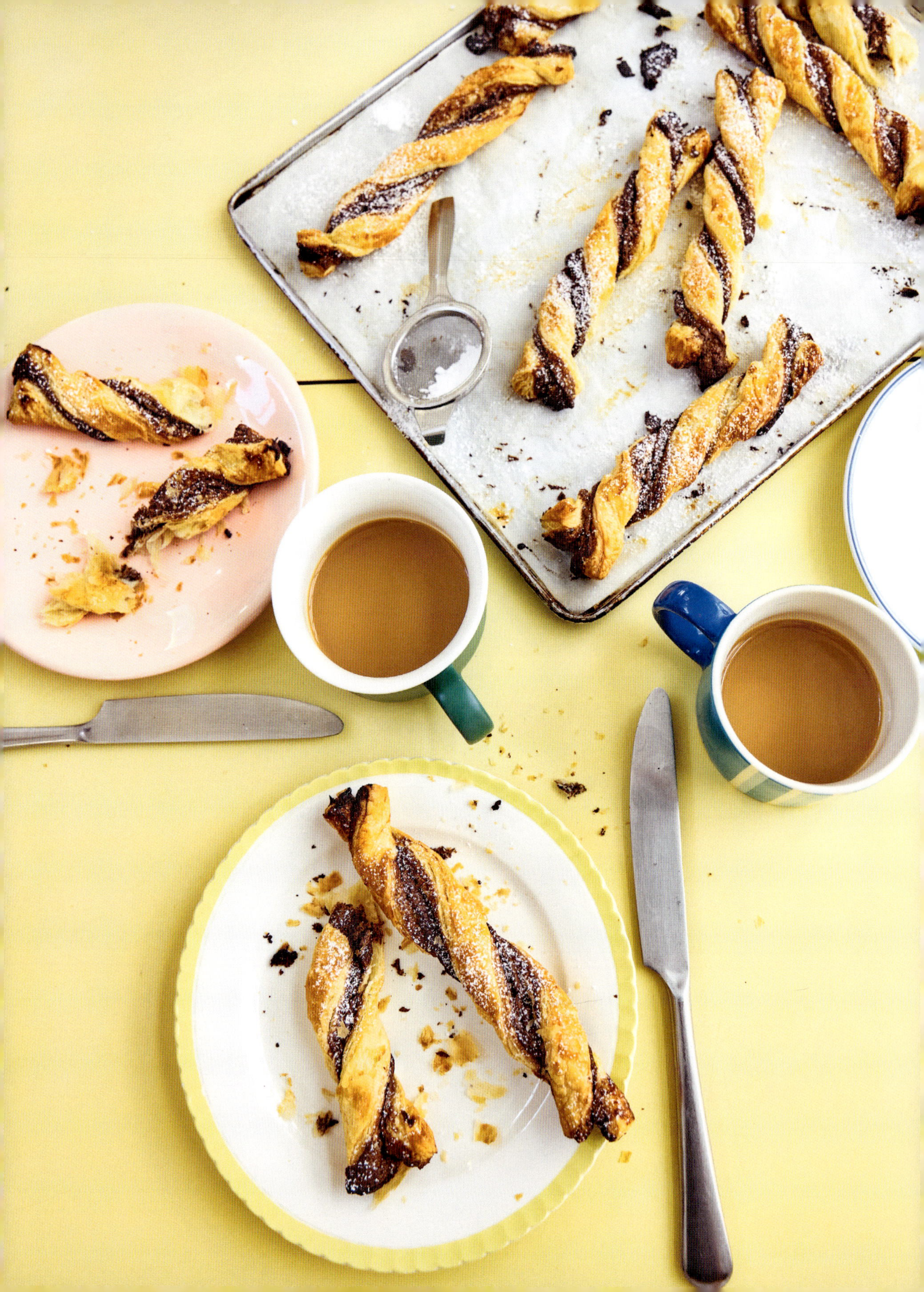

PREP TIME. 15 MINUTES / **COOK TIME.** 15 MINUTES / **MAKES.** 12

HANGOVER HELPERS

When I'm hungover, chocolate comes calling and especially so at breakfast! This recipe is a naughty combo of a pain-au-chocolat and a Nutella sandwich. Using only a couple of ingredients, you can whip these up in no time and they're showy enough to impress your mates out of their hangovers!

Nutella Twists

1. Preheat the oven to 400°F (200°C)
2. Unravel the puff pastry and cut it in half widthways.
3. Spread the Nutella across one half of the puff pastry, making sure you spread it evenly and to the edge.
4. Place the other piece of pastry on top and cut it into 12 long pieces, about the thickness of your index finger. Take each piece and twist it on both sides, in opposite directions, to achieve the twist shape.
5. Place onto a baking sheet lined with parchment paper. Use your finger, or a pastry brush if you happen to have one, to brush over some beaten egg and bake in the oven for 15 minutes.
6. Sieve or dust over some powdered sugar at the end and serve warm or cold.

1 sheet of pre-rolled puff pastry
½ cup Nutella
1 egg
Powdered sugar, for dusting

HANGOVER HELPERS

SERVES. 2 / **PREP TIME.** 10 MINUTES / **COOK TIME.** 40 MINUTES

This veg-packed frittata is the perfect way to start your day and keeps well in the fridge, setting you up for a week of healthy breakfasts. I've suggested the veg to use in the recipe, but this is really adaptable so feel free to use up whatever you have to hand.

Five-a-Day Veggie Frittata

① Preheat the oven to 350°F (180°C) and place a large frying pan over medium heat.

② Slice the bell pepper, mushrooms and red onion.

③ Pour 2 tablespoons of the vegetable oil into the hot frying pan and add the mushrooms. Season with salt and pepper and cook for 2 minutes or until they are nice and golden brown.

④ Add the bell peppers and onion and cook for a further 2 minutes. An additional tablespoon of oil might be necessary here if the pan looks quite dry.

⑤ Finally, add the spinach and the tomatoes and cook for an extra minute, or until the spinach has wilted. Taste, season with salt and pepper, if needed, and set aside.

⑥ Crack your eggs into another frying pan with a metal handle (not a plastic one otherwise it'll melt in the oven) or an ovenproof dish (roughly 10½ x 4-inches [27 x 17cm]), season with salt and pepper and beat with a fork until smooth.

⑦ Add in all the veggies and mix to combine before sprinkling your grated Parmesan cheese on top.

⑧ Bake in the oven for 30–35 minutes until it is golden brown and cooked all the way through (no bits of runny egg in the center!). Remove from the oven and enjoy.

Ingredients
1 red bell pepper
3½ oz (100 g) chestnut mushrooms (around 7 mushrooms)
½ red onion
3 tbsp vegetable oil
2½ oz (70 g) spinach, washed
Handful of cherry tomatoes
6 eggs
¾ oz (21 g) Parmesan cheese, grated
Sea salt and black pepper

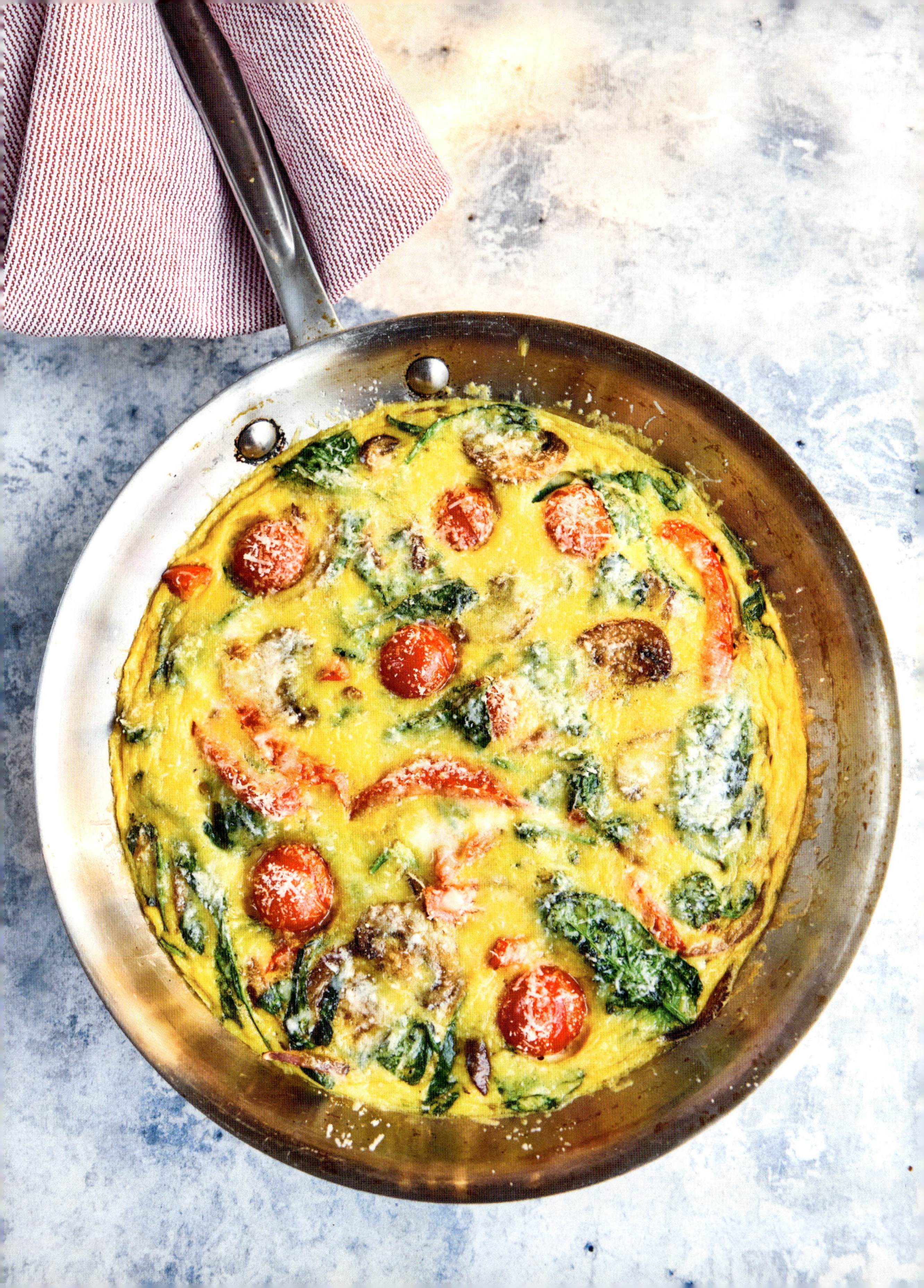

FOOD IN A FLASH

Instead of picking up a frozen pizza on your way home, how about choosing one of the easy and delicious recipes from this chapter? Comforting One-Pot Mac 'n' Cheese, a 15-minute Thai Chicken Curry, Pineapple and Pork Tacos, Sausage and Leek Gnocchi and more. They are all cheap, tasty, truly satisfying meals that are perfect for any day of the week.

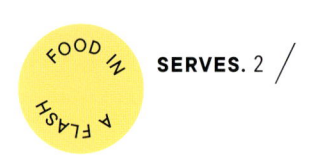

SERVES. 2 / **PREP TIME.** 5 MINUTES / **COOK TIME.** 15 MINUTES

FOOD IN A FLASH

Making mac 'n' cheese can be fiddly. Multiple saucepans, colander... The mess can pile up. Not anymore. This mac 'n' cheese is a one-pan game changer and takes barely 10 minutes. There are no strict rules here, so feel free to go off-piste and add fried bacon or mushrooms or whatever leftovers you have to hand.

One-Pot Mac 'n' Cheese

3 cups milk
6 oz (170 g) macaroni
2 tbsp cornstarch
3½ oz (100 g) Cheddar cheese
½ tsp mustard (optional)
¼ cup breadcrumbs
Sea salt and black pepper

① Put milk and macaroni into a saucepan. Bring it up to a gentle simmer, and continue to simmer for 10 minutes, stirring frequently to stop the pasta sticking to the pan. Don't let the milk boil.

② Meanwhile, mix the cornstarch with 2 tablespoons of cold water in a bowl until smooth. Grate the cheese and set aside.

③ Once the pasta is cooked, pour in the cornstarch, mix and stir continuously until the sauce thickens and just starts to bubble. Add in the cheese and mustard, if using, and season with salt and pepper. Add in additional milk to loosen it up, if necessary.

④ Preheat the broiler to its highest setting.

⑤ Pour the mac 'n' cheese into an ovenproof dish, top with the breadcrumbs and place under the broiler until it is golden brown. Watch it closely as this only takes about a minute.

⑥ Serve up and enjoy!

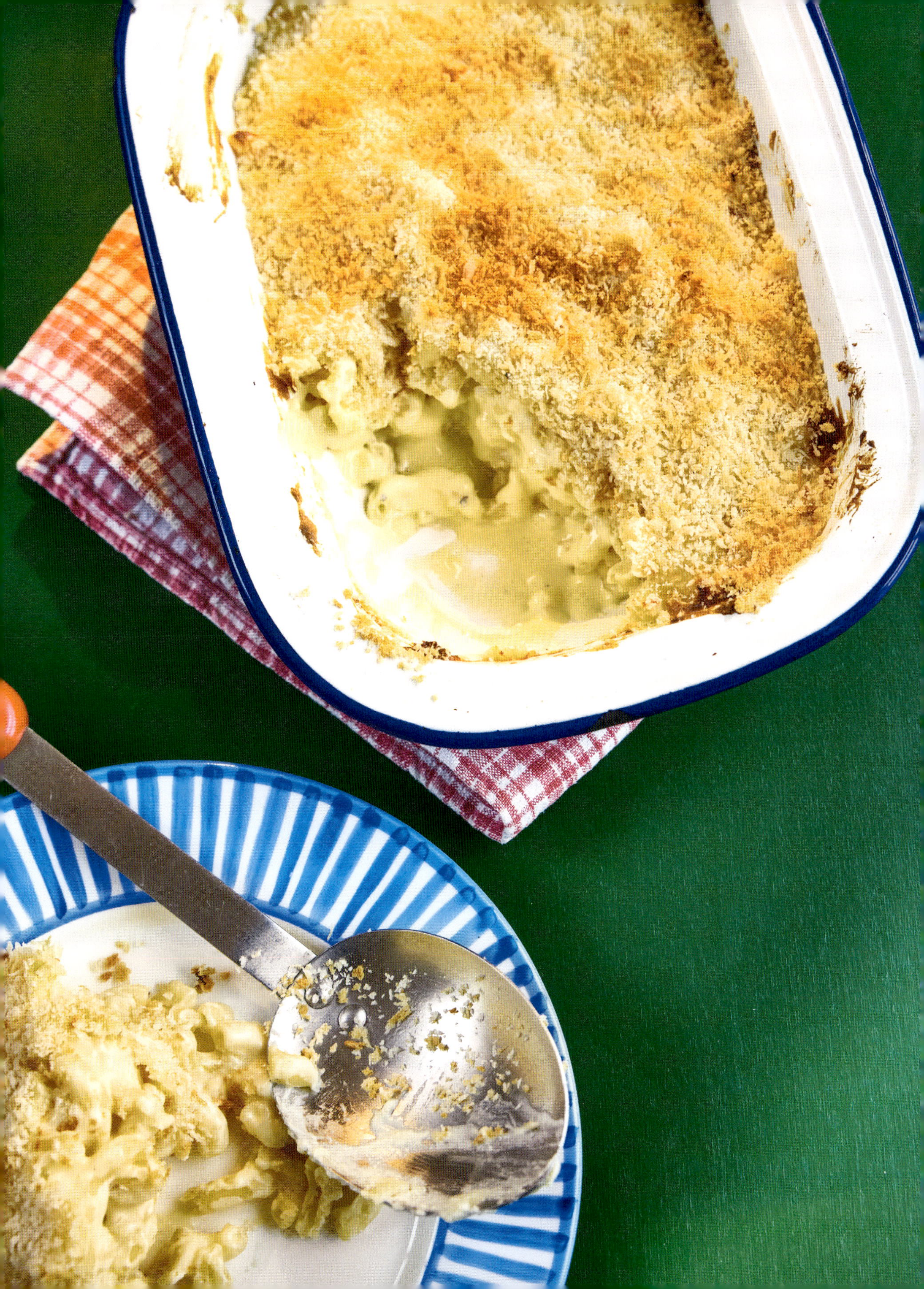

68

PREP TIME. 30 MINUTES / COOK TIME. 15 MINUTES / SERVES. 4

FOOD IN A FLASH

Bored of salad? You needn't be. Crunchy veg paired with a rich peanut dressing and curried chicken. Watch out for cheap peanut butters because they tend to be heavy on palm oil. This dish deserves 100% peanuts and so do you.

Chicken Satay Salad

① In a large bowl, mix together the coconut milk, spices, lime juice and a generous amount of salt and pepper. Add the chicken thighs and mix together so they're nicely combined, cover and marinate for at least half an hour or overnight in the fridge.

② For the salad, just roughly chop the lettuce, halve the tomatoes and use a veg peeler to slice the carrots and cucumber into lovely ribbons. Place in a bowl and set aside for later.

③ To make the dressing, it couldn't be simpler: just combine all the ingredients with ⅓ cup of water and whisk them together until you have a nice smooth dressing.

④ Preheat your broiler to its highest setting.

⑤ Take the chicken out of the marinade bowl and lay the thighs onto a baking sheet. Place under the broiler for 10 minutes until the chicken is nicely charred and cooked through. Let it rest for 5 minutes, and then chop into bite-size chunks.

⑥ Put the salad in a bowl, add all of the dressing and use two dessert spoons to mix it through.

⑦ Then top with the chicken and serve with extra lime wedges to squeeze over.

8 chicken thighs, skinless and boneless
3 baby gem lettuces
7 oz (200 g) cherry tomatoes
2 carrots
1 cucumber
Sea salt and black pepper

FOR THE CHICKEN MARINADE

¾ cup coconut milk
1 tbsp mild curry powder
1 tbsp ground turmeric
Juice of 1 lime

FOR THE DRESSING

1 cup smooth peanut butter
2½ tbsp honey
2½ tbsp light soy sauce
4 tbsp sesame oil
Juice of 1½ limes (save the other ½ for garnish)

SERVES. 2 **PREP TIME.** 15 MINUTES / **COOK TIME.** 5 MINUTES

FOOD IN A FLASH

This dish epitomizes 'Food in a Flash'. Once the pork first hits the hot wok, you'll be sitting down to enjoy delicious food within 5 minutes. Chillax.

Sam's Drunken Noodles

1. Start by chopping up your red onion and red bell pepper into thumb-sized pieces and set aside in a bowl. Then grate your ginger and garlic, slice your chilli and put into another bowl.

2. Roughly chop 2 slices of pineapple, reserving the juice from the can (use the other half of the can for the Pork and Pineapple Tacos recipe on page 74) and thinly slice the spring onions.

3. For the sauce, it's really simple. Just combine all of the ingredients listed and mix it up until the cornstarch is all mixed in and there are no lumps.

4. Thinly slice your pork, season with salt and pepper and now you're ready to start frying.

5. Pour the vegetable oil into a very hot wok and cook the pork for 2 minutes until it's nice and golden brown.

6. Remove the pork from the wok, trying to keep the oil in the wok, and add the red pepper and onion. Stir-fry them for about a minute and then add in your garlic, chilli and ginger and cook for a further 30 seconds.

7. At this point, if the pan looks a little dry, you can always add a touch more vegetable oil.

8. Finally, add in the noodles, pineapple, the sauce and the pork. Give it a toss so it's nicely combined, garnish with the spring onions and you're done.

1 red onion
1 red bell pepper
1 thumb-sized piece of fresh ginger
3 cloves of garlic
1 red chilli
1 x 8 oz (225 g) can of pineapple slices in juice (not syrup)
3 spring onions
2 pork blade steaks
2 tbsp vegetable oil
7 oz (200 g) straight-to-wok egg noodles
Sea salt and black pepper

FOR THE SAUCE

4 tbsp ketchup
3 tbsp pineapple juice from the can of slices
2 tbsp light soy sauce
1 tsp cornstarch

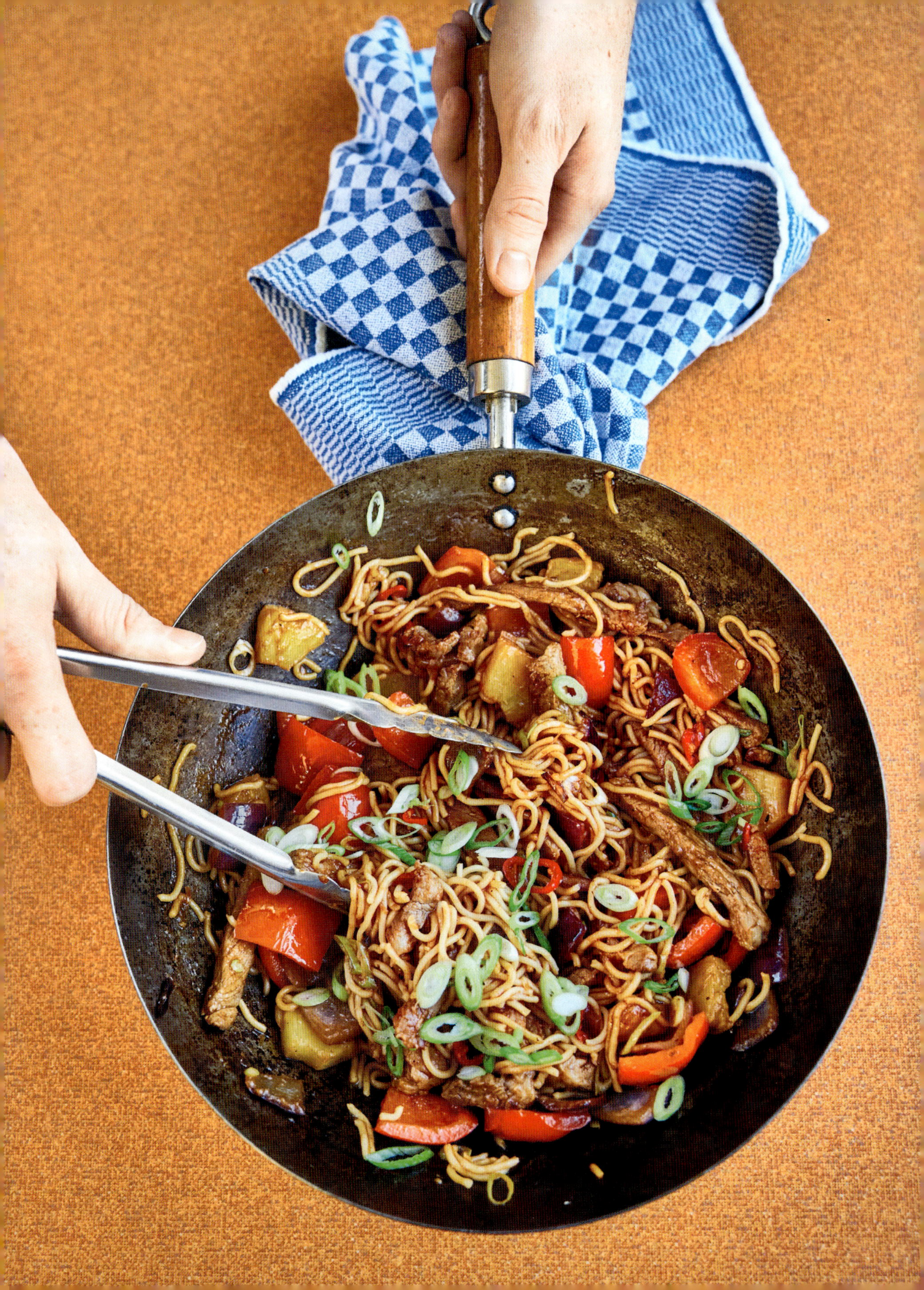

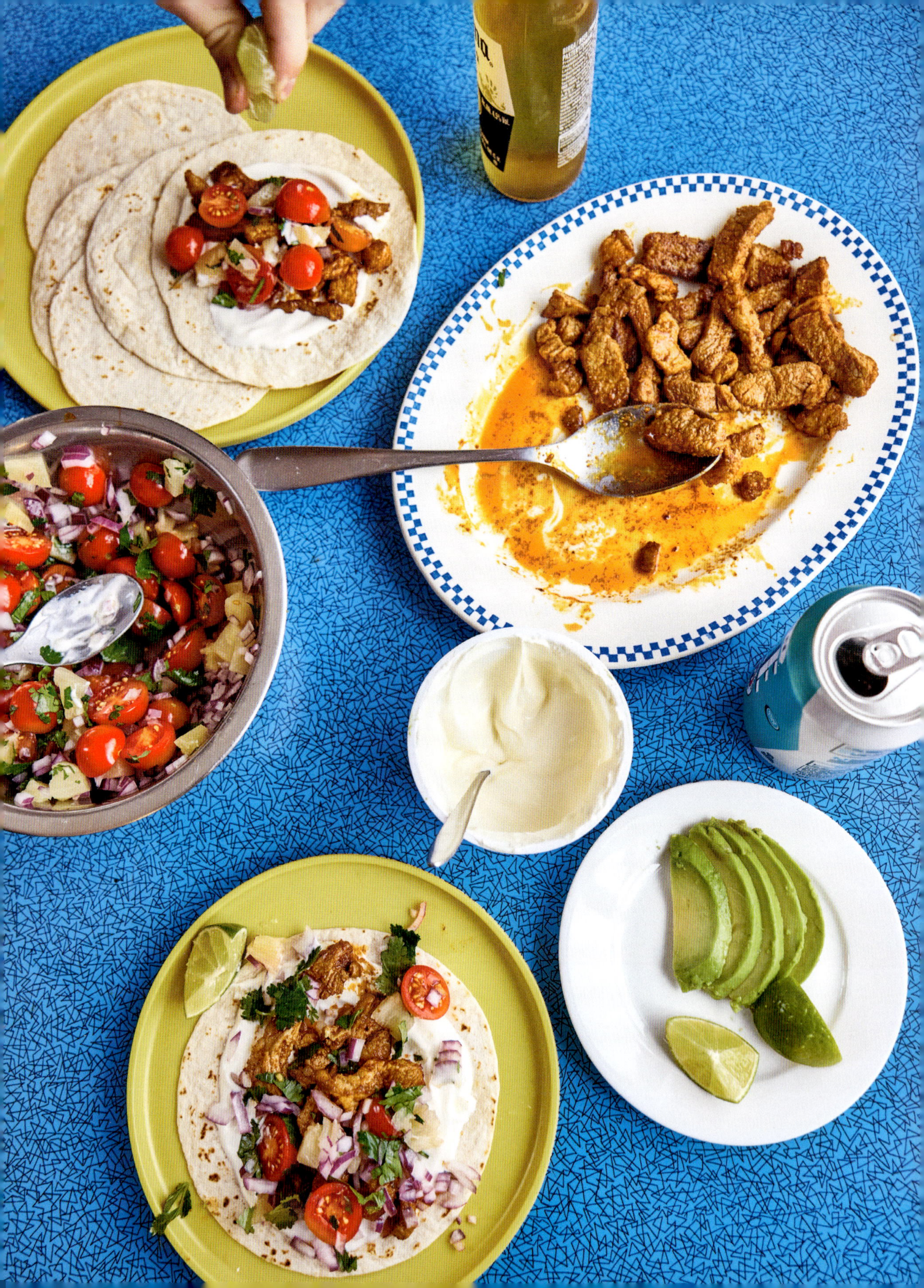

MAKES. 6 SMALL TACOS / **PREP TIME.** 15 MINUTES / **COOK TIME.** 5 MINUTES

FOOD IN A FLASH

Turn the leftovers from Sam's Drunken Noodles (see page 70) into this tropical winner. Beautiful pork with tons of flavor pairs brilliantly with the zesty pineapple and tomato salsa, all combined in a lovely warm tortilla. This dish comes together very easily and is perfect for a hot summer's day served with a few cold BEROs.

PORK & Pineapple Tacos

① Start by thinly slicing the pork. Mix 3 tablespoons of the olive oil with the smoked paprika, cumin and coriander in a medium bowl. Add the pork to the marinade and mix well. Season with salt and pepper and set aside.

② Clean your chopping board and then halve the cherry tomatoes, dice the red onion and roughly chop 2 slices of pineapple and the cilantro.

③ Add that into a bowl with the remaining olive oil, the juice of half the lime (keep the other half for garnish) and season with salt and pepper. Mix it up and set aside.

④ A final bit of prep before we start cooking. Cut around the avocado stone lengthways and open the avocado up. Remove the stone with a spoon and scoop out the flesh. Cut each half into six pieces and leave to one side.

⑤ In a very hot frying pan, cook the pork for 3–4 minutes or until it's golden brown and cooked through.

⑥ Warm the tortillas in the microwave by placing them on a microwave-safe plate and draping a damp piece of kitchen paper over the top. Heat for 30 seconds to a minute until they are warm and soft.

⑦ To serve up, spread some sour cream onto a tortilla, top with the pork, spoon on the pineapple salsa and garnish with the avocado and lime.

2 pork blade steaks
4 tbsp olive oil
1 tbsp smoked paprika
1 tsp ground cumin
1 tsp ground coriander
7 oz (200 g) cherry tomatoes
½ red onion
1 x 8 oz (225 g) can of pineapple slices in juice (not syrup)
Handful of cilantro
1 lime
1 avocado
6 small tortillas
½ cup sour cream
Sea salt and black pepper

SERVES. 2 / **PREP TIME.** 10 MINS / **COOK TIME.** 5 MINS

FOOD IN A FLASH

This one is showy, but it's also easy, quick and surprisingly cheap. A perfect lunch using Britain's finest ingredients that comes together in minutes and wouldn't look out of place in a restaurant. Boom.

BROILED MACKEREL + FENNEL & APPLE SLAW

① Preheat the oven to its highest broiler setting.

② Finely slice the fennel, red onion and apple and add them to a bowl. Season with salt and pepper and squeeze over the lemon juice.

③ Add in enough mayonnaise to bring it all together and finish with some chopped parsley.

④ Drizzle the vegetable oil over the mackerel fillets and season with salt on both sides.

⑤ Place the fish into a roasting pan, skin side up, and put it underneath the broiler for 3–5 minutes, depending on how hot your broiler is, until the skin is crisp and the fish flakes easily.

⑥ Once the skin is nice and crispy, serve it immediately with the fennel and apple slaw.

1 bulb of fennel
½ red onion
1 Granny Smith apple
Juice of ½ lemon, keep the other half to garnish
2 tbsp mayonnaise
Handful of chopped parsley
1 tbsp vegetable oil
4 mackerel fillets
Sea salt and black pepper

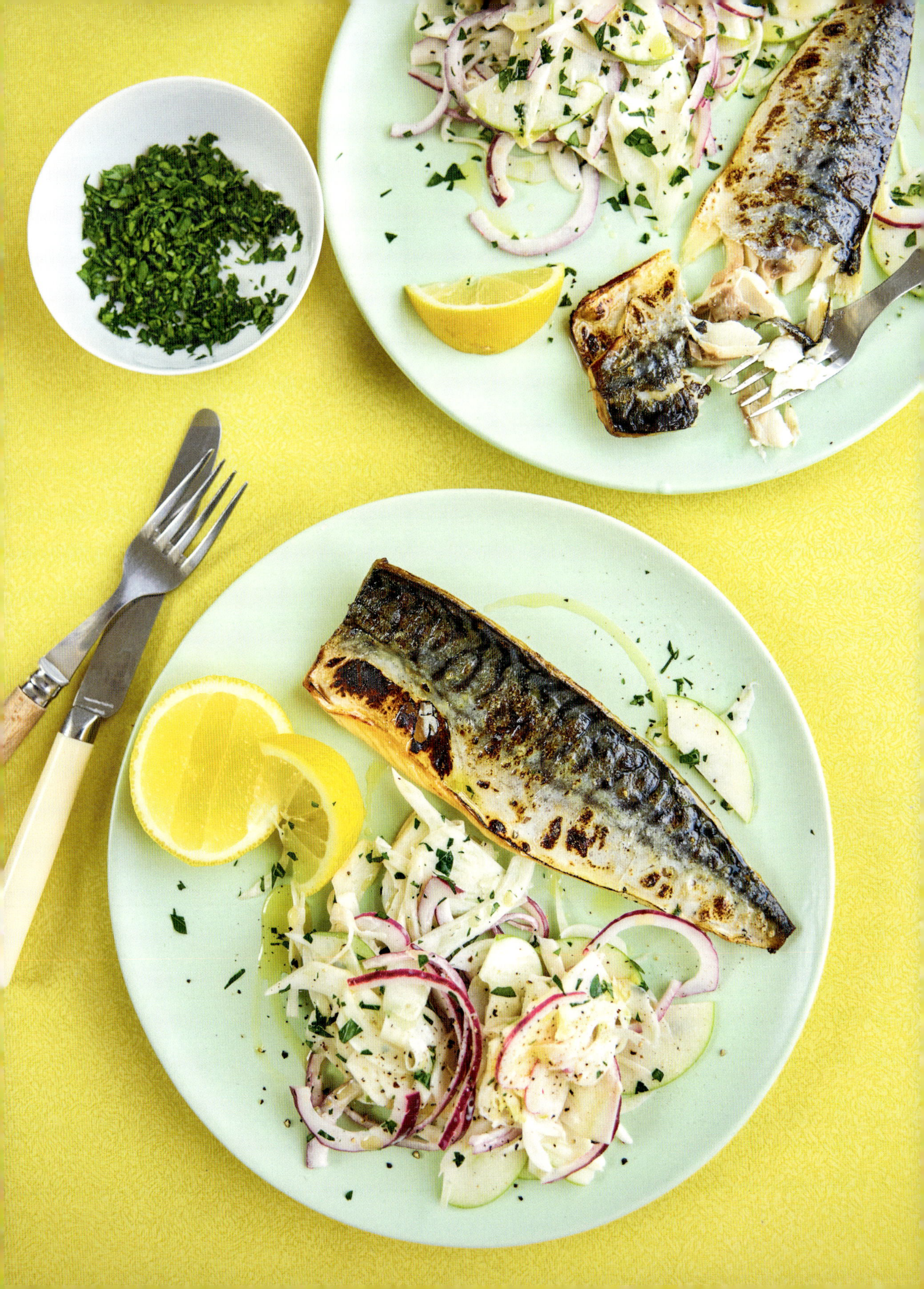

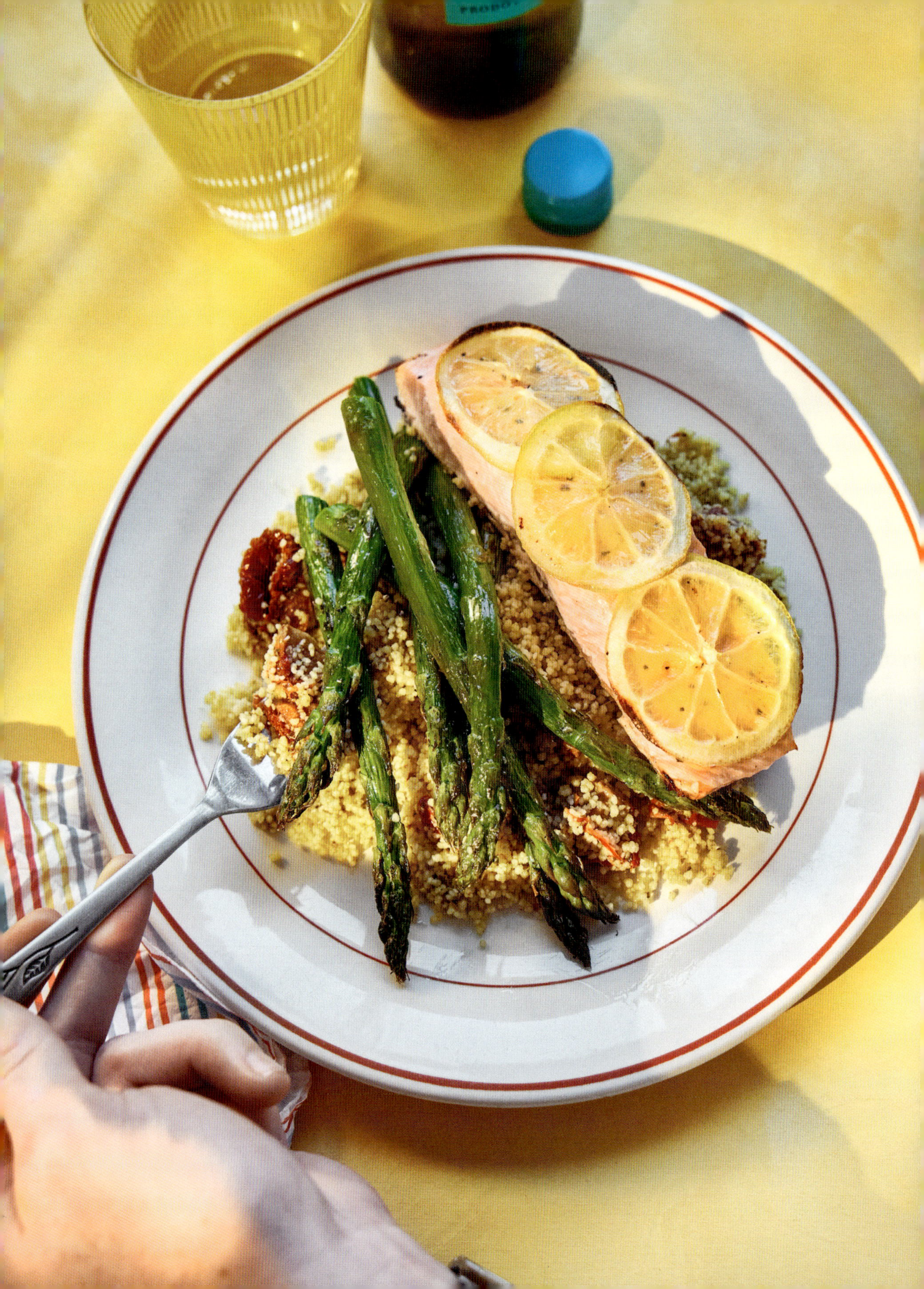

PREP TIME. 10 MINUTES / **COOK TIME.** 10 MINUTES / **SERVES.** 2

FOOD IN A FLASH

Another of my go-tos, especially when I'm too tired to cook but still want to eat something healthy and delicious. The richness of the salmon with crisp asparagus pairs brilliantly with fresh, vibrant pesto couscous. Just let the oven do the work, so you can figure out what to watch on Netflix and pour yourself a glass of something cold.

Roasted Salmon & Asparagus + Pesto Couscous

① Preheat your oven to 400°F (200°C).

② Arrange your asparagus in a roasting pan and place the salmon fillets on top. Drizzle over the olive oil and season with salt and pepper.

③ Thinly slice half the lemon and add the slices onto the salmon fillets. Place the butter on the lemon slices and bake for 10 minutes.

④ As soon as your salmon is in the oven, put your couscous in a bowl and pour in enough boiling water to cover, around ½ cup. Quickly cover tightly with plastic wrap or tin foil and set aside until the salmon is ready.

⑤ Remove the plastic wrap and fluff up the couscous with a fork. Roughly chop the sun-dried tomatoes and stir them through the couscous along with the pesto. Season with salt, pepper and a squeeze of lemon juice.

⑥ Pile the couscous onto the plates and then add the asparagus. Top with the salmon and garnish with some lemon wedges.

Ingredients
8 oz (180 g) asparagus (around 16 spears)
2 small salmon fillets
2 tbsp olive oil
1 lemon, plus a couple of wedges
1½ tbsp butter
4 oz (120 g) couscous
Handful of sun-dried tomatoes
6 tsp basil pesto
Sea salt and black pepper

SERVES. 2 / **PREP TIME.** 5 MINUTES / **COOK TIME.** 15 MINUTES

FOOD IN A FLASH

Minimum effort… maximum satisfaction. Simple ingredients only, but still packs a punch. This dish is ready in the time it takes your pasta to cook. Perfect for when time is pressing and you want to impress.

Speedy Seafood Spaghetti

① Put the spaghetti into a pan of salted boiling water and use tongs to bend the spaghetti into the water. Cook according to the package instructions.

② In the meantime, you can mince your garlic, chop your parsley and halve your tomatoes.

③ Once the pasta is cooked, reserve a cup of pasta water, then drain the pasta and set aside while you make the sauce.

④ Drizzle the olive oil into a hot frying pan, add your garlic and tomatoes and cook for a couple of minutes until they start to break down.

⑤ Follow it in with the prawns, harissa and mussels and sauté for a few minutes or until the shrimp turn pink and the mussels open.

⑥ Squeeze over the lemon juice and add in your pasta. Don't be afraid to add some pasta water as well, as the starchy water will help the sauce stick to the pasta.

⑦ Finish with the chopped parsley. Taste and season with some salt and pepper and a little more harissa, if you fancy, and enjoy.

6 oz (180 g) spaghetti
2 cloves of garlic
Handful of parsley
5 oz (150 g) cherry tomatoes
2 tbsp olive oil
5 oz (150 g) raw shrimp
2–3 tsp harissa paste
5 oz (150 g) raw mussels
Juice of ½ lemon
Sea salt and black pepper

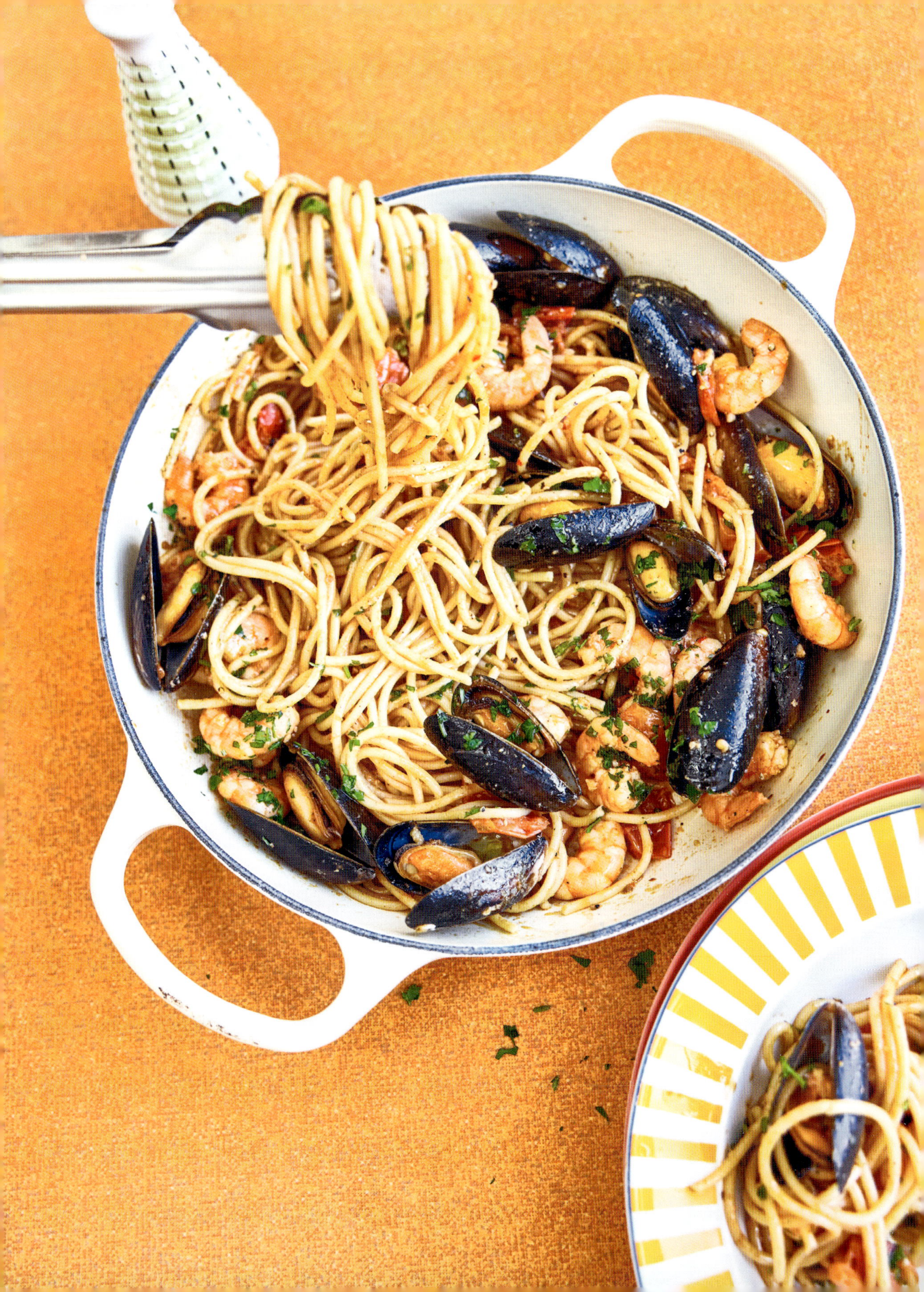

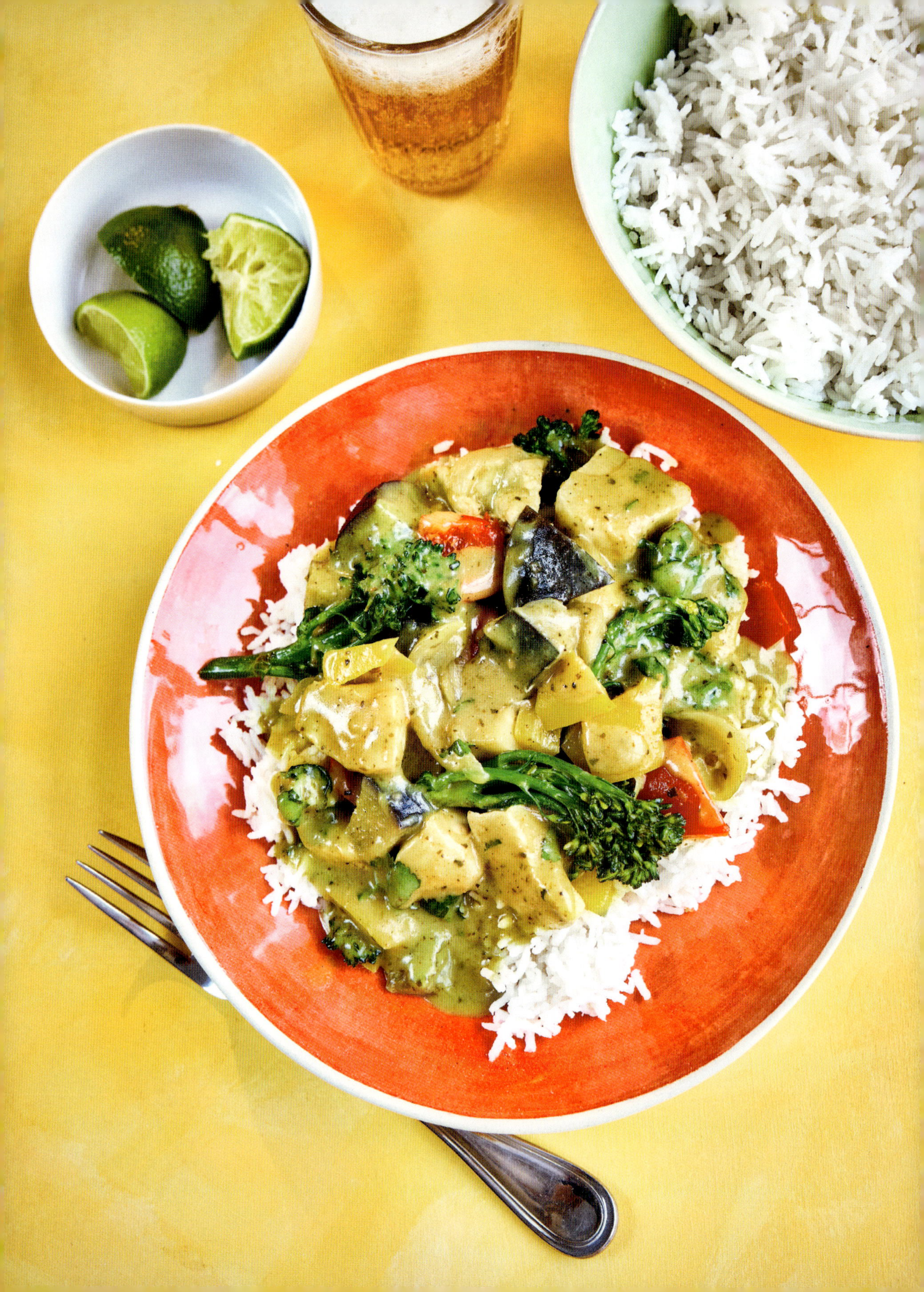

PREP TIME. 5 MINUTES / **COOK TIME.** 15 MINUTES / **SERVES.** 2-3

FOOD IN A FLASH

I was lucky enough to spend some time in Thailand as a kid and fell in love with the beaches, the people and, especially, the food! This fragrant, zesty curry is a favorite the world over and for good reason. It's super simple to prepare, packed with flavor and will bring sunshine to your plate whatever the weather.

15-Minute Thai Chicken Curry

① Slice your onion and fry in a saucepan with the vegetable oil. Season with a pinch of salt and cook over medium to high heat for 5 minutes until it's starting to caramelize.

② Meanwhile, chop up your bell peppers, eggplant and chicken into bite-sized pieces.

③ Once the onion is golden, add in the Thai curry paste and fry for 2 minutes. Pour in the coconut milk and bring to a simmer.

④ Once simmering, add in the chicken and eggplant and simmer for 5 minutes. Now add in your bell peppers and broccolini and cook for a further 2 minutes. (I like my veg to be nice and crunchy in this dish, but you can cook it for longer if you like it softer.)

⑤ Finish with lots of chopped cilantro, season with lime juice, fish sauce, sugar, salt and pepper, and you're ready to serve.

½ onion
1 tbsp vegetable oil
2 bell peppers
½ eggplant
2 chicken breasts
6-7 oz (170-200 g) jar of Thai green curry paste (or 1-2 tbsp if using a Thai brand)
1 x 13.5 oz (398 ml) can of coconut milk
10 pieces of broccolini
Handful of chopped cilantro
Juice of 1 lime
1½ tbsp fish sauce
1 tbsp sugar
Sea salt and black pepper
5 oz (150 g) cooked rice, to serve (see page 22)

SERVES. 4 / **PREP TIME.** 10 MINUTES / **COOK TIME.** 20 MINUTES

FOOD IN A FLASH

This one-pan veggie bonanza is a perfect mid-week meal. Loaded full of beautiful Mediterranean vegetables, and can we show a little love for the orzo, please? A pasta too long in the shadow of spaghetti and rigatoni. Its time has come!

Ratatouille Orzo

① Dice your onion, bell peppers, zucchini and eggplant into a small dice.

② Pour the vegetable oil into your largest frying pan over a medium heat. Once hot, add in your veggies, season with salt and pepper and cook for 4 minutes.

③ Meanwhile, you can mince your garlic and add that into the pan with the cherry tomatoes and cook for a further minute.

④ Add in the orzo, chopped tomatoes and stock and bring it up to the boil. Reduce the heat to low, place a lid on top and simmer for 8 minutes.

⑤ Taste and season the orzo, then tear the mozzarella into small pieces and scatter them over the top of the orzo. Place the lid back on and cook for 2 more minutes.

⑥ Finish with some fresh basil and a healthy amount of Parmesan, and your one-pot veggie wonder is ready.

Ingredients
1 red onion
2 red and/or yellow bell peppers
1 zucchini
½ eggplant
2 tbsp vegetable oil
2 cloves of garlic
Handful of cherry tomatoes
8 oz (225 g) orzo
1 x 15.5 oz (439 g) can of chopped tomatoes
1 cup vegetable stock
1 ball of fresh mozzarella
Bunch of basil
Handful of grated Parmesan cheese
Sea salt and black pepper

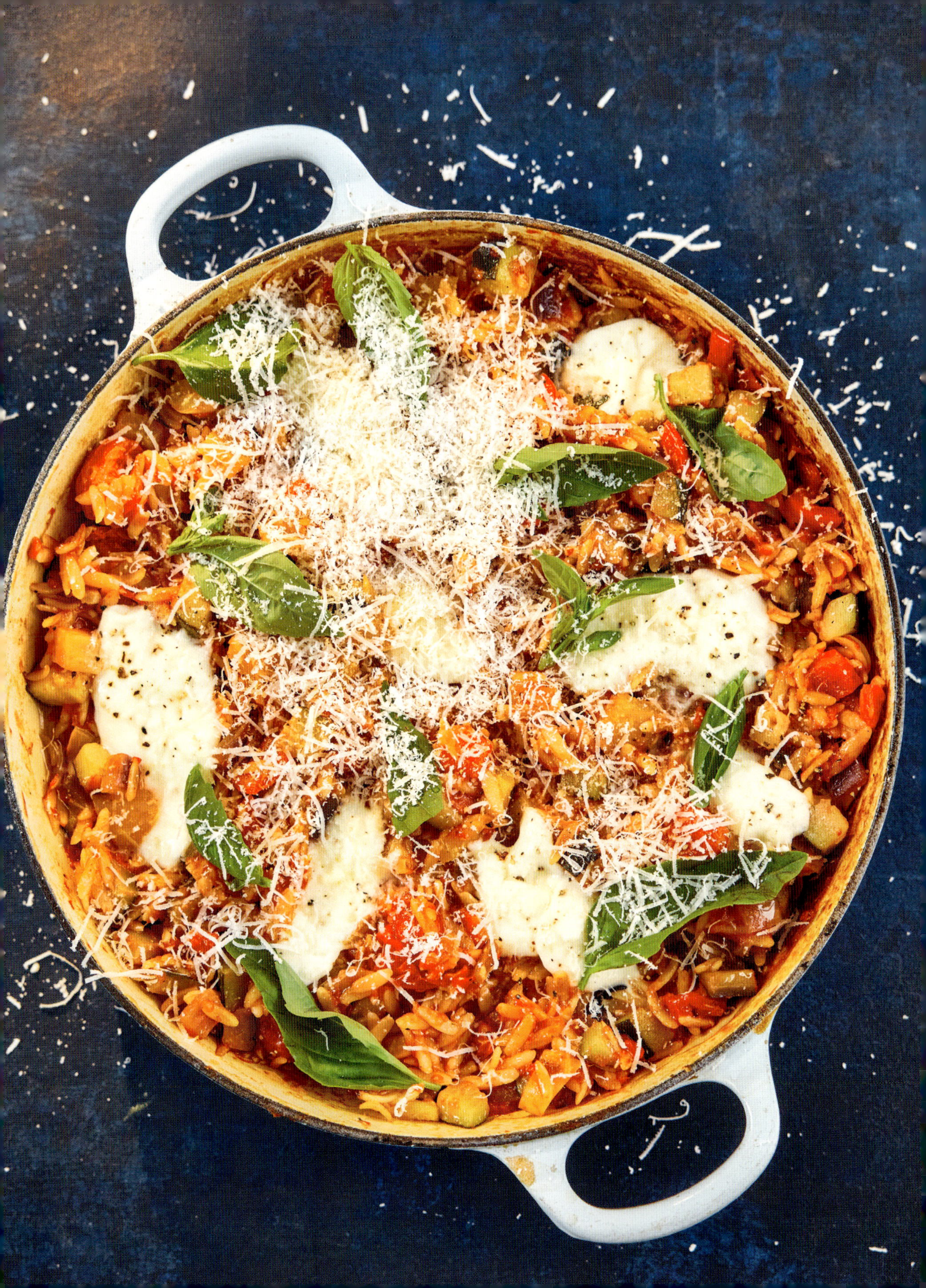

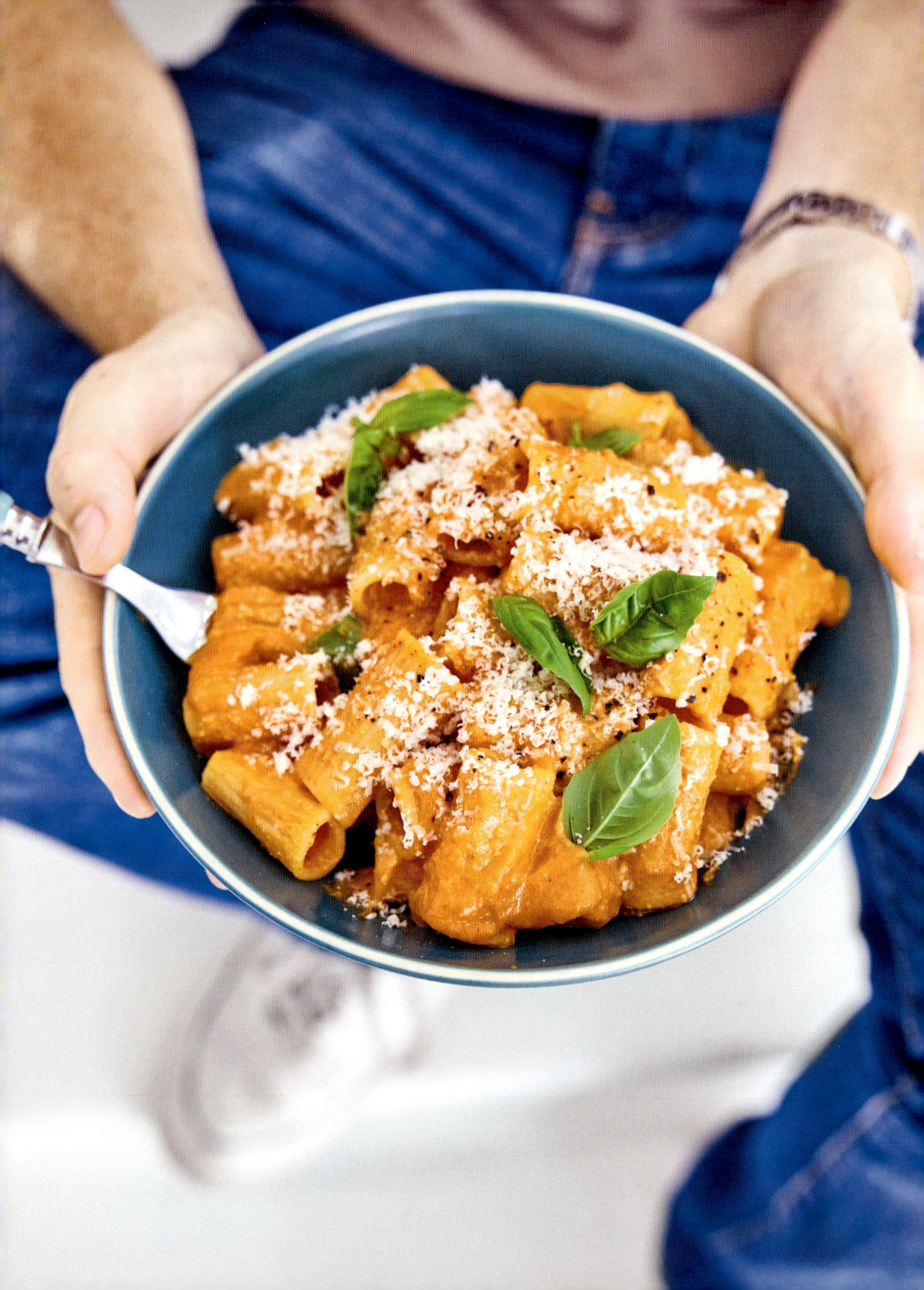

PREP TIME. 5 MINUTES / **COOK TIME.** 30 MINUTES / **SERVES.** 2

FOOD IN A FLASH

Some things are just meant to be together... Ross and Rachel, Batman and Robin, Harry and Sally... And similarly, garlic, chilli and fresh tomatoes. A match made in heaven.

Tomato & Mascarpone Rigatoni

① Preheat your oven to 400°F (200°C).

② Halve your tomatoes, lightly crush the garlic with the back of a knife just to break the skin and halve the chilli.

③ Add them all into a roasting pan, drizzle over the olive oil and season with salt and pepper. Place in the oven and roast for 30 minutes.

④ Bring a pan of salted water up to a boil and cook your pasta according to the packet instructions. Drain the cooked pasta and save a ladle of pasta water.

⑤ Remove the tomatoes from the oven. Put the tomatoes, half the chilli and the mascarpone into a jug; squeeze out the roasted garlic from its skin and add too. Don't forget to pour in all the roasting juices.

⑥ Use a hand blender to blitz to a smooth purée. Taste and check for seasoning. If you'd like it spicier, add in the remaining chilli to boost the spice levels.

⑦ Add the sauce to the cooked pasta with the Parmesan. Tear in the fresh basil and season with salt and pepper. If the sauce feels a little too thick, add a splash of pasta water.

⑧ Serve up with some more fresh basil and the grated Parmesan.

6 large beefsteak tomatoes (or 8 medium)
8 cloves of garlic, unpeeled
1 red chilli
2 tbsp olive oil
1 lb (454 g) rigatoni
1½ oz (50 g) mascarpone
Large handful of grated Parmesan cheese, plus extra to serve
Handful of basil, plus a few leaves to serve
Sea salt and black pepper

FOOD IN A FLASH

SERVES. 2 / **PREP TIME.** 10 MINUTES / **COOK TIME.** 15 MINUTES

One-pot dishes are low on effort (and washing up!) but can be big on flavor. Gnocchi keeps for ages in the fridge and is super quick to prepare. A tasty, versatile ingredient for days when time is pressing. Veggie sausages will work just as well, so swap those in if you're meat-free.

One-Pot Sausage & Leek Gnocchi

① Slice your mushrooms, cut your sausages into four pieces each and mince your garlic. Heat 1 tablespoon of the vegetable oil in a large pan over high heat. Add in the mushrooms and sausages and brown them for 3–4 minutes.

② Meanwhile, trim off the woody ends of the leeks. Slice the leeks in half and wash them well in the sink, then thinly slice.

③ Once the mushrooms and sausages are nicely browned, remove them from the pan and set aside on a plate. Add the other 2 tablespoons of vegetable oil to the pan and lower the heat to medium. Add the leeks to the pan with a touch of salt and sauté for 5 minutes.

④ Add in the garlic and cook for 1 minute, then put the mushrooms and sausages back in the pan. Pour in the wine and chicken stock and bring to a boil.

⑤ Add the gnocchi and simmer for 2 minutes.

⑥ Finish with the cream, Parmesan and parsley and season with salt and pepper.

3½ oz (100 g) chestnut mushrooms (around 6 mushrooms)
4 sausages
2 cloves of garlic
3 tbsp vegetable oil
2 leeks
¼ cup white wine
1 cup chicken stock
10 oz (283 g) gnocchi
3 tbsp heavy cream
3 tbsp Parmesan cheese, grated, plus extra to serve
Handful of chopped parsley
Sea salt and black pepper

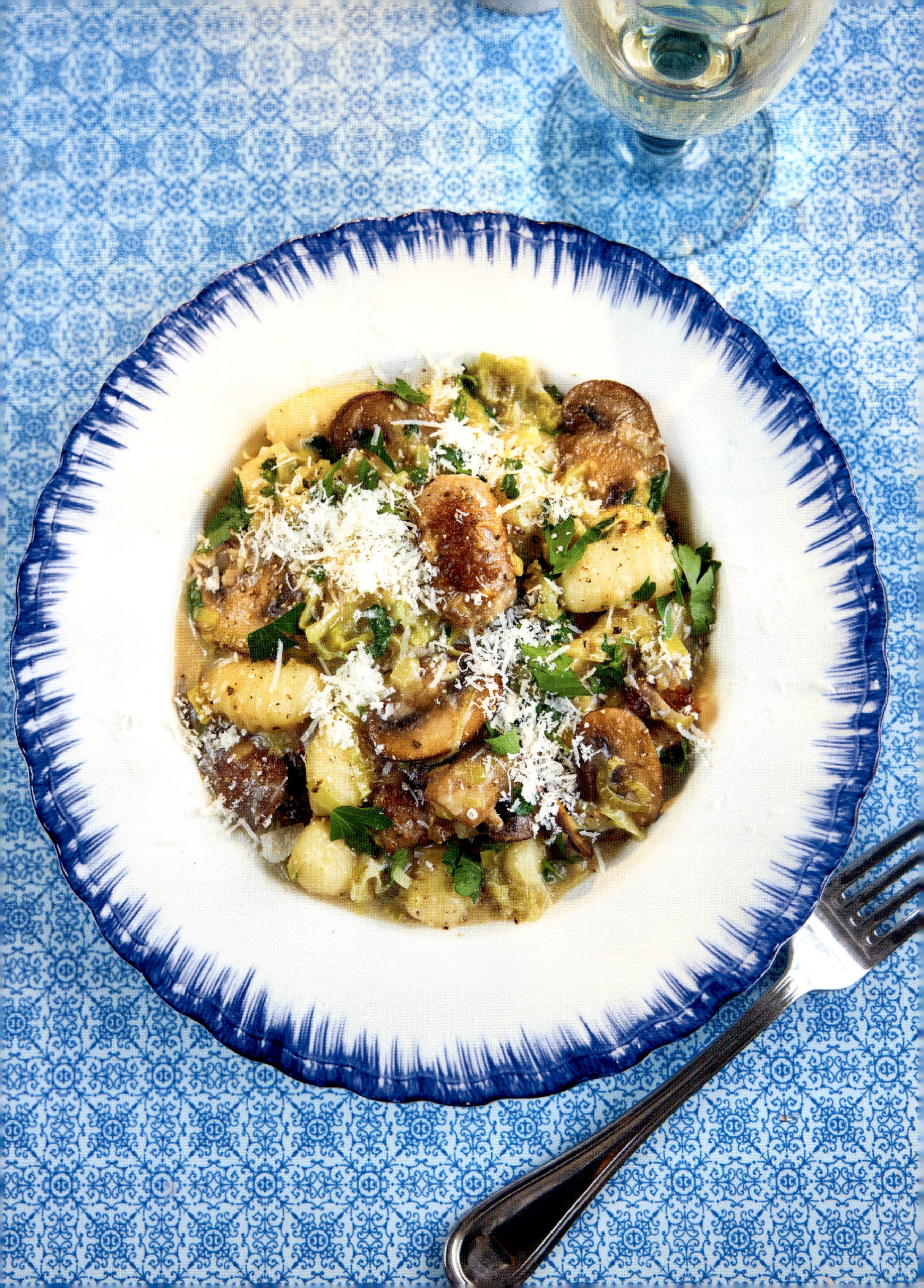

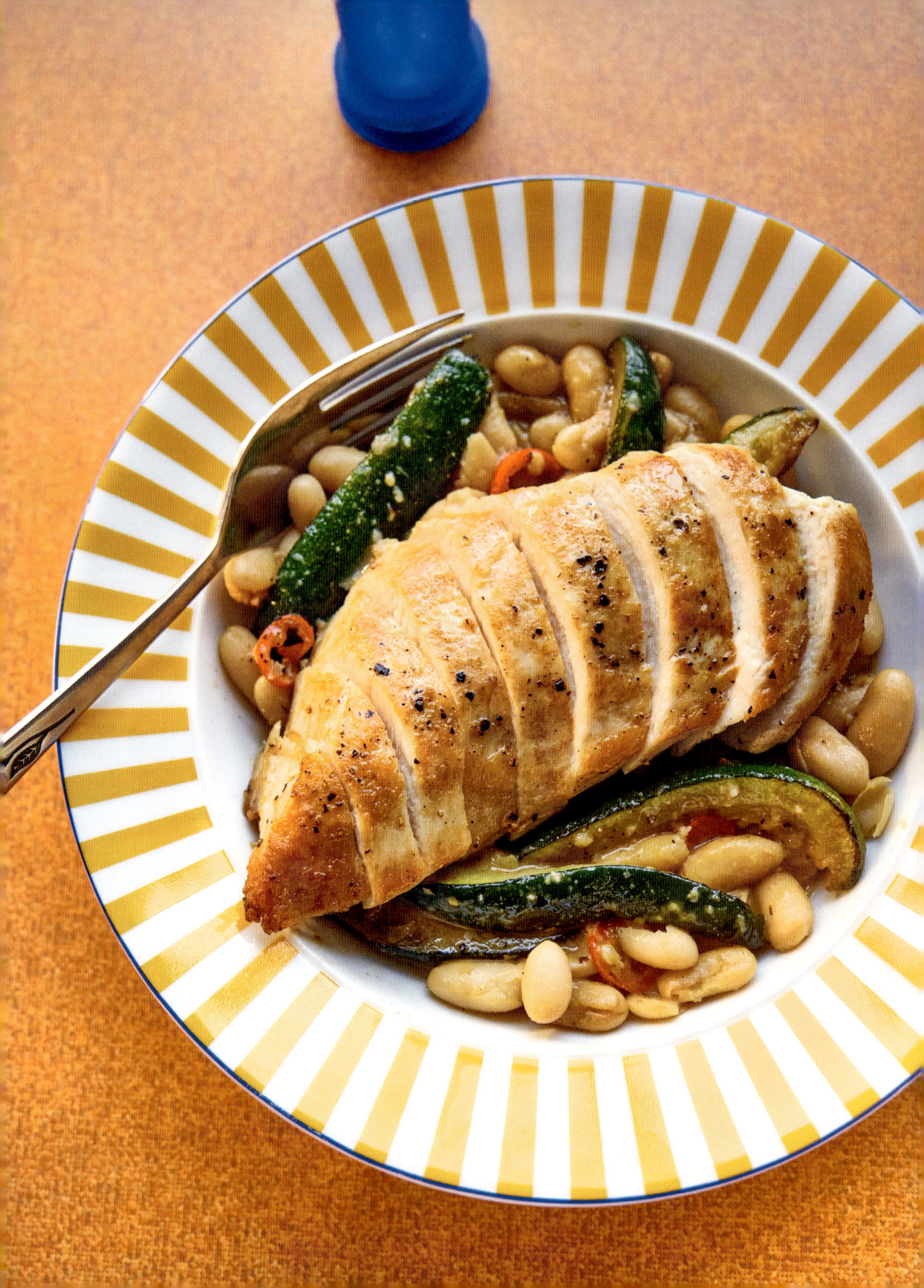

PREP TIME. 5 MINUTES / **COOK TIME.** 15-20 MINUTES / **SERVES.** 2

FOOD IN A FLASH

One word here – comfort. A beautiful stew, super healthy and nourishing and packed with goodness. It's also got a big punch of protein if you're after those gains!

Pan-Fried Chicken Breast
+ a Zucchini & Bean Stew

① Preheat your oven to 350°F (180°C).

② Top and tail the zucchini and cut them into small wedges. Thinly slice your chilli and garlic and weigh out the chicken stock, white wine and butter.

③ Place a frying pan over high heat with 1 tablespoon of vegetable oil. Season the chicken with salt and pepper on both sides and once the pan is nice and hot, cook the chicken for 3 minutes on one side or until it is nice and golden brown.

④ Flip the chicken over and cook for a further minute before adding half of the butter. Allow the butter to melt and spoon it over the chicken breasts. Transfer the chicken breasts to a roasting pan (pouring any butter from the pan over the chicken) and finish the cooking in the oven for 7–10 minutes, or until cooked through.

⑤ Place the pan back on the heat with the other tablespoon of vegetable oil and add in the zucchini. Season with salt and pepper and cook for 2–3 minutes, or until it is nice and golden.

⑥ Add the chilli and garlic and cook for 1 minute before adding in the drained cannellini beans, wine and chicken stock. Bring it up to a boil and reduce the liquid until the sauce can coat the back of a spoon.

⑦ Finish it with the remaining butter, stirring until the butter has melted and thickened the sauce, then squeeze in the juice of half the lemon and season with salt and pepper.

⑧ Pile the gorgeous zucchini and bean stew onto two plates, carve your chicken and place on top. Garnish with a wedge of lemon and enjoy.

2 small or 1 large zucchini
½ red chilli
2 cloves of garlic
½ cup chicken stock
2 tbsp white wine (optional but highly recommended)
3 tbsp butter
2 tbsp vegetable oil
2 chicken breasts
1 x 15.5 oz (439 g) can of cannellini beans
1 lemon
Sea salt and black pepper

SERVES. 4 / **PREP TIME.** 15 MINUTES / **COOK TIME.** 35 MINUTES

FOOD IN A FLASH

Spicy, packed with veg and ready in a flash, this is the perfect low-effort, big-flavor meal that will knock your socks off. Definitely one to add to the weekly meal plan.

JERK CHICKEN TRAY BAKE + a BROCCOLI & CORN SALAD

1. Preheat your oven to 400°F (200°C).
2. Put the vegetable oil and the jerk seasoning into a bowl and mix to combine.
3. Roughly chop your red onions, then arrange on a large baking sheet with the chicken and pour over the marinade. Get your hands in there and mix it up to make sure the seasoning is evenly spread.
4. Season the chicken with salt and pepper on both sides and bake in the oven skin side up and for 25–30 minutes, or until the chicken is cooked through.
5. For the broccoli and corn salad, chop the broccoli into little bite-sized florets and put them into a bowl with the corn. Thinly slice the spring onions and add them along with the crème fraîche. Season with salt, pepper and the lemon juice. Mix it to combine and set aside.
6. Once the chicken is cooked, take out and turn the oven to its highest broiler setting. Broil the chicken for 3–4 minutes, or until you get lovely crispy skin.
7. Pile the salad onto each plate. Top with the chicken and onions and don't forget to spoon over all the lovely roasting juices from the pan.

6 tbsp vegetable oil
3 tbsp jerk seasoning
3 red onions
2 lb (1 kg) chicken thighs and drumsticks, skin on and bone in
1 large broccoli
3 spring onions
¾ cup corn kernels
4 oz (113 ml) crème fraîche
Juice of ½ lemon
Sea salt and black pepper

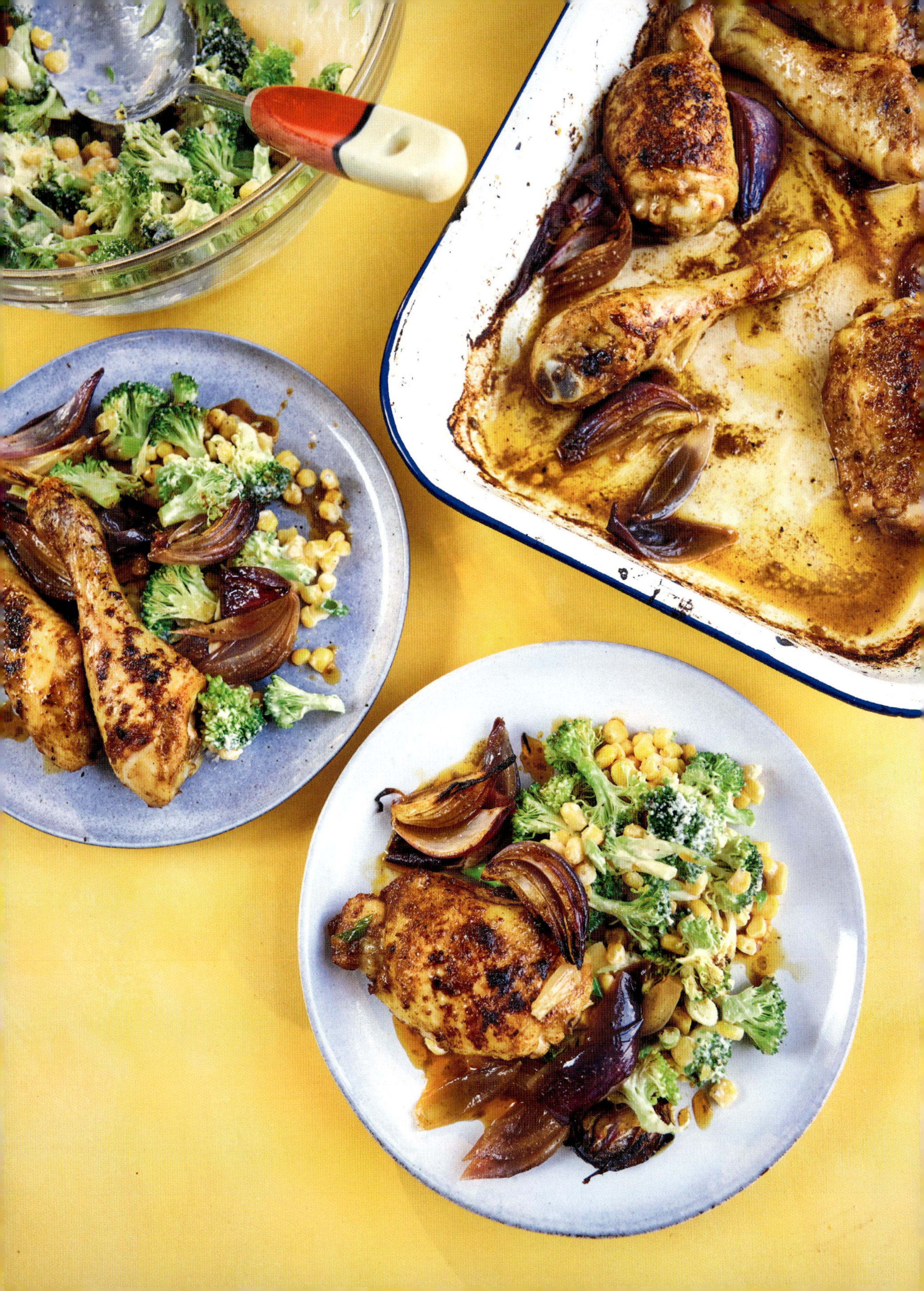

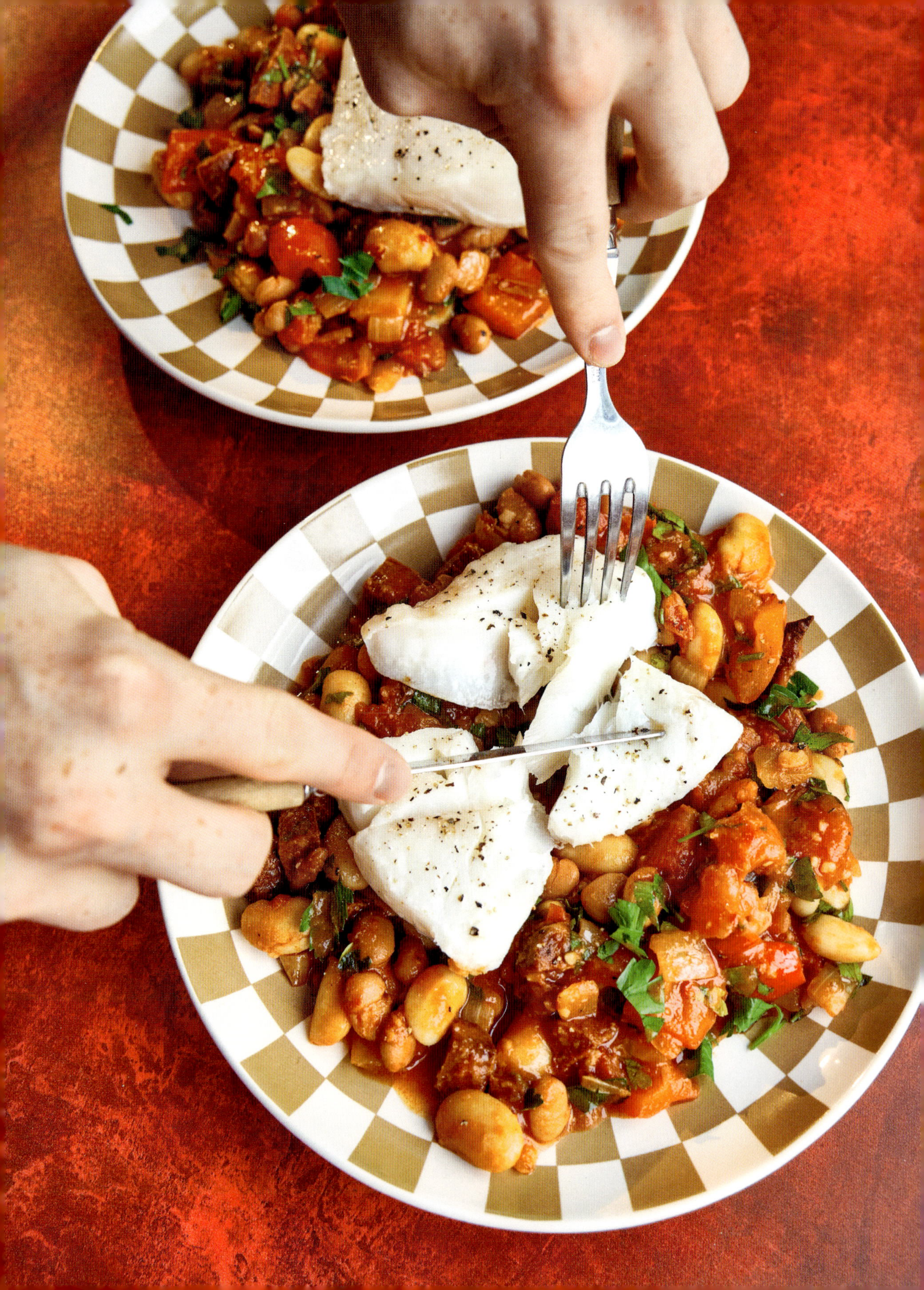

PREP TIME. 10 MINUTES / **COOK TIME.** 20 MINUTES / **SERVES.** 4

FOOD IN A FLASH

A great, quick meal that keeps on giving. Any leftovers can be given a quick makeover by topping with a fried egg for a banging breakfast the next day.

ROASTED COD + a spicy sausage cassoulet

1. Preheat your oven to 350°F (180°C).
2. Remove the skin of the chorizo and roughly chop. Put into a cold saucepan and place on a medium to low heat for 5 minutes, or until the chorizo is sizzling and the oil has rendered out of it.
3. In the meantime, you can roughly dice the bell peppers and onion and mince your garlic.
4. Add all the veggies in with the chorizo, season with salt, pepper, paprika and chilli flakes, and cook down for 5 more minutes.
5. While the veg softens, we can pat the fish dry with some kitchen paper. Drizzle with the vegetable oil and season with salt and pepper on each side.
6. Once the veg is softened, add in the drained beans, along with the chopped tomatoes and ¾ cup of water. Mix to combine and simmer for 10 minutes.
7. Place the fish on a baking pan and bake for 8–10 minutes. You'll know it's cooked when the fish flakes when pressed.
8. Finally, check the seasoning of the cassoulet, add in the chopped parsley and serve up with the fish on top.

1 ring of chorizo
1 red bell pepper
1 yellow bell pepper
1 onion
2 cloves of garlic
1 tbsp smoked paprika
1 tsp chilli flakes
4 cod fillets, skinless
2 tbsp vegetable oil
1 x 15.5oz (439 g) can of pinto beans, drained
1 x 15.5oz (439 g) can of butter beans, drained
1 x 15.5oz (439 g) can of chopped tomatoes
Handful of chopped parsley
Sea salt and black pepper

FOOD IN A FLASH

SERVES. 4   **PREP TIME.** 10 MINUTES / **COOK TIME.** 30 MINUTES

Sure, veggies will love this dish, but carnivores need to get on board, too. You can absolutely make your own béchamel (see page 26 for the recipe) but there's no shame in buying a jar if time is against you.

Spinach & Mushroom Tart

① Preheat your oven to 350°F (180°C).

② Quarter the mushrooms and mince the garlic.

③ Pour the vegetable oil into a large saucepan and, once hot, add in the mushrooms. Season with salt and pepper and cook for 3 minutes until golden brown. Add the garlic and fry for 30 seconds, then add in the spinach and cook for a further minute, stirring until just wilted.

④ Taste and season the mushroom and spinach mixture and then tip it into a sieve. Use the back of a wooden spoon to push out any excess water from the spinach as this will dilute the flavor and lead to soggy pastry.

⑤ Unravel the puff pastry and, keeping it on the paper it came in, place it onto a large baking sheet. Using a knife, make a small incision to form a border about 1–1 ½ inch (2–3 cm) from the outside, being careful not to cut all the way through the pastry. Prick the pastry within the border with a fork in about ten places.

⑥ Spread all of the béchamel onto the base of the pastry (within the border) and season with salt and pepper. Sprinkle over the grated Parmesan.

⑦ Top with the drained mushroom and spinach mixture and bake for 20–25 minutes.

⑧ In the meantime, you have plenty of time to clean down the kitchen and dress the rocket in some olive oil.

⑨ Once the tart is golden brown and cooked through, garnish with the rocket and enjoy this lovely meal.

10 oz (275 g) chestnut mushrooms
2 cloves of garlic
2 tbsp vegetable oil
7 oz (200 g) spinach, washed
1 x 14 oz (396 g) package of ready-rolled puff pastry
½ cup white sauce from a jar or Sam's Béchamel Sauce (see page 26)
1½ oz (50 g) Parmesan cheese, grated
Handful of arugula
1 tbsp olive oil
Sea salt and black pepper

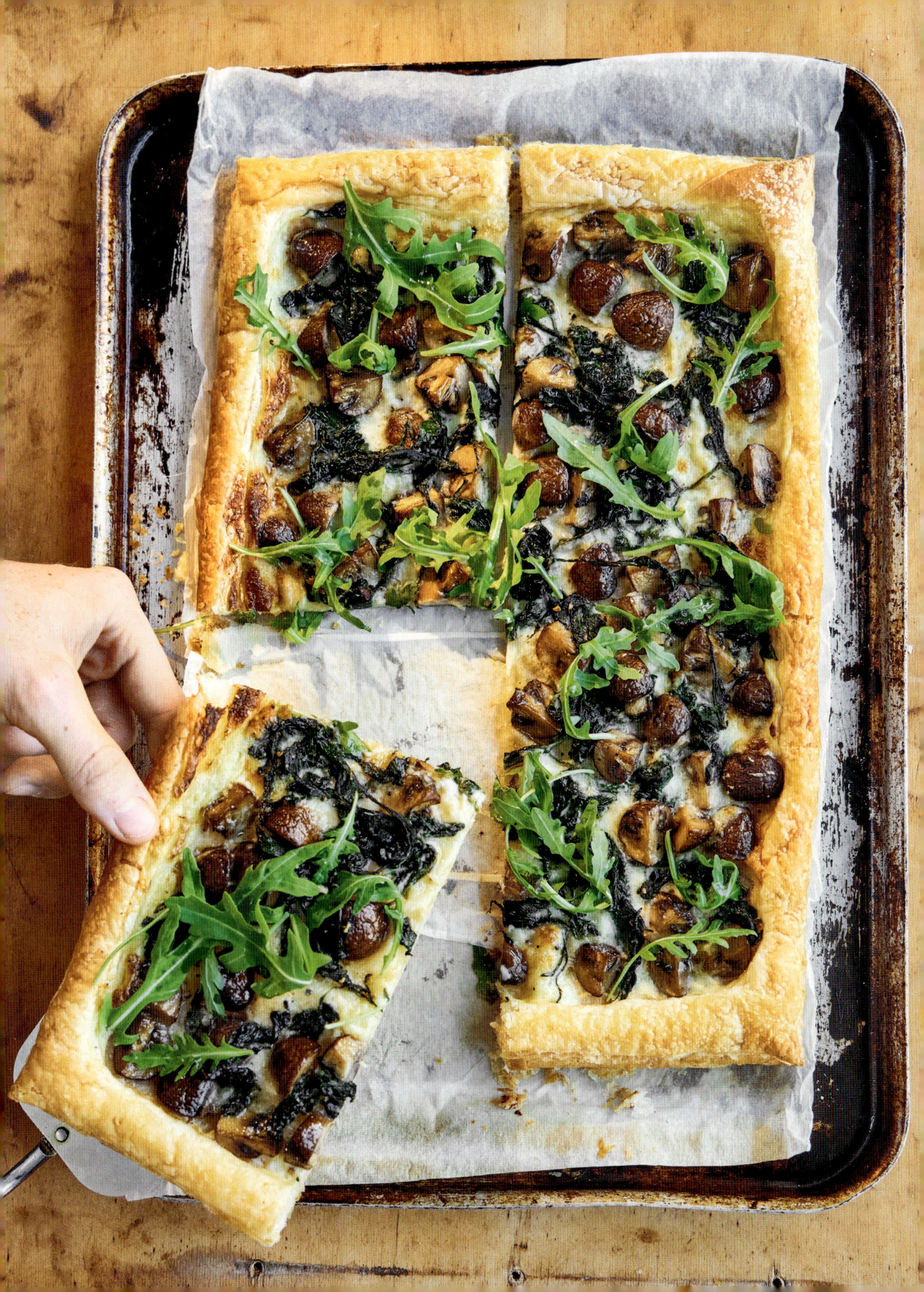

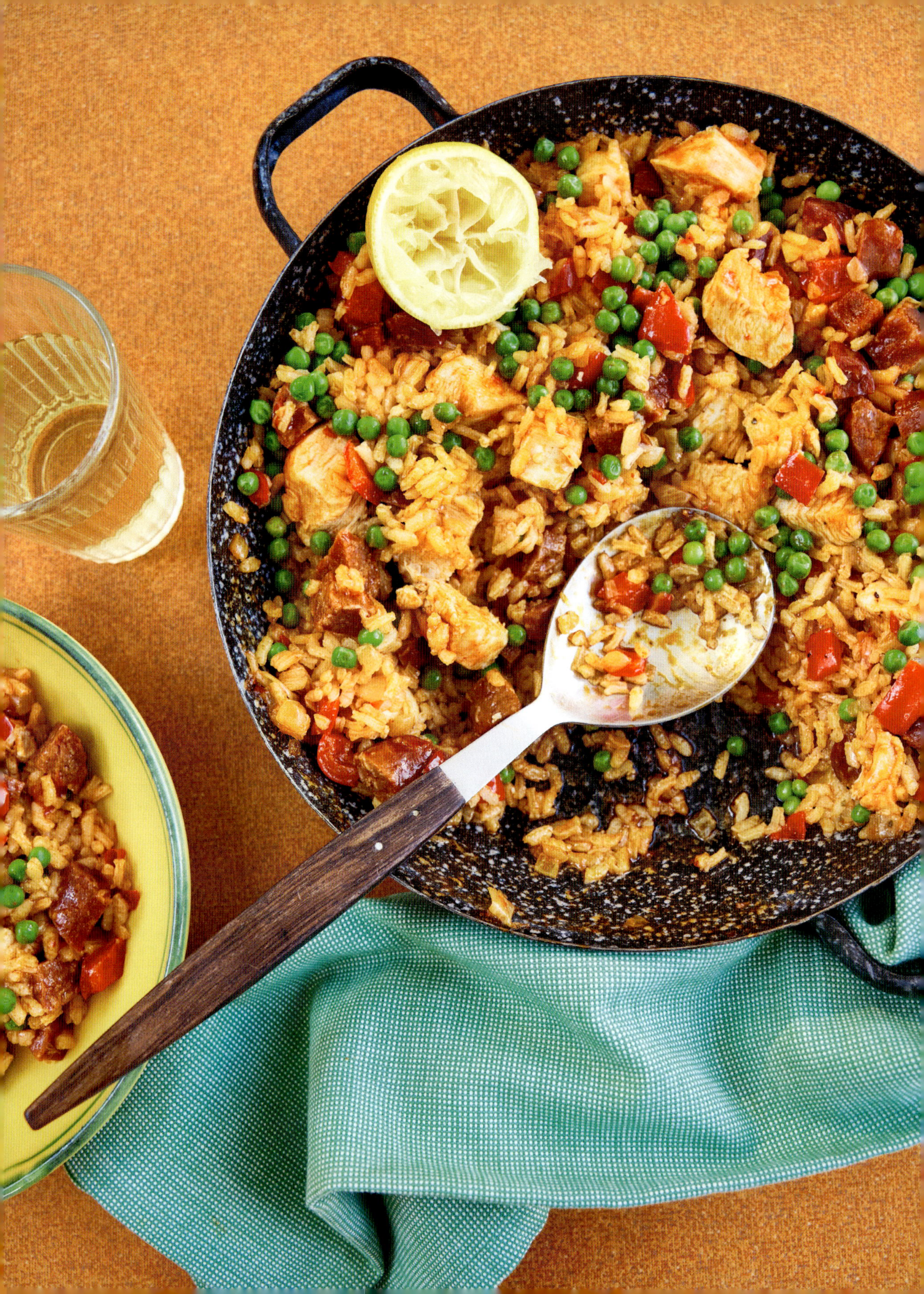

PREP TIME. 15 MINUTES / **COOK TIME.** 20 MINUTES / **SERVES.** 4

FOOD IN A FLASH

A classic dish that is packed with huge flavors and is sure to cause appreciative gasps and spontaneous rounds of applause (probably). We've steered free of seafood here to keep the cost down, but chicken and chorizo bring all the Spanish sunshine anyway. A fiesta and then a siesta. Nice.

Chicken & Chorizo Paella

① Remove the skin of the chorizo and dice it up along with the onion and red bell pepper. Place a large saucepan over medium heat, pour in the vegetable oil and add in the chorizo, onion and red pepper. Season with salt and pepper and cook for 5 minutes.

② Mince the garlic and dice the chilli and add them into the saucepan along with the rice, paprika and tomato paste. Cook this off for 1 minute, stirring continuously.

③ Pour in the chicken stock and bring to a boil. Simmer for 5 minutes.

④ Cut the chicken into bite-sized pieces and add it to the paella. Reduce the paella to a simmer and cook, stirring occasionally, for a further 8 minutes or until the chicken is cooked and the rice is just tender.

⑤ Add in the peas and the lemon juice and cook for a further 2 minutes. Taste, season with salt and pepper and serve up.

1 ring of spicy chorizo
1 white onion
1 red bell pepper
1 tbsp vegetable oil
3 cloves of garlic
½ red chilli
1⅓ cup paella rice
1 tbsp paprika
1 tbsp tomato paste
2¼ cup chicken stock
3 chicken breasts
1 cup frozen peas
Juice of ½ lemon
Sea salt and black pepper

SERVES. 6 / **PREP TIME.** 10 MINUTES / **COOK TIME.** 20 MINUTES

FOOD IN A FLASH

Fish pie rocks but boy it's a faff. Too many steps and too many pans. So, here's my cheat version to make everything easy and just as tasty-tastic.

Speedy Fish Pie

① Chop the woody ends off the leek and slice down the middle. Remove the outer layer and rinse under some running water to remove any dirt. Thinly slice and put into a saucepan over medium heat with the vegetable oil. Season with salt and cook for 8 minutes, stirring occasionally to prevent it from burning.

② Once soft, add in all the white sauce and bring to a boil.

③ Season the fish with salt and pepper, add it to the sauce and simmer for 2–3 minutes, until the fish is just cooked. If the sauce seems a little too thick, then add a splash of milk.

④ Add in the cheese, taste and season and place the mix into an ovenproof dish.

⑤ Add the melted butter and a splash of milk to the mash in its tray and give it a good mix with a spoon until it is smooth and creamy.

⑥ Preheat the broiler to medium-high.

⑦ Spoon the mash over the pie and spread it out. Place it under the broiler for 5–10 minutes until it's golden brown and crispy.

1 leek
1 tbsp vegetable oil
1 x 15 oz (425 g) jar of white sauce or 1 batch of Sam's Béchamel Sauce (see page 26)
2 x 12 oz (340 g) packages of fish pie mix
Splash or 2 of milk
1½ oz (50 g) Cheddar cheese, grated
2 tbsp butter, melted
5½ cup prepared mashed potatoes or my Mash (see page 28)
Sea salt and black pepper

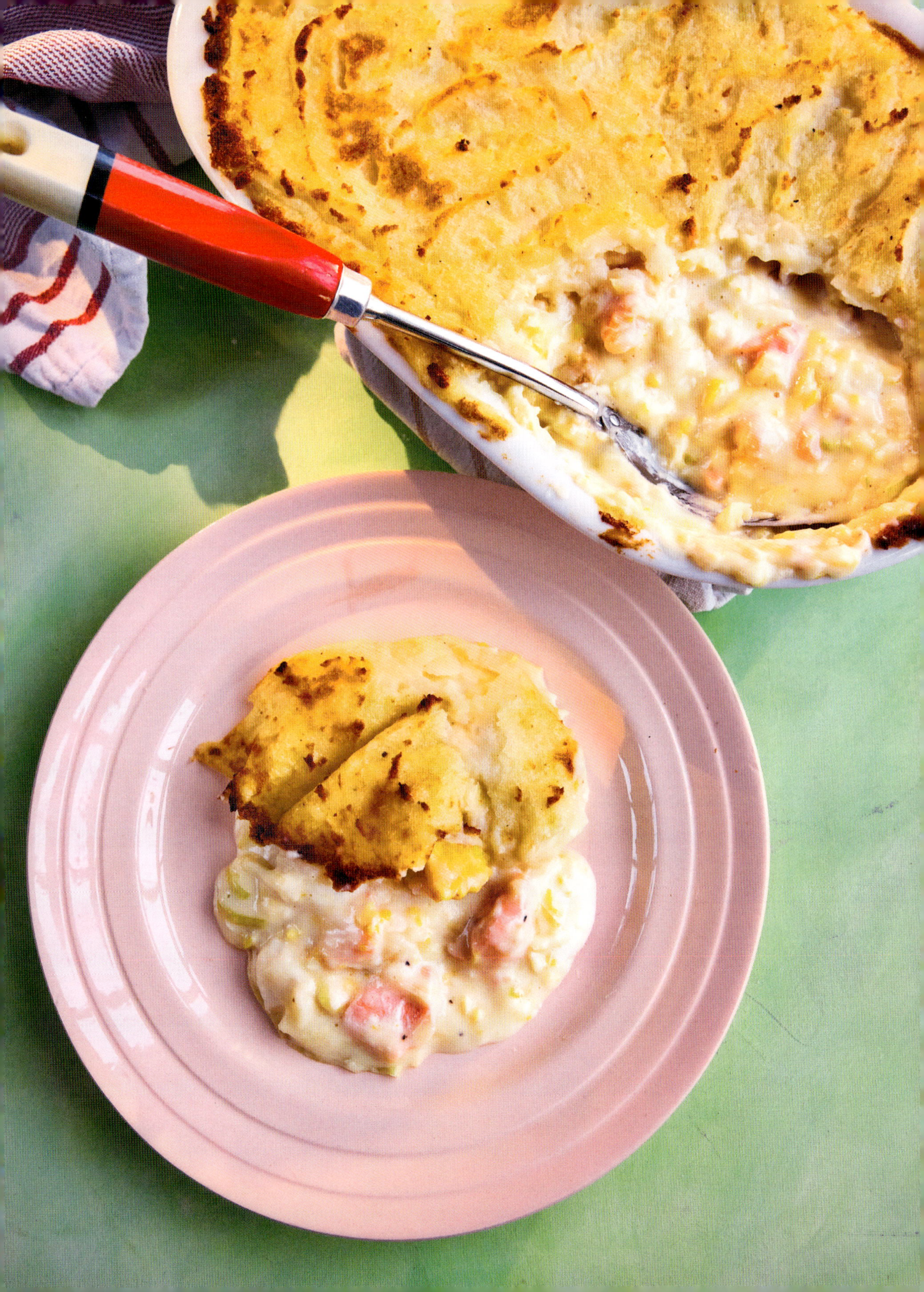

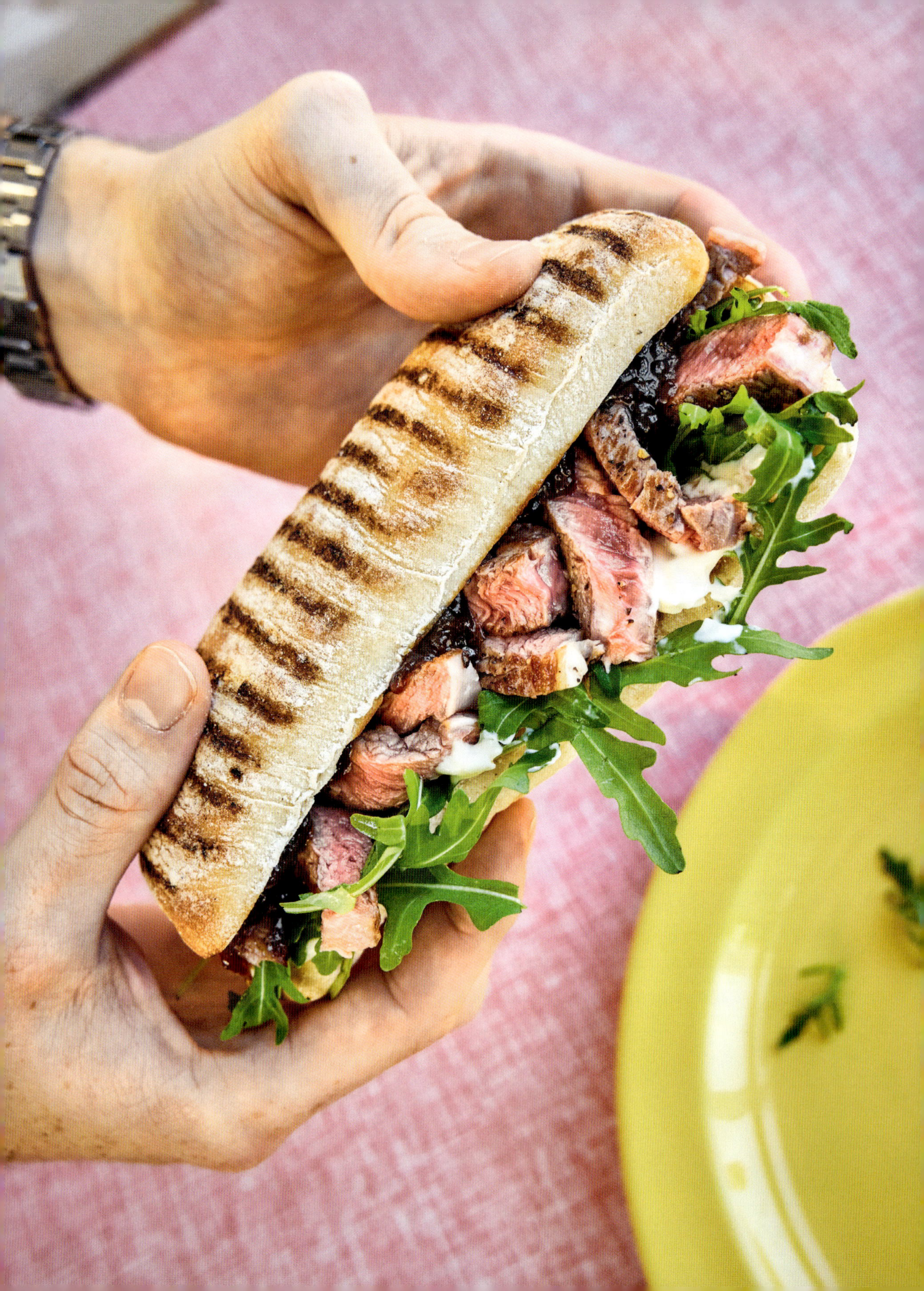

PREP TIME. 5 MINUTES / **COOK TIME.** 5 MINUTES / **SERVES.** 2

FOOD IN A FLASH

Steak doesn't need to be expensive. Minute steak works fine here and if you treat it nicely, you'll get the luxury of a more expensive cut. Top Tip: It is essential that your steak is at room temperature before cooking. Remove from the fridge at least half an hour before cooking, to ensure a great sear and caramelization.

Steak Sandwich

2 tbsp mayonnaise
1 tsp horseradish sauce
2 panini or ciabatta loaves
1 medium sirloin steak (roughly ½ in [1 cm]) or 2 thin sirloin steaks
1 tbsp vegetable oil
5 tbsp caramelized onion chutney
Handful of arugula
Sea salt and black pepper

① Preheat the oven to 325°F (160°C).

② Combine the mayo and horseradish sauce.

③ Halve the panini or ciabatta loaves and toast in the oven for 10 minutes.

④ Season the steak with salt and pepper and preheat your frying pan over high heat.

⑤ Pour in the oil and once it's smoking, cook the steak for 90 seconds on each side (if using a smaller, thinner steak, cook for 45 seconds on each side). Rest on a chopping board for 3–5 minutes.

⑥ Spread the horseradish mayo on the base of the sandwich and spread the chutney on the top half of the bread.

⑦ Carve the steak and place into the sandwiches before topping with the rocket.

SERVES. 2 / **PREP TIME.** 20 MINUTES / **COOK TIME.** 12–15 MINUTES

FOOD IN A FLASH

I call this dish a no-conversation meal because everyone is too busy eating to talk! It has the perfect balance of flavors and textures: sweet, salty, spicy. A guaranteed conversation killer, so ideal for dining with people you don't like!

Sesame Soy Chicken

1 red bell pepper
½ red onion
1 thumb-sized piece of fresh ginger
3 cloves of garlic
2 spring onions
1 tbsp sesame seeds, plus extra for garnish
¼ cup light soy sauce
¼ cup light brown sugar
1½ tbsp ketchup
1 tbsp cornstarch
2 chicken breasts
3 tbsp vegetable oil
Cooked rice, to serve (see page 22)

1. Start off by getting all the prep out of the way. Thinly slice the red bell pepper and red onion, place in one bowl and set aside. Grate the ginger and garlic, place in a second bowl and set aside. Thinly slice the spring onions and place in a third bowl, add the sesame seeds and set aside.

2. Put the soy sauce, brown sugar, ketchup, 3 tablespoons of water and the cornstarch into a bowl, mix to combine then set aside.

3. Chop the chicken into bite-sized chunks.

4. Pour 2 tablespoons of the vegetable oil into a screaming-hot frying pan and cook your chicken for 3–4 minutes. Once golden brown and cooked through, remove from the pan and set aside.

5. Add the other tablespoon of oil into the pan and add the red bell pepper and red onion. Stir-fry for 1 minute. Add in the ginger and garlic and cook for a further 30 seconds.

6. Pour in the sauce, lower the heat to medium and let it reduce for around 3–5 minutes until it's nice and sticky.

7. Finally, add the cooked chicken back in with the spring onions and sesame seeds. Give it one final mix, garnish with some extra sesame seeds and serve with rice.

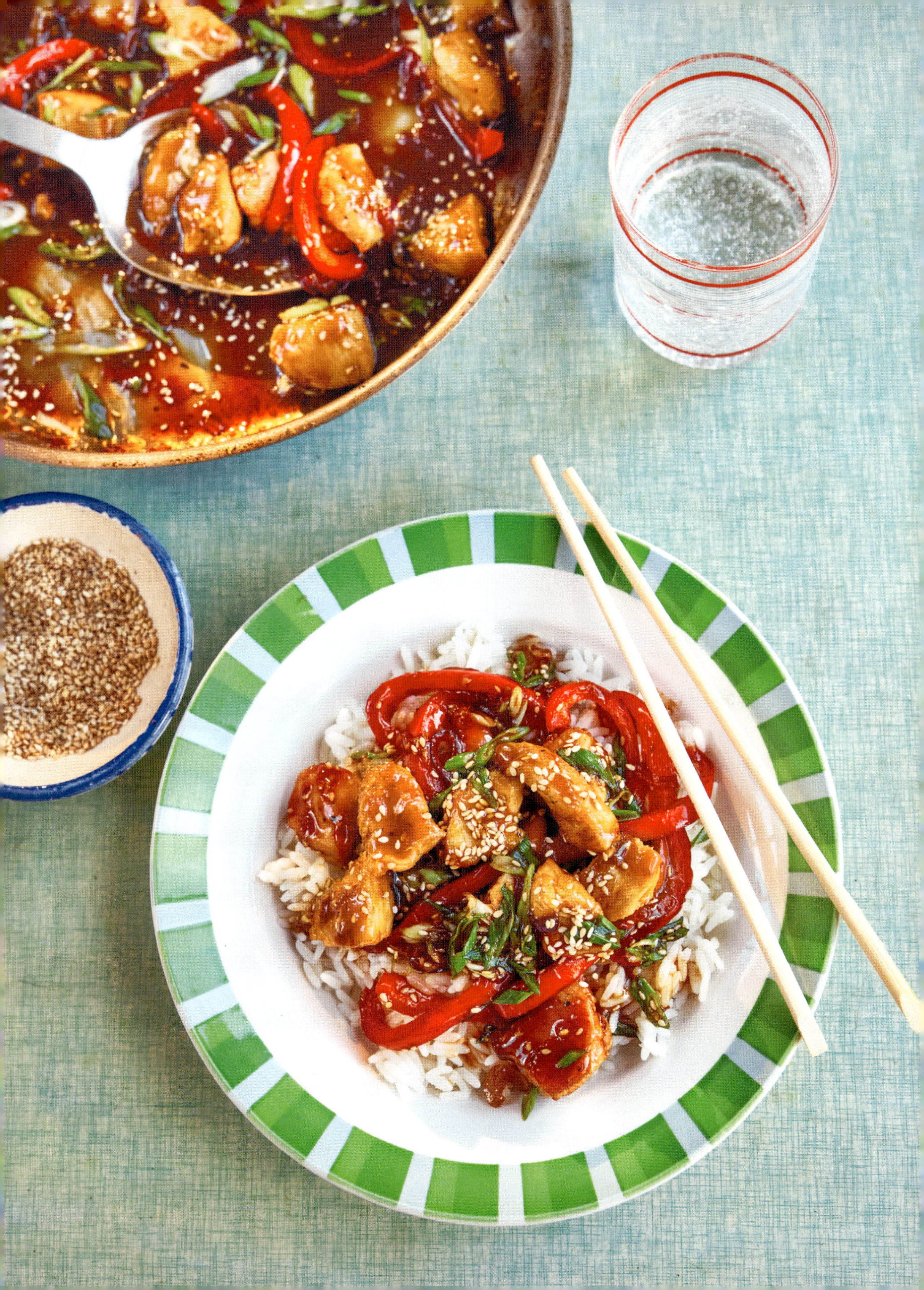

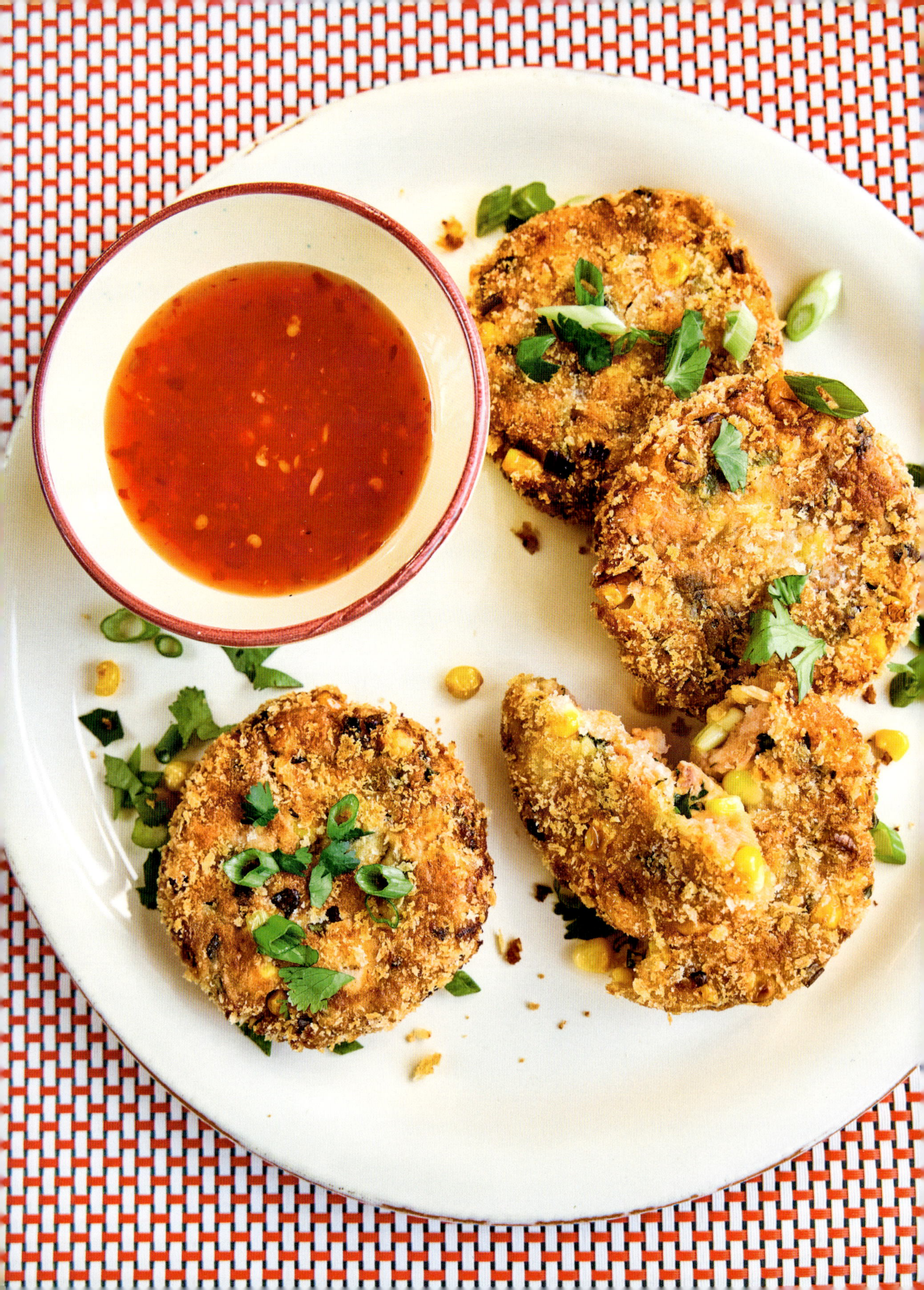

PREP TIME. 20 MINUTES / **COOK TIME.** 5 MINUTES / **MAKES.** 6 (A GOOD-SIZED LUNCH FOR 2)

FOOD IN A FLASH

Throwing food away is like throwing money away and it's not good for the conscience or the planet either. This is a great way of using up any leftover mashed potatoes and has the added bonus of being super tasty, too!

Thai Tuna & Sweetcorn Fishcakes

① Put the mash in a bowl along with the curry paste, tuna, flour and drained sweetcorn.

② Finely slice the spring onions and cilantro. Save one-third of the spring onions and cilantro for garnish and add the rest into the mashed potatoes. Finally, add the lime zest and juice, season generously with salt and pepper and mix to combine.

③ Lightly flour the chopping board and drop six blobs of the mix onto it. With a slightly damp hand, press down on the fishcakes to flatten and form round patties about ½ inch (1 cm) thick.

④ Put the breadcrumbs in a shallow bowl or plate and press each fishcake into the breadcrumbs until it is well coated.

⑤ Preheat a large frying pan over high heat and pour in the vegetable oil. Once hot, gently lower each fritter into the hot oil. Leave to cook for 2 minutes on each side, or until golden brown all over.

⑥ Once golden brown on each side, place on a tray with a sheet of kitchen paper to remove any excess oil. Serve with some sweet chilli sauce on the side, the rest of the lime cut into wedges and garnish with the remaining cilantro and spring onions.

¾ cup leftover prepared mashed potatoes or my Mash (see page 28)

3 heaped tbsp Thai red curry paste

1 x 5 oz (141 g) can of tuna

½ cup all-purpose flour, plus extra for dusting

3½ oz (100 g) canned sweetcorn, drained

5 spring onions

Small handful of cilantro

2 limes (zest of 2, juice of ½), plus wedges to garnish

½ cup breadcrumbs (I used panko)

5 tbsp vegetable oil

Sweet chilli sauce, to serve

Sea salt and black pepper

Fakeaway

FAVORiTeS

We all crave a takeaway from time to time. Even when our bank balance is saying no, our hearts and our tastebuds are saying yes! When that happens, come straight to this chapter I guarantee you will thank me. With these simple recipes, you can even make a night of it with friends. Serve up everything from Butter Chicken, Speedy Pizzas and Piri Piri Chicken Burgers to Movie Night Nachos and more.

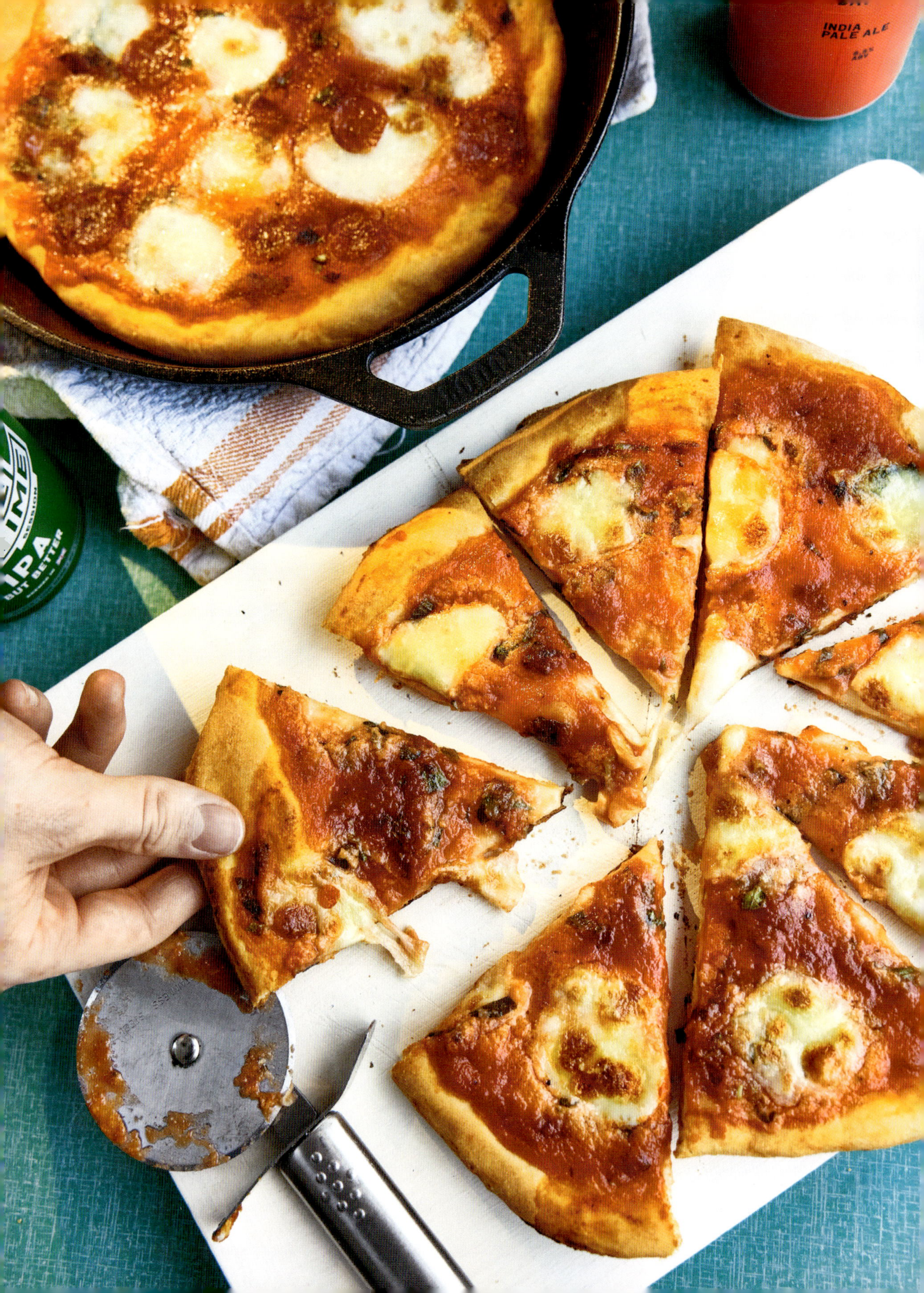
INDIA PALE ALE
IPA
BUT BETTER

PREP TIME. 15 MINUTES / **COOK TIME.** 15 MINUTES / **SERVES.** 2 X 10-INCH (25 CM) PIZZAS

FAKEAWAY FAVORITES

There's a reason that pizza is the world's most popular dish, but making the dough from scratch can mean hours and hours of prep. This clever recipe swaps out the yeast for self-rising flour instead, meaning you can whip up wicked pizzas in barely 30 minutes.

Speedy Pizza

① Preheat the oven to 400°F (200°C).

② Mix the flour, yogurt and 1 tablespoon of the olive oil together until it forms a rough dough. If it's too dry, add in a few tablespoons of water to bring it together.

③ Transfer the dough to a lightly-floured worktop and knead for a couple of minutes until it's nice and smooth. Place into a clean bowl and set aside while you prep everything else.

④ For the sauce, just combine the passata, 1 tablespoon of the olive oil, garlic and fresh basil. Mix it up and season with salt and pepper.

⑤ Cut your mozzarella into small pieces, patting them dry on a piece of kitchen paper and prep the toppings of your choice.

⑥ Preheat a large frying pan (a 10-inch (25 cm) pan is ideal) over high heat.

⑦ Cut the dough in half and roll out one piece as thin as possible to match the size of your frying pan.

⑧ Place the dough into the frying pan and spread on the tomato sauce, leaving a ½-inch (1 cm) border around the edge. Top with the mozzarella, sprinkle over the Parmesan and add the toppings of your choice. Use a pastry brush or a bit of paper towel dipped in olive oil to brush a little oil onto the crust around the edge.

⑨ Use a spatula to lift up the pizza and once the bottom is nice and golden brown, slide it either directly onto the wire rack of the oven or onto a large baking tray and cook for 10 minutes until the mozzarella has melted and the crust is golden. Repeat with the remaining piece of dough.

---

2 ⅓ cup self-rising flour

⅔ cup Greek yogurt

2 tbsp olive oil

⅔ cup tomato passata

½ clove of garlic, minced

Bunch of basil, roughly chopped

1 ball of mozzarella

Handful of grated Parmesan cheese

Sea salt and black pepper

FOR THE TOPPINGS

Salami/pepperoni

Ham and pineapple

Onions, mushrooms and peppers

Ham, olives and mushrooms

Peppers and goat's cheese

Garlic butter, mozzarella and caramelized onions

FAKEAWAY FAVORITES

SERVES. 2 **PREP TIME.** 20 MINUTES / **COOK TIME.** 20 MINUTES

Clean, healthy and packed full of goodness, a poke bowl is a choose your own flavor adventure with a difference. Use this base recipe as a starting point and add whatever else you have to hand to really make this recipe your own.

Salmon Poke Bowl

1. Place the rice into a saucepan and cover with 1 cup of water. Season with salt and bring to the boil. Once boiling, place a lid on top, turn the heat to low and simmer for 12 minutes.

2. In the meantime, dice the cucumber and mango. Thinly slice the spring onion and avocado and grate the carrot.

3. For the dressing, just combine all the ingredients together in a bowl.

4. Pat the salmon fillets dry with some kitchen paper and season with salt.

5. Pour the vegetable oil into a frying pan over medium heat and cook the salmon fillets skin side down for around 3½ minutes or until the skin is golden brown and crispy.

6. Carefully flip the salmon and cook for another 2½ minutes before adding the butter and removing from the heat.

7. Load the rice into bowls and drizzle over some of the dressing. Top with the fish and all the veggies, drizzle over any remaining dressing, squeeze over the mayonnaise and add the sriracha.

¾ cup rice
½ cucumber
1 mango
3 spring onions
½ avocado
1 carrot
2 salmon fillets
1 tbsp vegetable oil
Knob of butter
¼ cup mayonnaise
1 tbsp sriracha
Sea salt and black pepper

FOR THE DRESSING

3 tbsp light soy sauce
1½ tbsp sesame oil
1½ tbsp rice vinegar
1½ tsp sriracha
1½ tsp honey
1 clove of garlic, grated
1 thumb-sized piece of fresh ginger, grated

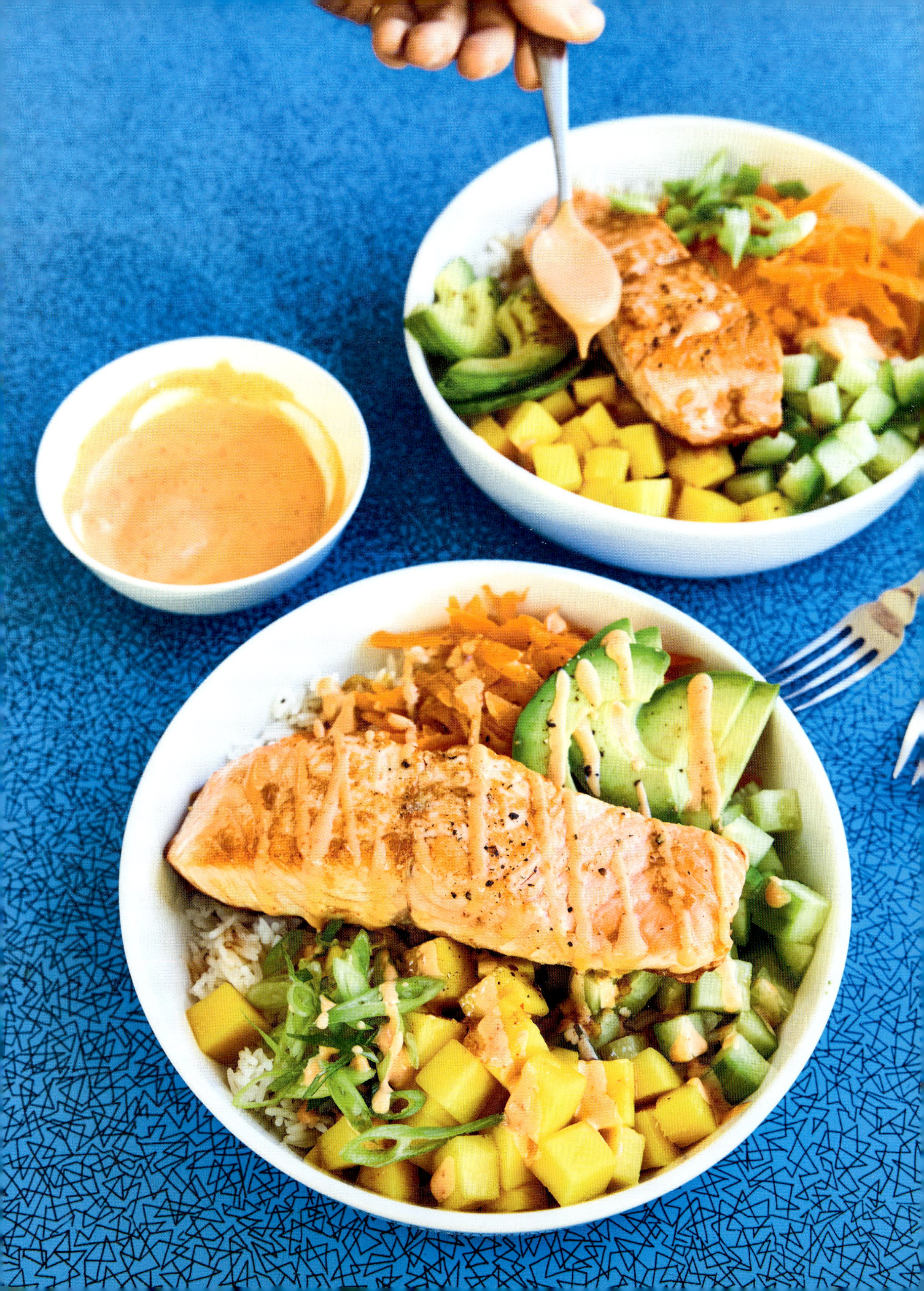

FAKEAWAY FAVORITES

SERVES. 2 **PREP TIME.** 10 MINUTES **COOK TIME.** 20 MINUTES

A great middle-of-the-table dinner for a night in with friends or family that is full of flavor but light on prep. Have recipe cards on hand because people will ask!

Cajun Chicken + Spicy Rice

① Preheat your oven to 350°F (180°C).

② Start by mixing 3 tablespoons of the vegetable oil and the Cajun seasoning. Pour this marinade onto the chicken breasts and make sure they are nicely coated. Season the chicken breasts with salt and pepper on both sides and set aside to marinate.

③ Now you can roughly dice your bell peppers and onion. Put them into a deep pan over medium heat with 2 tablespoons of the vegetable oil and salt and pepper and sweat that down.

④ After about 3 minutes of cooking, add in your minced garlic, harissa paste, tomato paste and rice and cook for a further minute.

⑤ Pour in the chicken stock and bring it up to a boil. Once boiling, lower the heat, put a lid on (or cover with a baking sheet) and simmer for 12 minutes.

⑥ Meanwhile, heat the remaining 2 tablespoons of the oil in a large frying pan over medium heat. Fry your chicken breasts for 3 minutes on each side or until you achieve a nice golden brown color all over.

⑦ Add in the butter and transfer the chicken (along with all the roasting juices) to a baking dish. Bake in the oven for 5–7 minutes, until cooked through.

⑧ Once the rice is cooked, stir in the peas to warm through, and add parsley and lemon juice.

⑨ Check for seasoning and place the chicken breasts on top of the rice. Spoon over some of the buttery juices from the chicken pan and serve it in the middle of the table for everyone to dig in.

7 tbsp vegetable oil
3 tbsp Cajun seasoning
4 chicken breasts
1 red bell pepper
1 yellow bell pepper
½ onion
2 cloves of garlic, minced
1 tsp harissa paste
1 tbsp tomato paste
1½ cup rice
2 cups chicken stock
3½ tbsp butter
⅔ cup frozen peas
Handful of chopped parsley
Juice of 1 lemon
Sea salt and black pepper

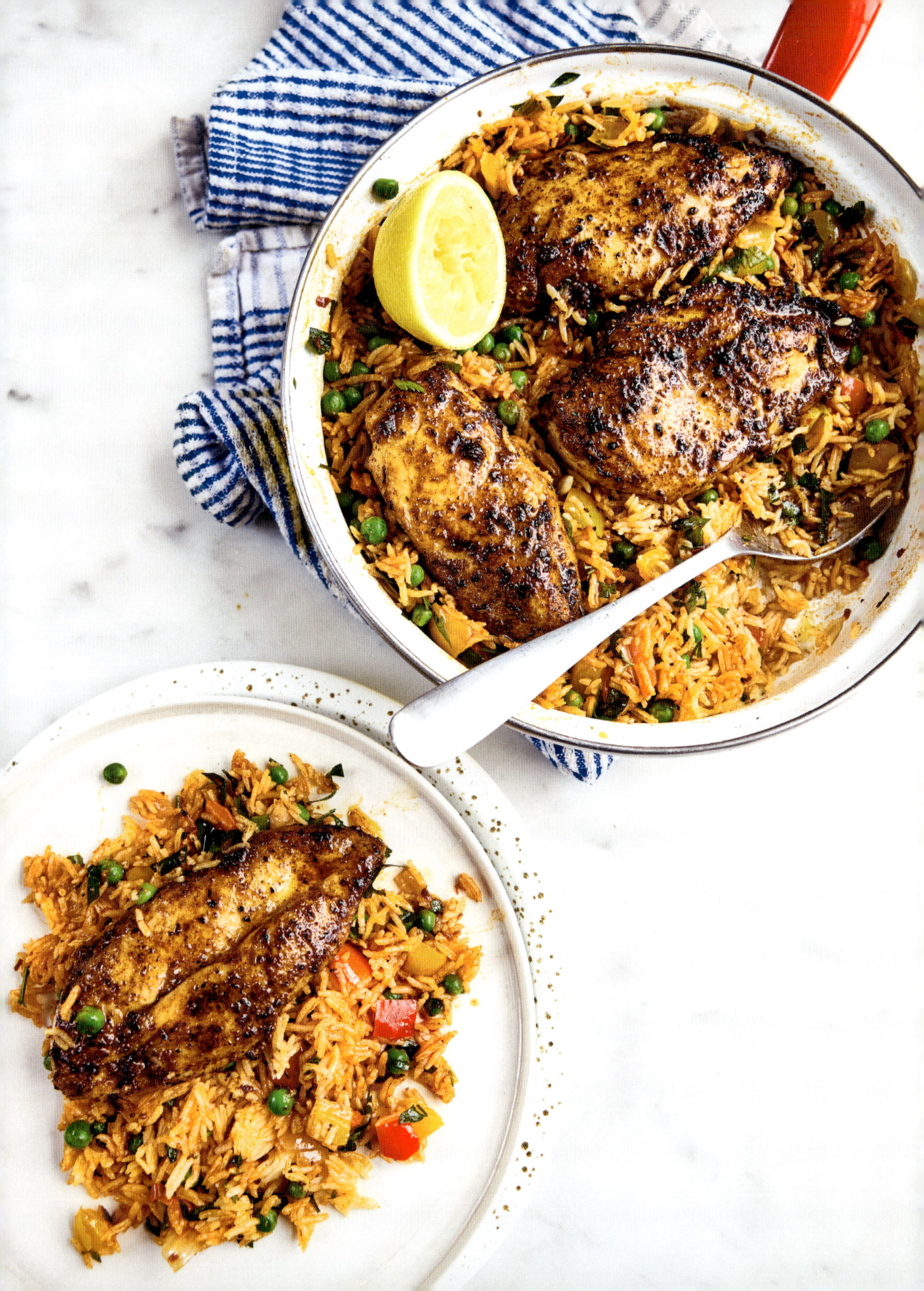

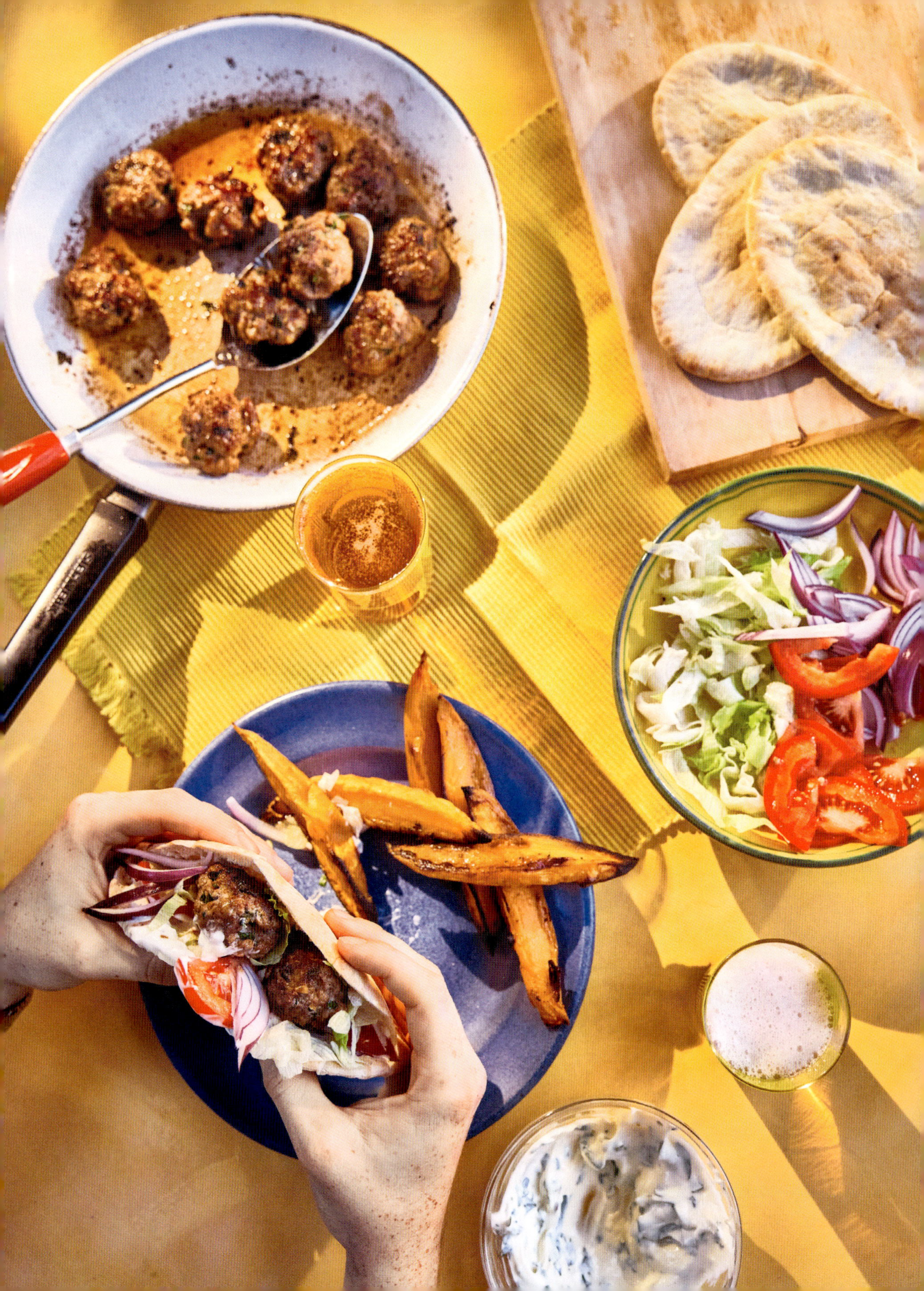

PREP TIME. 25 MINUTES / **COOK TIME.** 30 MINUTES / **SERVES.** 2 VERY HUNGRY PEOPLE

FAKEAWAY FAVORITES

A kebab is a wonderful thing that deserves more than being eaten at a bus stop at 3 a.m. Make this simple recipe at home and you'll soon be enjoying this Turkish classic on nights in just as much as nights out.

Spiced Lamb Kebab + Sweet Potato Wedges

① Preheat your oven to 425°F (220°C).

② Peel and chop your sweet potatoes into thick wedges. Drizzle them in the vegetable oil and season with salt and pepper.

③ Place onto a baking sheet and bake for 25–30 minutes, turning them once or twice, until they are cooked and starting to color.

④ In the meantime, mince the garlic, chop the parsley and set both aside.

⑤ Combine the ground lamb with all of the spices, some salt and two-thirds of the garlic and parsley, saving some for the aioli.

⑥ Once it's nicely combined, shape your ground lamb into 12 koftas (roughly 2½–3 inches [6–7 cm] long) and season them on both sides with salt and pepper.

⑦ Fry the koftas in the oil in a large frying pan over medium to high heat for 7–8 minutes, or until cooked through. Keep turning the koftas during the cooking so they brown evenly on all sides.

⑧ Quickly combine the mayonnaise with the rest of the garlic and parsley. Finely slice your tomato, red onion and lettuce.

⑨ Once the wedges are golden brown, turn the oven off and add the pitta breads for a minute or two to warm through.

⑩ To assemble, load the pita breads with lots of aioli and a couple of koftas and top with the lovely salad. Serve with the sweet potato wedges.

4 cloves of garlic
Handful of parsley
1 lb (454g) ground lamb
2 tsp ground cumin
1 tsp ground coriander
1 tsp paprika
2 tbsp vegetable oil
⅔ cup mayonnaise
1 beefsteak tomato
½ red onion
½ iceberg lettuce
4 pita breads
Sea salt and black pepper

FOR THE SWEET POTATO WEDGES

2 large sweet potatoes
2 tbsp vegetable oil

FAKEAWAY FAVORITES

SERVES. 2   **PREP TIME.** 5 MINUTES / **COOK TIME.** 15 MINUTES

The classics are classics for a reason and this one is a favorite of mine. Bacon, eggs and Parmesan all come together to make a deliciously rich, slippery coating for perfectly cooked spaghetti. Quick, easy and impressive. What's not to love?!

Spaghetti Carbonara

3½ oz (100g) spaghetti
3 eggs (1 whole egg and 2 yolks)
1½ oz (50g) Parmesan cheese, grated
3 strips of bacon (streaky or back bacon or lardons, preferably smoked)
1 tbsp vegetable oil
Sea salt and black pepper

1. Put the spaghetti into a pan of salted boiling water and use tongs to bend the spaghetti into the water. Cook according to the package instructions.

2. Put 1 whole egg along with 2 egg yolks in a small bowl. Add in the grated Parmesan and a generous pinch of black pepper. Mix to combine.

3. When the pasta is nearly cooked, slice the bacon into thin pieces and fry in a frying pan with the vegetable oil over a high heat for a few minutes until golden brown and crispy.

4. When the pasta is cooked and the bacon is crispy, use some tongs to take the pasta straight out of the water and into the pan and take off the heat.

5. Stir in the egg mixture and mix it around. If it's too thick, Add a tablespoon or two of the leftover pasta water and mix to combine until you have the desired consistency.

6. Plate up and enjoy.

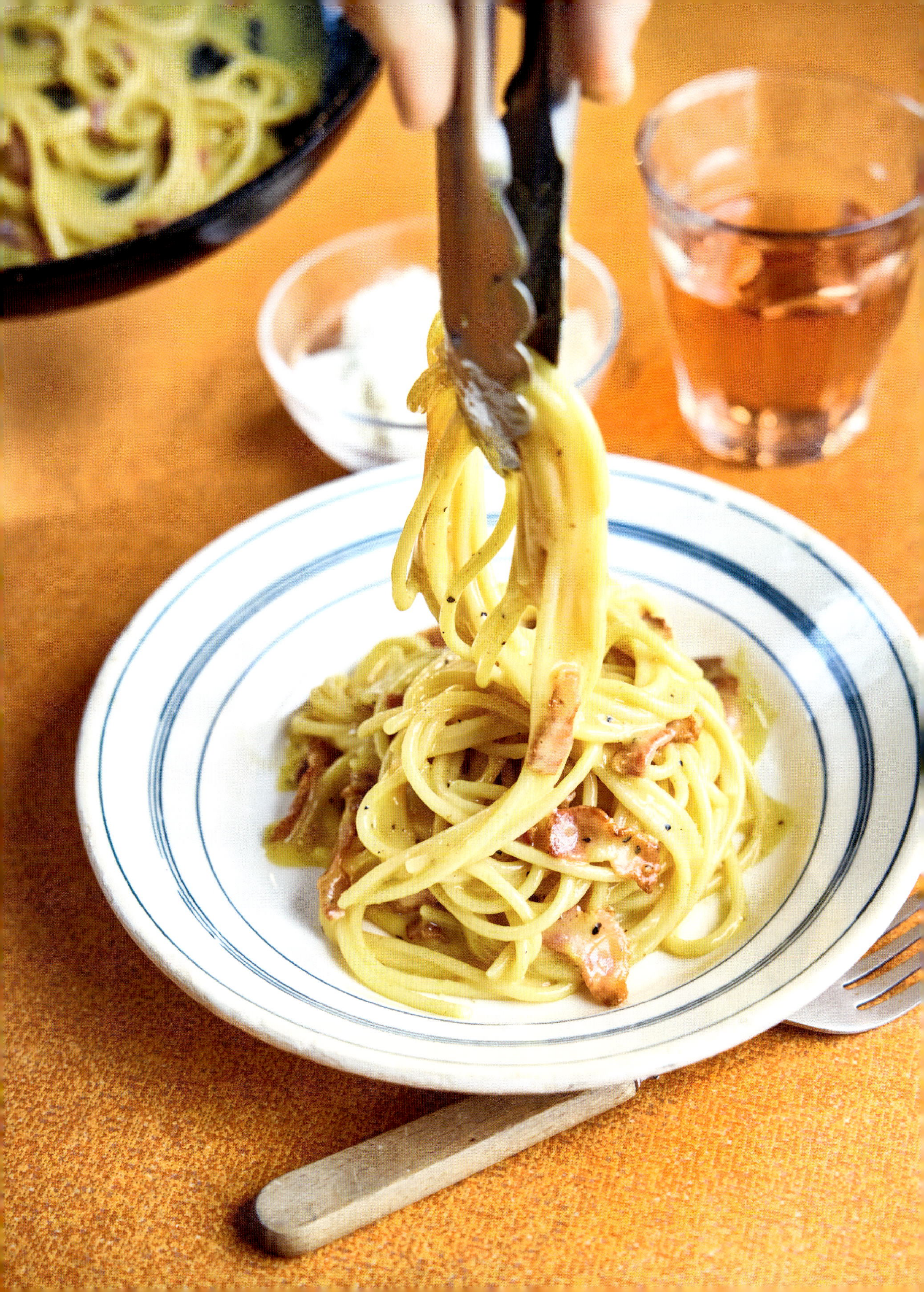

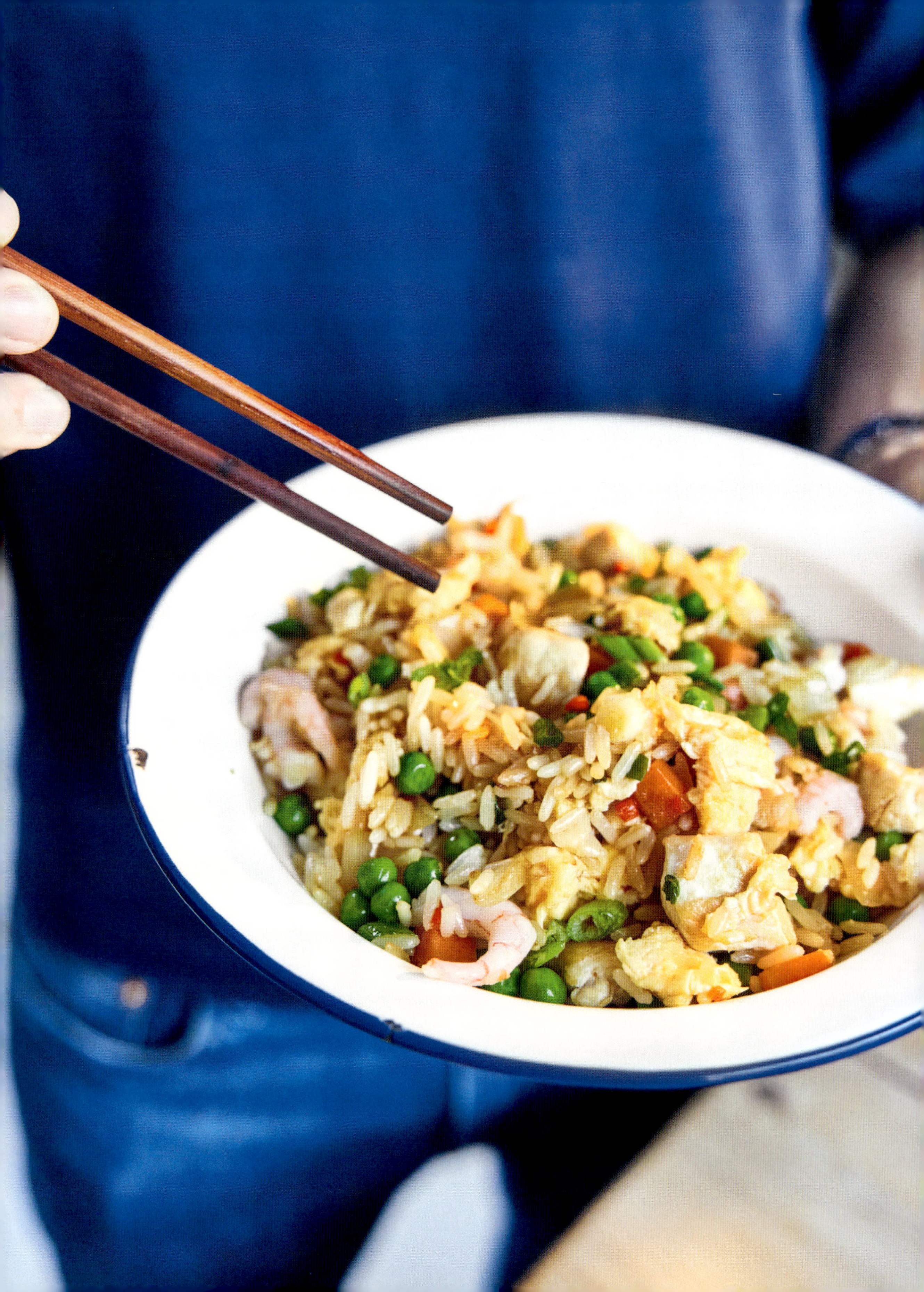

PREP TIME. 10 MINUTES / **COOK TIME.** 25 MINUTES / **SERVES.** 2

FAKEAWAY FAVORITES

It wouldn't be a Fakeaway chapter without this naughty number. A true Team Holland go-to and a great user-upper of all your leftovers. Don't be shy. Express yourself and make it your own.

Special Fried Rice

① Use leftover rice or go to page 22 for how to cook rice.

② Now, it's time for the prep. Finely dice the onion and carrot and thinly slice the spring onions. Place that all into one bowl, saving the green parts of the spring onion for garnish. Grate the ginger and garlic and dice the chilli, if using, and add to a separate bowl.

③ Finally, dice up the chicken breast into small chunks. Season with salt and preheat the wok – if you have one – or saucepan – if you don't – over high heat.

④ Pour 2 tablespoons of the vegetable oil into the wok and add the chicken. Leave it to cook for 3 minutes before pushing the chicken to one side of the pan and cracking the egg into the empty half of the pan. Scramble the egg in the pan and cook for a further minute before scooping everything out of the pan and transferring to a plate.

⑤ Pour the remaining 2 tablespoons of vegetable oil into the pan and stir-fry the vegetables for 2–3 minutes until the carrot has just started to soften. Add in the garlic, ginger and chilli and fry until fragrant (usually 30 seconds to a minute).

⑥ Now add the cooled cooked rice into the hot wok. Use a wooden spoon to break up the rice into smaller bits. Add the frozen peas and stir fry for 1–2 minutes until defrosted.

⑦ Finally, add the chicken and egg, prawns and the green parts of the spring onion along with the soy sauce and sesame oil and cook this until everything is nicely combined.

⑧ Taste and season with some more salt or soy sauce and serve.

2 ⅓ cup cooked leftover rice
½ white onion
1 carrot
3 spring onions
1 thumb-sized piece of fresh ginger
3 cloves of garlic
½ red chilli (optional)
1 chicken breast
4 tbsp vegetable oil
1 egg
½ cup frozen peas
3 oz (80g) small cooked prawns
1 tbsp light soy sauce
1 tsp sesame oil
Sea salt

SERVES. 4 | **PREP TIME.** 15 MINUTES | **COOK TIME.** 45 MINUTES

FAKEAWAY FAVORITES

Inspired by the world's most popular restaurant, this is my take on the perfect takeaway burger, layered up with all the good stuff and served with deliciously crunchy squashed potatoes.

SMASHED BURGERS + SMASHED POTATOES

1. Preheat your oven to 350°F (180°C).
2. Place your potatoes into a pan. Cover with cold water and season with salt. Simmer for 10–15 minutes, until just tender.
3. Mix the burger sauce ingredients together and set aside.
4. Dice the onion, slice your gherkins and set them aside.
5. Drain your potatoes and then, using something flat (a spatula, glass, potato masher or the bottom part of a saucepan), lightly crush the potatoes flat. You want them flattened and split open but still in one piece.
6. Put them into a roasting pan, drizzle with 4 tablespoons of the vegetable oil, season with salt and pepper and roast them in the oven for 30 minutes.
7. Split your ground beef into four balls and, just like with the potatoes, use something flat to smash them down less than ½ inch (1cm) thick. Season them with salt and pepper on both sides.
8. Once your potatoes are cooked, turn the oven off and place your burger buns inside to warm through. Now start preheating your frying pan over a high heat.
9. Once smoking, add in the remaining 2 tablespoons of oil and cook the patties for 2 minutes on one side, then give them a flip and cook until they are nicely caramelized. Add a slice of American cheese onto each patty and place a lid on top for the last minute of cooking.
10. Slather the burger sauce onto each side of the bun. Top with the burger and garnish with the gherkins and diced onion.

1 lb (454 g) new potatoes
½ white onion
2 gherkins
6 tbsp vegetable oil
1 lb (454 g) ground beef
4 burger buns
4 slices of American cheese
Sea salt and black pepper

FOR THE BURGER SAUCE
4 tbsp ketchup
4 tbsp mayonnaise
1 heaped tsp yellow mustard

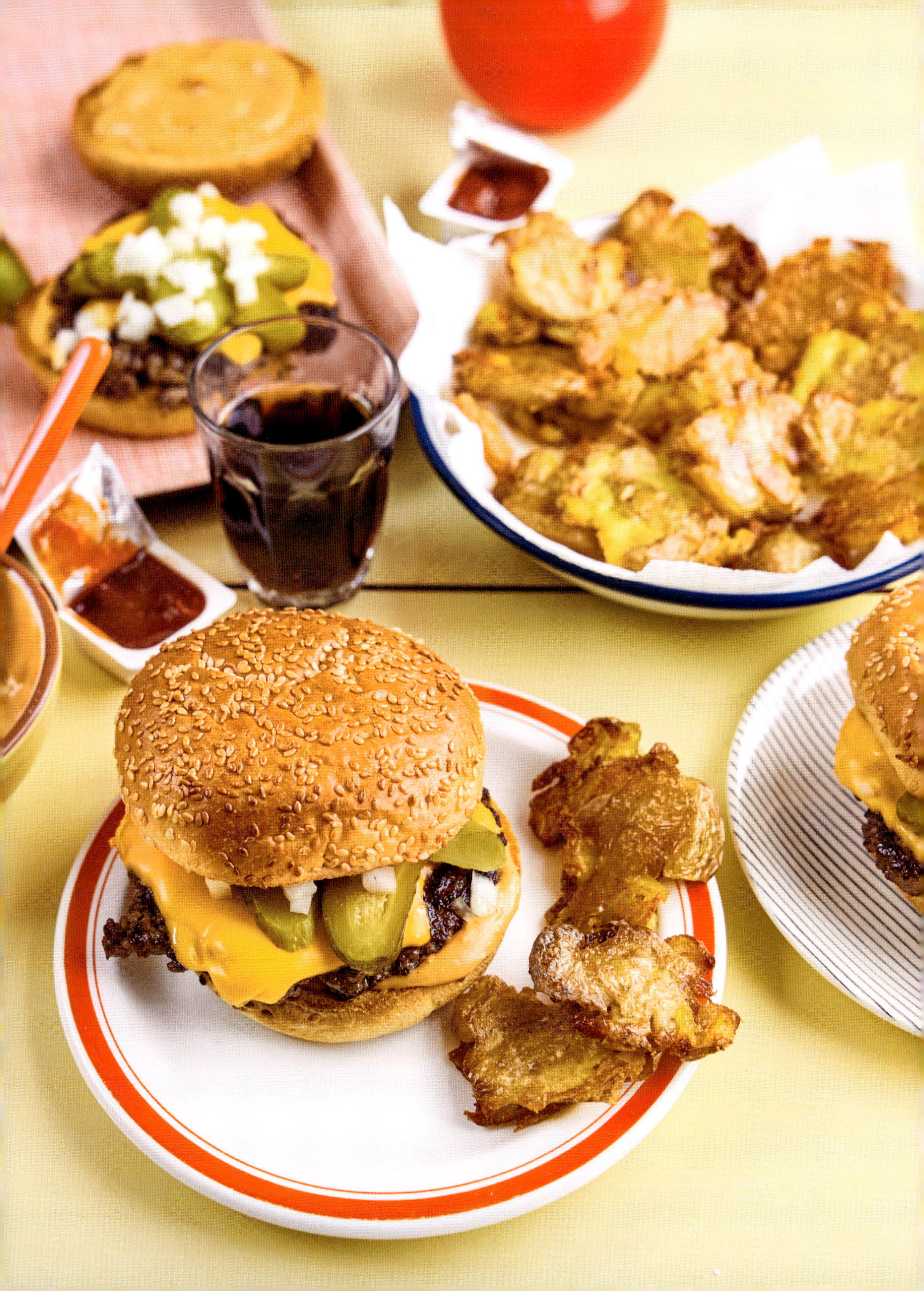

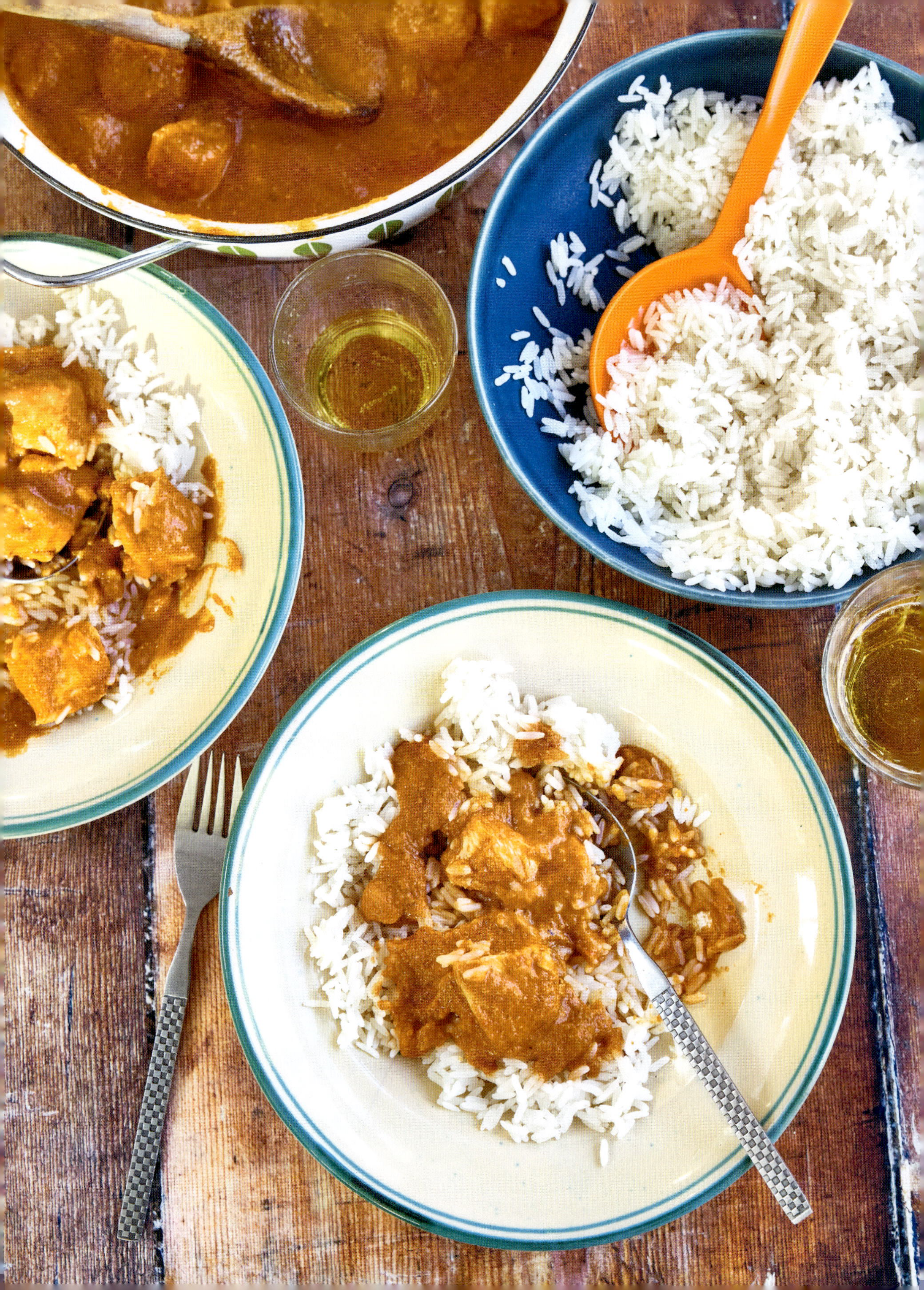

PREP TIME. 15 MINUTES / **COOK TIME.** 1 HOUR / **SERVES.** 4

FAKEAWAY FAVORITES

Rich, creamy, just a hint of spice, there's a reason why butter chicken is near the top of the UK's favorite curries. This makes a big batch that feeds four, so is perfect for a Friday night with friends, but will equally keep in the fridge for up to four days if you want to treat yourself over a few nights.

BUTTER CHICKEN

1. Thinly slice the onion and place a large saucepan with 1 tablespoon of the vegetable oil over medium heat. When the pan is hot, add the onion, season with salt and cook for 10 minutes until nicely caramelized.

2. Roughly chop the ginger, chilli and garlic. Add them into the pan and cook for 1 minute.

3. Add in the remaining tablespoon of oil and the tomato paste, spices and some salt and cook for another minute.

4. Stir in the chopped tomatoes, fill the can up halfway with water and add it to the pan, too. Bring it up to a boil, place a lid on top, reduce to a simmer and cook for 30 minutes.

5. While the sauce is cooking, you have time to dice up the chicken into large bite-size pieces. Season with salt and pepper and set aside.

6. After 30 minutes use a hand blender to blitz to a smooth sauce. Add in the chicken, butter and cream and simmer for 12 minutes until the chicken is cooked and the sauce has thickened up.

7. Take a piece of chicken out and cut into it to see if it's cooked. It should be white all the way through. Taste and season the curry with more salt, if needed, and serve with rice.

1 large or 2 small onions
2 tbsp vegetable oil
1 thumb-sized piece of fresh ginger
1 red chilli
3 cloves of garlic
1½ tbsp tomato paste
1 tbsp ground cumin
1 tbsp ground coriander
½ tbsp garam masala
1 tbsp ground turmeric
½ tbsp chilli powder
1 x 15.5 oz (439 g) can of chopped tomatoes
4 chicken breasts
5 tbsp butter
⅓ cup cream
Sea salt and black pepper
Cooked rice, to serve (see page 22)

SERVES. 2 / **PREP TIME.** 15 MINUTES / **COOK TIME.** 7 MINUTES

FAKEAWAY FAVORITES

Another speedy and delicious Japanese classic that can be made at home at a fraction of the cost of eating out, and you don't even need to sit with strangers to enjoy it!

Yaki Udon

① Start by getting everything prepped. Slice your bell pepper, sugar snap peas, onion and mushrooms and place into one bowl. Grate the ginger and garlic, slice the chilli and put into a separate bowl.

② Combine all the ingredients for the sauce and set aside.

③ Finally, thinly slice the chicken, place in another bowl, marinate in 1 tablespoon of soy sauce and season with pepper. Now, we are ready to start cooking.

④ Pour 1 tablespoon of the vegetable oil into a hot wok set over very high heat and stir-fry the chicken for 2 minutes.

⑤ Push the chicken to one side of the pan. Crack an egg into the empty bit of pan and scramble it. Transfer the chicken and scrambled egg to a plate.

⑥ Put the wok back on the heat and fry your veggies in the remaining tablespoon of vegetable oil for 2 minutes. Add in the ginger, garlic and chilli and fry for a minute, stirring constantly.

⑦ Finally, add in the noodles, cooked chicken, egg and sauce and give it a toss so it's nicely combined.

⑧ Leave it to cook for a minute or so, until the noodles have softened and are nicely coated in sauce. Meanwhile, slice the spring onions and add them into the dish at the last minute.

⑨ Serve up and enjoy.

1 red bell pepper
2 oz (50g) sugar snap peas
½ white onion
4 chestnut mushrooms
1 thumb-sized piece of fresh ginger
3 cloves of garlic
1 red chilli
1 chicken breast
1 tbsp soy sauce
2 tbsp vegetable oil
1 egg
10 oz (300g) straight-to-wok udon noodles
3 spring onions
Sea salt and black pepper

FOR THE SAUCE

3 tbsp light soy sauce
2 tbsp oyster sauce
1 tbsp rice vinegar
1 tbsp sesame oil
1 tbsp sugar

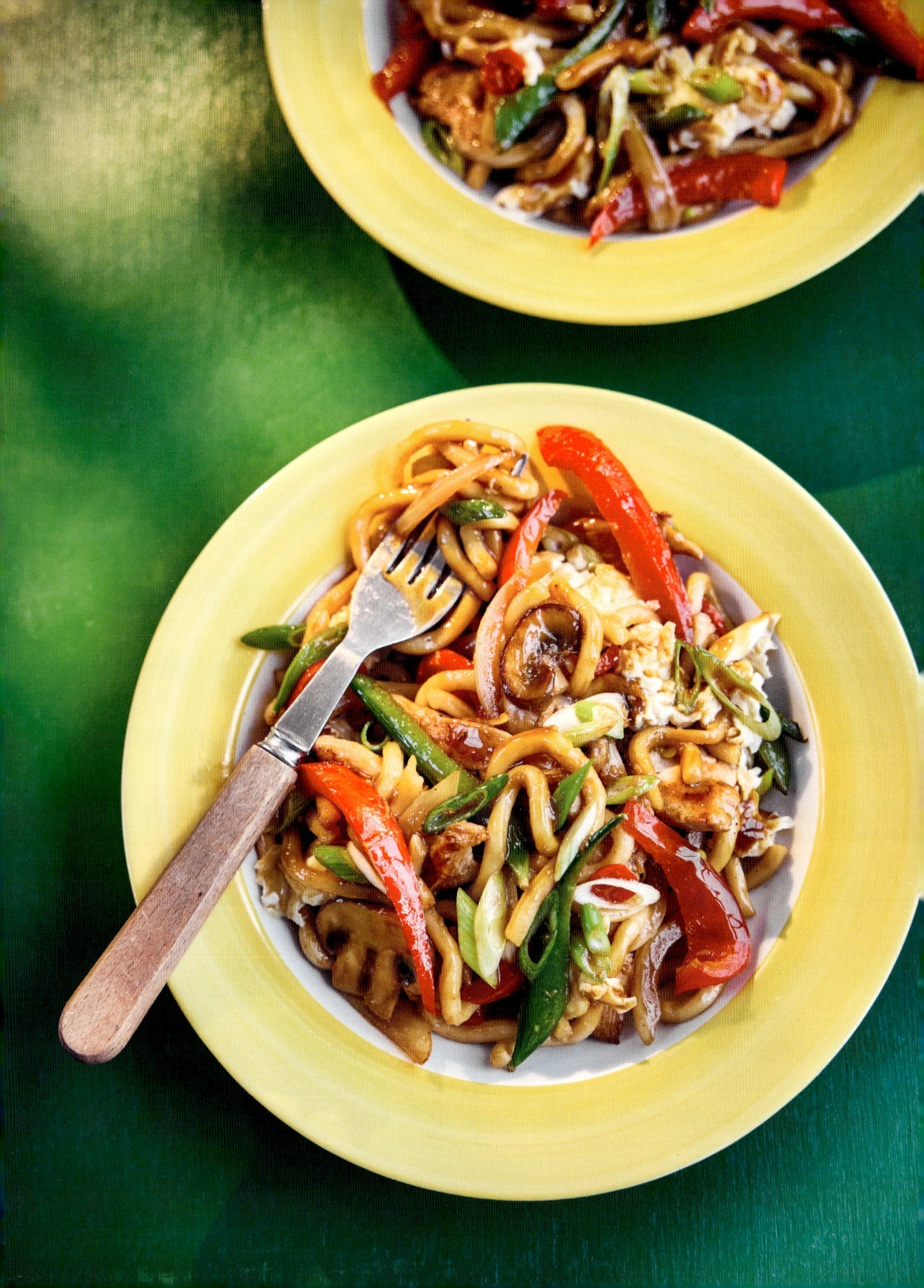

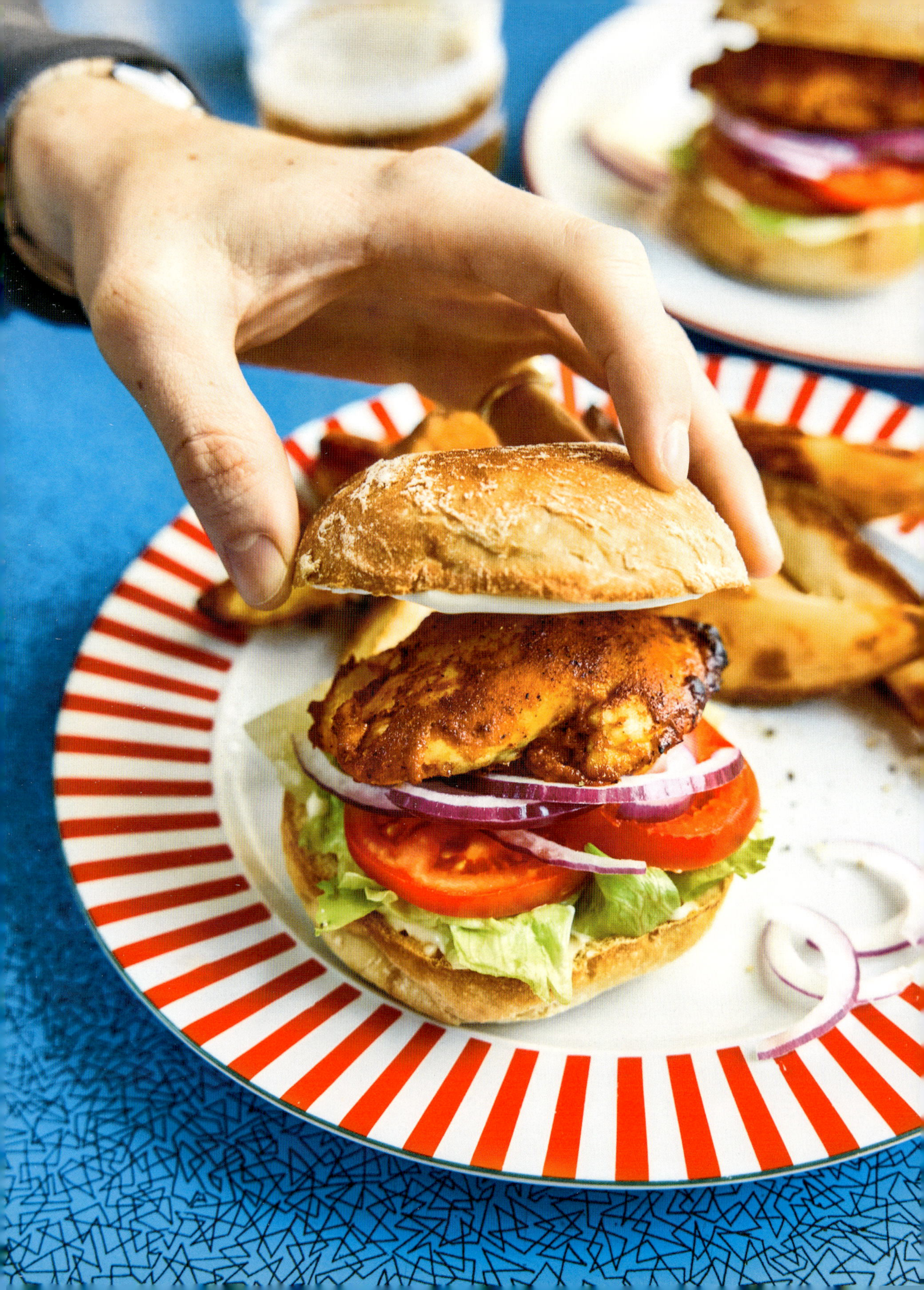

PREP TIME. 15 MINUTES + MARINATING / **COOK TIME.** 1 HOUR / **SERVES.** 2

FAKEAWAY FAVORITES

Tastier than your local chicken shop and half the price. The Portuguese flavors of spicy piri piri add real fire to this burger and the homemade chips are a definite step up from your average oven chip.

Piri Piri Chicken Burger + Homemade Oven Chips

① Place all the ingredients for the marinade into a blender and blitz till smooth.

② Add the chicken to the marinade and make sure it is nicely coated. Wrap in plastic wrap and leave to marinate in the fridge for at least 30 minutes. Ideally, if you have time, leave overnight.

③ Preheat the oven to 325°F (160°C). Pour the vegetable oil into a medium roasting pan and place it in the oven.

④ Cut the potatoes into wedges, put them in a saucepan, cover with cold water and season generously with salt. Bring to the boil and simmer for 5–10 minutes, or until they are parboiled and beginning to soften but not quite tender all the way through.

⑤ Once the potatoes are ready, drain in a colander and leave to steam dry.

⑥ Take the hot pan out of the oven and add your potatoes. Gently toss them in the pan to coat them in the oil and season with salt and pepper. Place in the oven and bake for 45 minutes, turning halfway through.

⑦ Once the potatoes have been in for 30 minutes, take your chicken out of the marinade and season with salt and pepper. Place on a baking sheet and bake for 15–20 minutes, or until cooked through.

⑧ Cut the bread in half and place in the oven for 1–2 minutes with the chicken to warm through and crisp up.

⑨ While everything cooks in the oven, thinly slice your tomato and red onion and tear the lettuce into bite-sized pieces.

⑩ Once the chicken is cooked, the chips are golden and the bread is crisp, take everything out of the oven and assemble your burgers. Spread some mayonnaise on both sides of the ciabatta, top with the lettuce, onion, tomato and chicken and serve.

4	chicken thighs, skinless and boneless
5 tbsp	vegetable oil
2 large or 4 medium	Maris Piper or Russet potatoes
2	ciabatta rolls, sliced in half lengthways
1	beefsteak tomato
½	red onion
¼	iceberg lettuce
	Sea salt and black pepper
	Mayonnaise, to serve

FOR THE MARINADE

2	roasted red peppers (from a jar)
6	cloves of garlic
2	red chillies
	Juice and zest of 1 lemon
1 tbsp	smoked paprika
1 tbsp	mixed herbs

FAKEAWAY FAVORITES

SERVES. 2 / **PREP TIME.** 20 MINUTES / **COOK TIME.** 10 MINUTES

Nights in are the new nights out. And they needn't be expensive. Binge some Netflix (other streaming services are available!) and chow down on delicious crunchy nachos with guac, sour cream, jalapeños and tomato salsa. Boom.

Movie Night Nachos

1. Preheat the oven to 350°F (180°C).
2. Start by making the guacamole. Halve the avocados and scoop the flesh into a bowl. Use a fork to smash into a smooth purée. Add the lime juice, minced garlic and cilantro and season with salt and pepper. Mix to combine and set aside.
3. For the tomato salsa, quarter the tomatoes and remove the seeds from inside. Roughly chop the flesh and put it into a bowl. Finely dice the red onion and add it to the tomatoes along with the chopped cilantro lime juice and olive oil and season with salt and pepper. Mix to combine and set aside.
4. Put the tortilla chips on a baking sheet and top with the mozzarella. Bake in the oven for 7–10 minutes.
5. Remove from the oven and scoop the nachos onto two plates.
6. Add blobs of guacamole, tomato salsa and sour cream all over the top. Garnish with some pickled jalapeños, lime wedges and more cilantro.
7. Crack open some beers, get the movie ready and enjoy!

---

4 oz (120 g) lightly salted tortilla chips

1 cup grated mozzarella

½ cup sour cream

FOR THE GUACAMOLE

2 avocados

Juice of ½ lime

1 clove of garlic, minced

Small handful of chopped cilantro

Sea salt and black pepper

FOR THE TOMATO SALSA

2 beefsteak tomatoes

½ red onion

Small handful of chopped cilantro

Juice of ½ lime

1 tbsp olive oil

TO SERVE

Pickled jalapeños

1 lime, sliced into wedges

Cilantro leaves

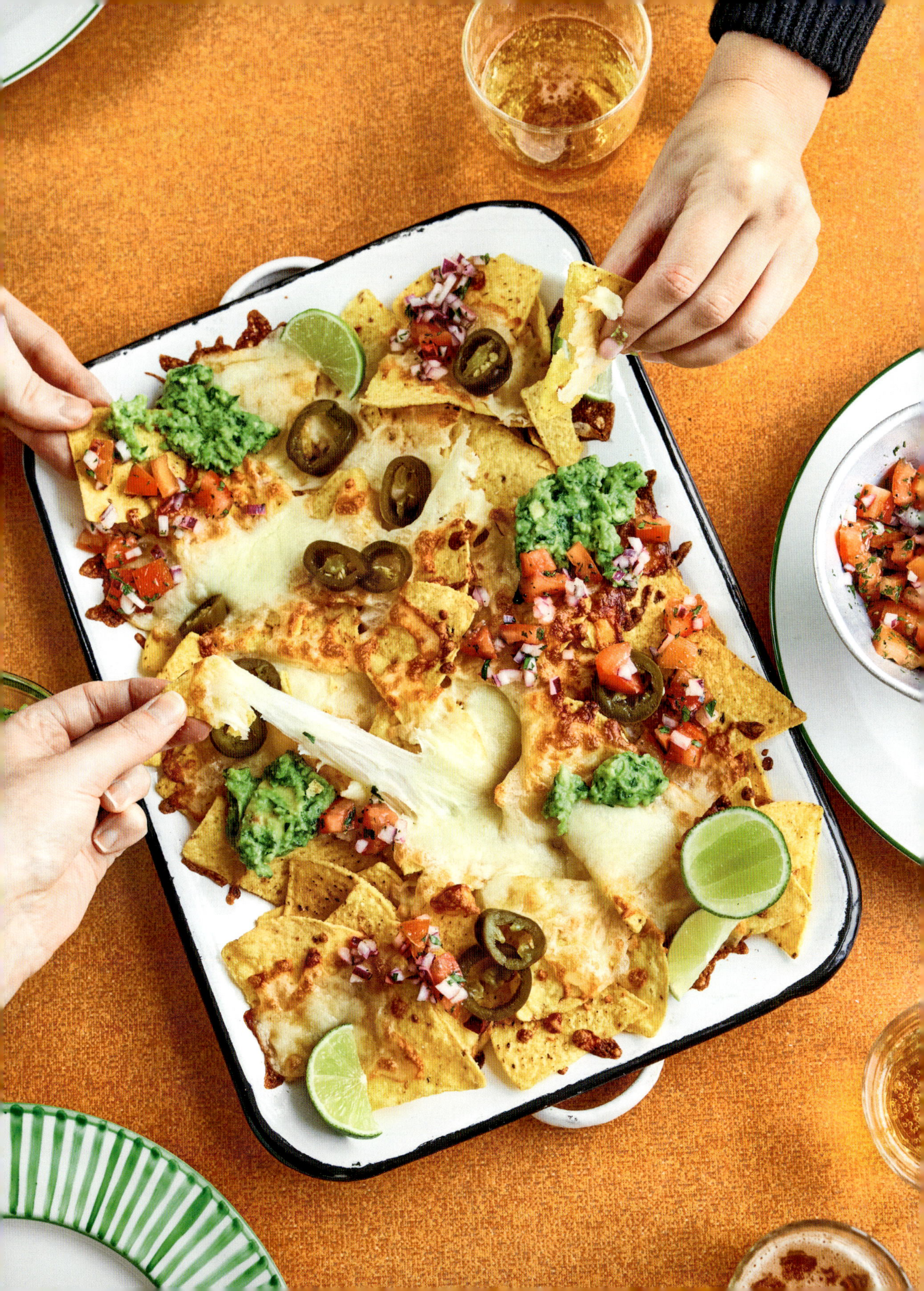

FAKEAWAY FAVORITES

SERVES. 4 / **PREP TIME.** 30 MINUTES / **COOK TIME.** 45 MINUTES

Waga who? Katsu curry is a lipsmacking Japanese classic of crunchy breaded chicken in a rich and spicy curry sauce that is surprisingly easy to make at home. You can buy panko breadcrumbs at any good supermarket, and they keep in a sealed container for ages, so add this to your repertoire and they definitely won't go to waste.

Chicken Katsu Curry

⅓ cup all-purpose flour
3 eggs
1 cup breadcrumbs (I use panko)
1 lb mini chicken breast fillets
¾ cup vegetable oil
Sea salt and black pepper
Cooked rice, to serve (see page 22)

FOR THE SAUCE

1 onion
2 carrots
1 thumb-sized piece of fresh ginger
5 cloves of garlic
2 tbsp vegetable oil
1 heaped tbsp mild curry powder
2 tbsp all-purpose flour
2½ cup chicken stock
2½ tbsp soy sauce

① To make the sauce, roughly chop the onion, carrots, ginger and garlic, add them to a hot saucepan with the vegetable oil and season with salt. Cook over medium heat for 5 minutes, then add the curry powder and flour and cook for 1 minute more.

② Pour in the chicken stock slowly, stirring to avoid lumps. Bring to the boil, then lower the heat and simmer for 20 minutes.

③ Clean up and get three large bowls, or large plates, and a baking sheet. Put the flour into one bowl, the well-beaten eggs into another and the breadcrumbs into the last one.

④ Season the flour with salt and pepper and add the chicken. Mix it round so all the chicken is coated in the flour. Shake off any excess flour and drop all of the chicken into the egg mixture. Mix it round so the egg can stick to the chicken and all the pieces are evenly coated.

⑤ Pick one chicken piece up and allow the excess egg to drip off before coating it in the breadcrumbs. Place it onto the baking tray. Do this with all the chicken and you'll be ready to fry.

⑥ Pour ⅔ cup vegetable oil into a large frying pan over medium heat and, once hot, add half the chicken and fry for 3–4 minutes on each side until golden brown and cooked through. Once cooked, remove the chicken to a plate lined with kitchen paper and loosely cover with foil to keep warm.

⑦ Repeat with the second half of the chicken, adding the remaining oil, if needed.

⑧ Use a hand blender to blend the sauce until smooth. Pour in the soy sauce, taste and season and keep warm.

⑨ To serve up, put some rice onto the base of the plate. Top with the chicken, pour over the sauce and dig in.

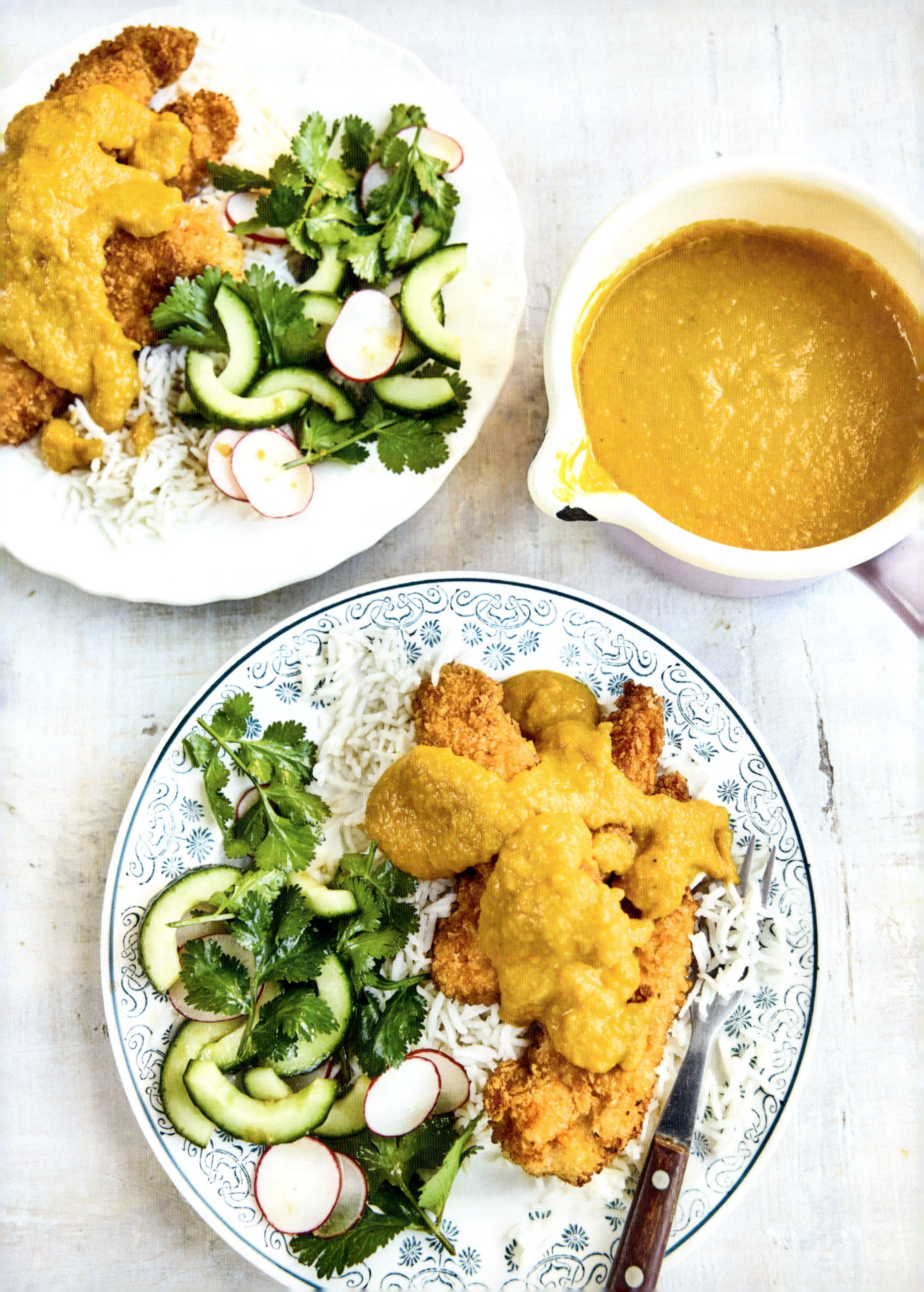

When Did I Last Eat A

Vegetables are delicious and super healthy, and yet too many of us are guilty of not munching on enough greens. This chapter aims to put that right with simple, flavor-packed recipes that make getting your five-a-day an absolute pleasure, from One-Tray Veggie Pasta and Saag Aloo Dhal to a classic and delicious Eggplant Parm.

vegetable?

SERVES. 4   **PREP TIME.** 15 MINUTES   **COOK TIME.** 40 MINUTES

WHEN DID I LAST EAT A VEGETABLE?

Cauliflower is a superfood that can pack just as much punch as any meat. Coated in paprika-and-cumin-spiked yogurt and roasted until rich and nutty, this recipe really makes your cauli shine! I like to serve this with flatbreads and Tzatziki (see page 185) for a dish that will have your guests clamoring for seconds.

ROASTED CAULIFLOWER TRAYBAKE

① Preheat the oven to 400°F (200°C).

② Cut your cauliflower into medium florets, and roughly chop the leaves. Cut the red onions into wedges.

③ In a mixing bowl, combine all of the yogurt marinade ingredients, mincing the garlic before adding it. Season well with salt and pepper.

④ Add the cauliflower florets and mix really well to make sure all the florets are coated in yogurt. Pour the florets into a large baking sheet, add the onion wedges, drizzle over 2 tablespoons of the olive oil and sprinkle over some salt.

⑤ Roast in the oven for 30 minutes, turning the veg once, until the cauliflower is starting to char and the onions are cooked and caramelized.

⑥ Meanwhile, pour the remaining tablespoon of olive oil into a mixing bowl and add the drained chickpeas and cauliflower leaves along with the smoked paprika, cumin and coriander. Mix well and season with salt and pepper.

⑦ After 30 minutes, add the chickpeas and cauli leaves to the baking sheet and mix to combine all the elements. Return to the oven and roast for a further 10 minutes.

⑧ Drizzle with olive oil and a good squeeze of lemon juice, scatter over the mint, if using, and serve with tzatziki and warm flatbreads.

---

1 large cauliflower, including the leaves

2 red onions

3 tbsp olive oil, plus extra for drizzling

1 x 15.5 oz (439 g) can of chickpeas, drained

½ tsp smoked paprika

½ tsp ground cumin

½ tsp ground coriander

Juice of 1 lemon

Small handful of chopped mint (optional)

Sea salt and black pepper

FOR THE YOGURT MARINADE

⅓ cup Greek yogurt

2 large or 4 small cloves of garlic

1 tsp smoked paprika

1 tsp ground cumin

1 tsp ground coriander

TO SERVE

Tzatziki (see page 185)

4 pita breads or Greek flatbreads

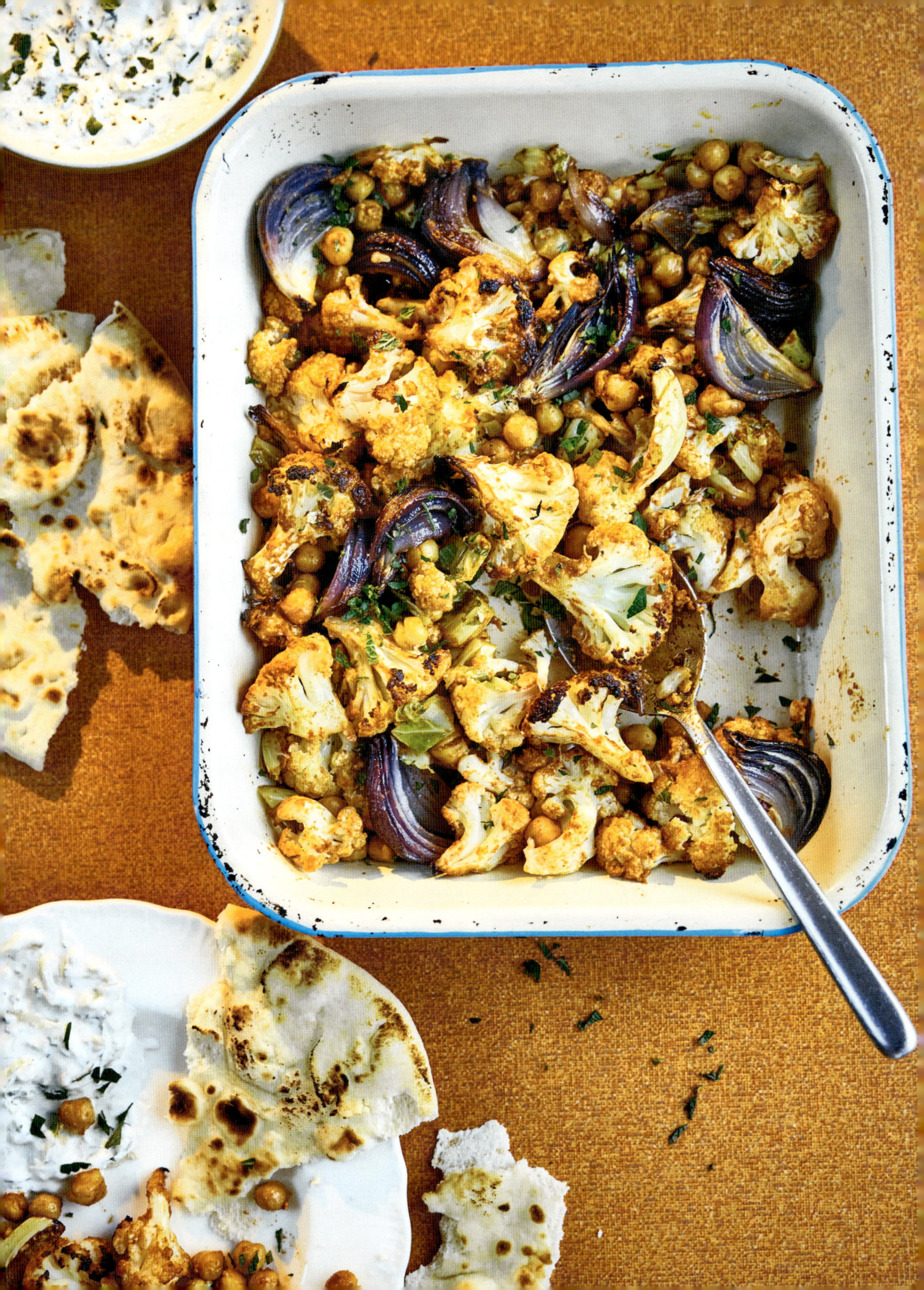

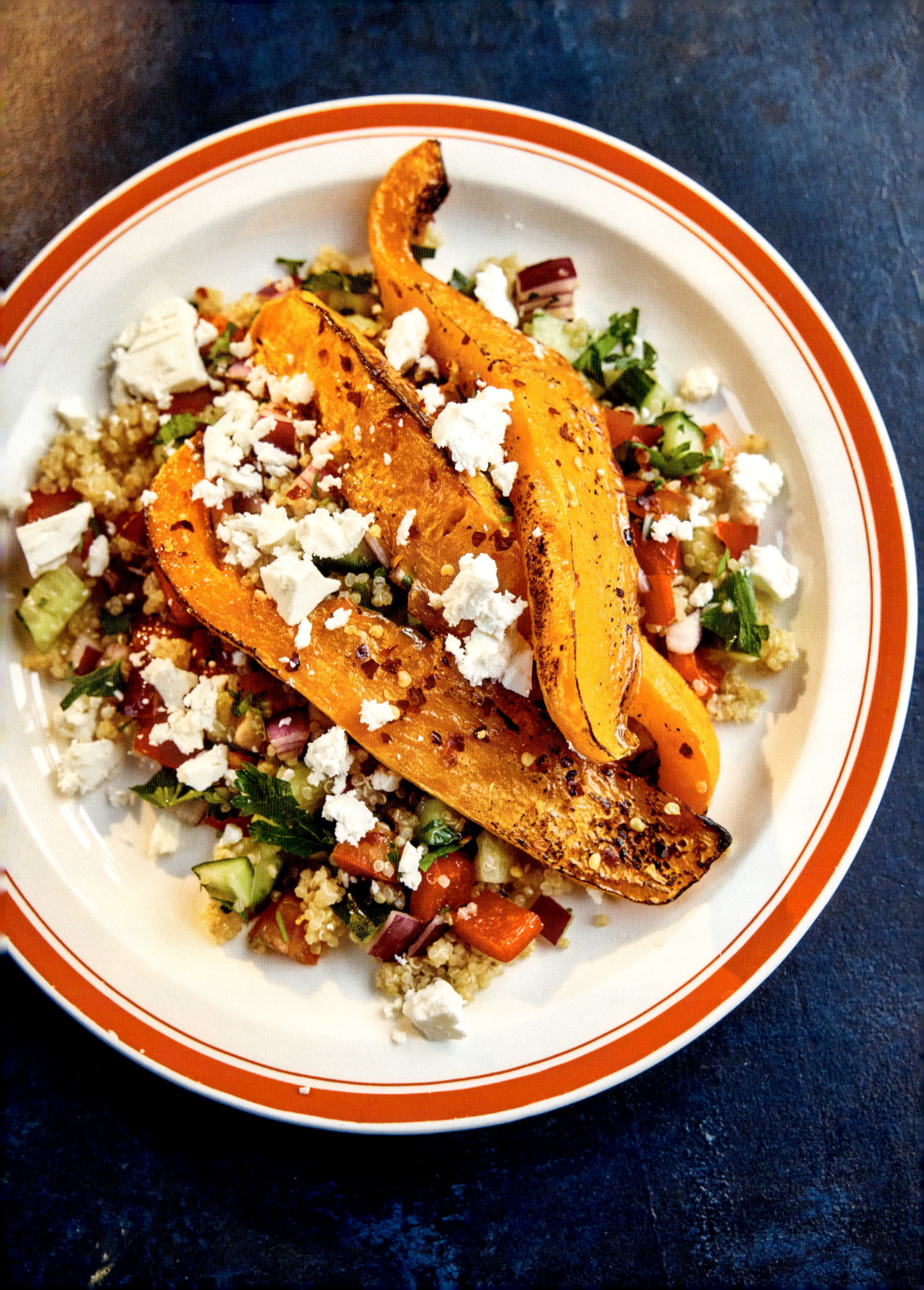

PREP TIME. 20 MINUTES / **COOK TIME.** 25 MINUTES / **SERVES.** 4 AS A MAIN, OR 8 AS A BBQ SIDE DISH

WHEN DID I LAST EAT A VEGETABLE?

A superfood salad that is also super wholesome, super versatile, super easy and, most importantly, super delicious! This is another recipe that can be adapted to suit what you have to hand, so go for a fridge forage and chuck in any bits that need using up. Save yourself some pennies, reduce food waste and eat something delicious.

Roasted Butternut Squash Salad
+ Quinoa & Feta

① Preheat the oven to 400°F (200°C).

② Cut your butternut squash in half and remove the skin with a vegetable peeler. Remove the seeds and chop into large wedges.

③ Place on a baking sheet, drizzle over the olive oil and season with salt and pepper. Place in the oven and bake for 20 minutes, turning the wedges over halfway through.

④ Remove from the oven, drizzle the wedges with honey and sprinkle over the chilli flakes, if using. Return to the oven for a further 5 minutes until the wedges are sticky and lightly charred.

⑤ Meanwhile, put the quinoa into a small saucepan and cover with ¾ cup cold water. Season with salt and bring to a boil over a medium heat.

⑥ Once boiling, place a lid on top, lower the heat and simmer for 12 minutes, and then remove from the heat and leave to stand for 5 more minutes.

⑦ For the salad, just roughly chop the tomatoes and cucumber. Chop the parsley and dice the bell pepper and red onion. Sling that all into a big bowl. Crumble in the feta and give it a good mix. Dress it in the olive oil and white wine vinegar and season with salt and pepper. Add in the quinoa and give it one final toss.

⑧ Place a healthy amount onto a plate and top with the roasted butternut squash.

1 medium butternut squash
2 tbsp olive oil
2 tbsp runny honey
Pinch of chilli flakes (optional)
⅔ cup quinoa
Sea salt and black pepper

FOR THE SALAD

3 beefsteak tomatoes
1 cucumber
Handful of parsley
1 red bell pepper
1 red onion
7 oz (200 g) feta cheese
2 tbsp olive oil
2 tbsp white wine vinegar

WHEN DID I LAST EAT A VEGETABLE?

SERVES. 2 **PREP TIME.** 15 MINUTES **COOK TIME.** 10 MINUTES

Everyone loves a burger, and this tasty veggie version uses simple ingredients with big flavors that come together in no time. This makes two burgers but is really easy to scale up if word gets out that you're cooking!

Veggie Burgers

① Drain the chickpeas and place them into a large bowl. Finely dice half the red onion, shred the parsley and mince the garlic and add these into the chickpeas bowl with the egg and breadcrumbs. Season with ½ teaspoon salt, a good amount of black pepper and the curry powder. Use a potato masher to crush it into a coarse paste and then shape the mixture into two patties.

② Pour the vegetable oil into a hot pan over medium heat and cook the patties for 3–4 minutes on each side until golden, then set aside.

③ Cut the burger buns in half and place cut side down in the frying pan for a couple of minutes to toast. Add some mayonnaise to each bun, then the lettuce, tomato and thinly sliced red onion. Top with the burger patties and place the lid on top.

④ I normally enjoy these wonders with some Sweet Potato Wedges (see page 115).

1 x 15.5 (439 g) can of chickpeas
½ red onion
Handful of parsley
3 cloves of garlic
1 egg
⅓ cup breadcrumbs
1½ tbsp mild curry powder
2 tbsp vegetable oil
2 burger buns
Handful of shredded lettuce
1 beefsteak tomato, sliced
Mayonnaise
Sea salt and black pepper

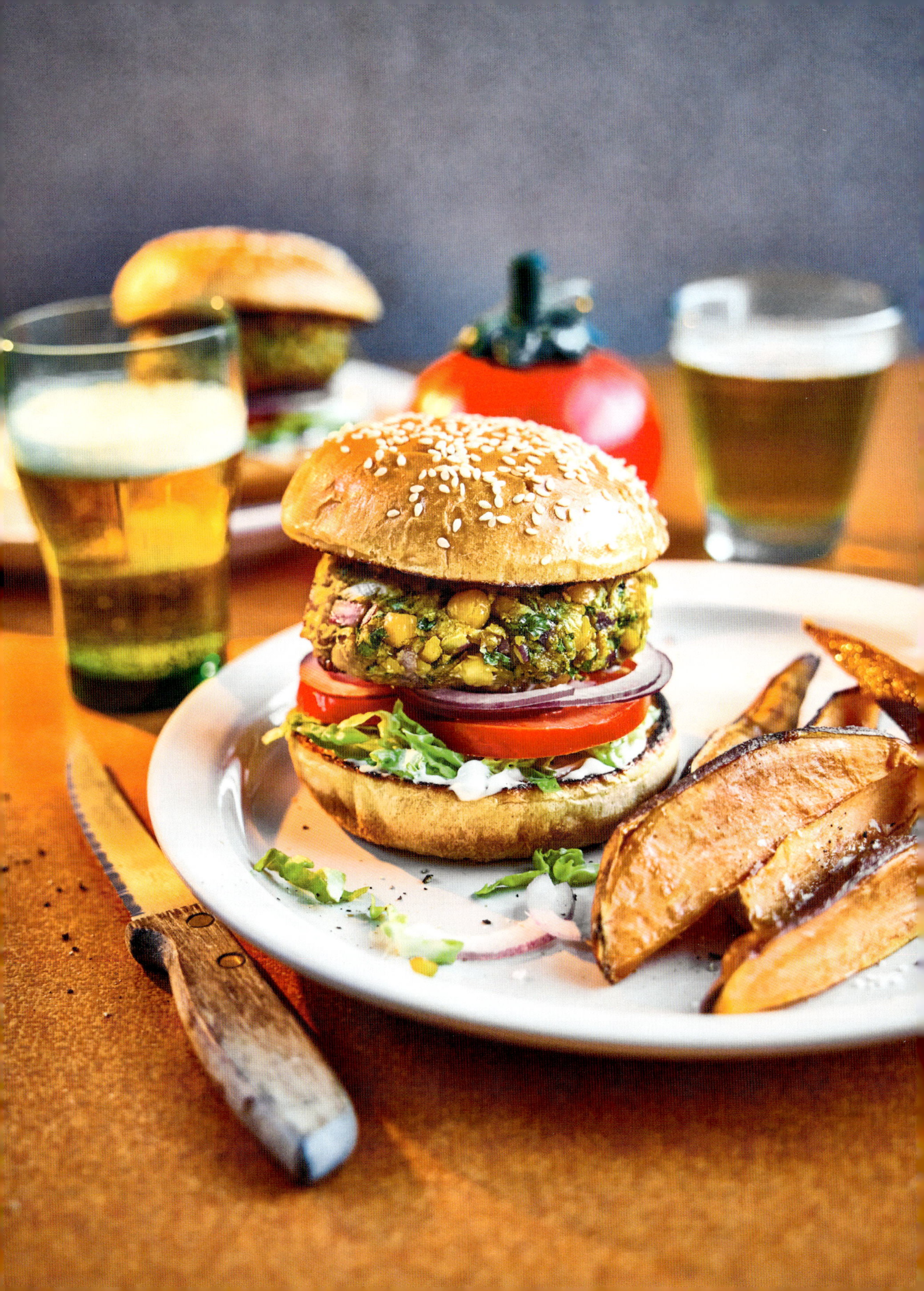

SERVES. 2 / **PREP TIME.** 25 MINUTES / **COOK TIME.** 20 MINUTES

WHEN DID I LAST EAT A VEGETABLE?

This light and fresh veggie main is packed with flavor and is a wonderful for those summer days when you want something light and healthy. What I love about this dish is that you can prep it during the day, ready to finish in the oven when hunger calls.

STUFFED ZUCCHINI + HOMEMADE GARLIC BREAD

① Preheat your oven to 350°F (180°C).

② Cut your zucchini in half lengthways. With the zucchini cut side up, use a small knife to score a crosshatch pattern, making sure to not cut into the skin on either side of the zucchini or cut all the way through to the bottom.

③ Season generously with salt and pepper and leave for 5 minutes to extract some of the moisture.

④ Pat your zucchini dry with a piece of paper towel. Heat the oil in the frying pan over high heat and fry the zucchini flesh side down for 2–3 minutes or until they are nice and golden brown. Place a weight on top of the zucchini (this could be a smaller frying pan) while frying to ensure you get a nice even color. Then put the zucchini on an baking sheet and bake for 7 minutes.

⑤ In the meantime, you can chop your parsley and mince the garlic.

⑥ For the garlic butter, just mix together the softened butter with ½ teaspoon of the minced garlic, a pinch of the parsley and some salt and pepper. Slice the ciabatta in half horizontally and spread the butter onto the cut sides ready for the oven.

⑦ Once the zucchini come out of the oven, use a teaspoon to scrape out the flesh and place into a bowl. Add in the feta, sunflower seeds, pumpkin seeds, remaining garlic and parsley and the lemon zest and mix to combine.

⑧ Refill the zucchini shells with the new filling and bake the zucchini and garlic bread for another 10 minutes.

⑨ Once the bread is heated through and the zucchini are golden, you're ready to plate up and serve with a salad on the side.

2 zucchini	
2 tbsp vegetable oil	
3½ oz (100 g) feta cheese	
3 tbsp sunflower seeds	
3 tbsp pumpkin seeds	
Zest of ½ lemon	

FOR THE GARLIC BREAD

Small handful of chopped parsley	
3 cloves of garlic	
2 tbsp butter, softened	
1 small loaf of ciabatta bread	
Sea salt and black pepper	
Salad leaves, to serve	

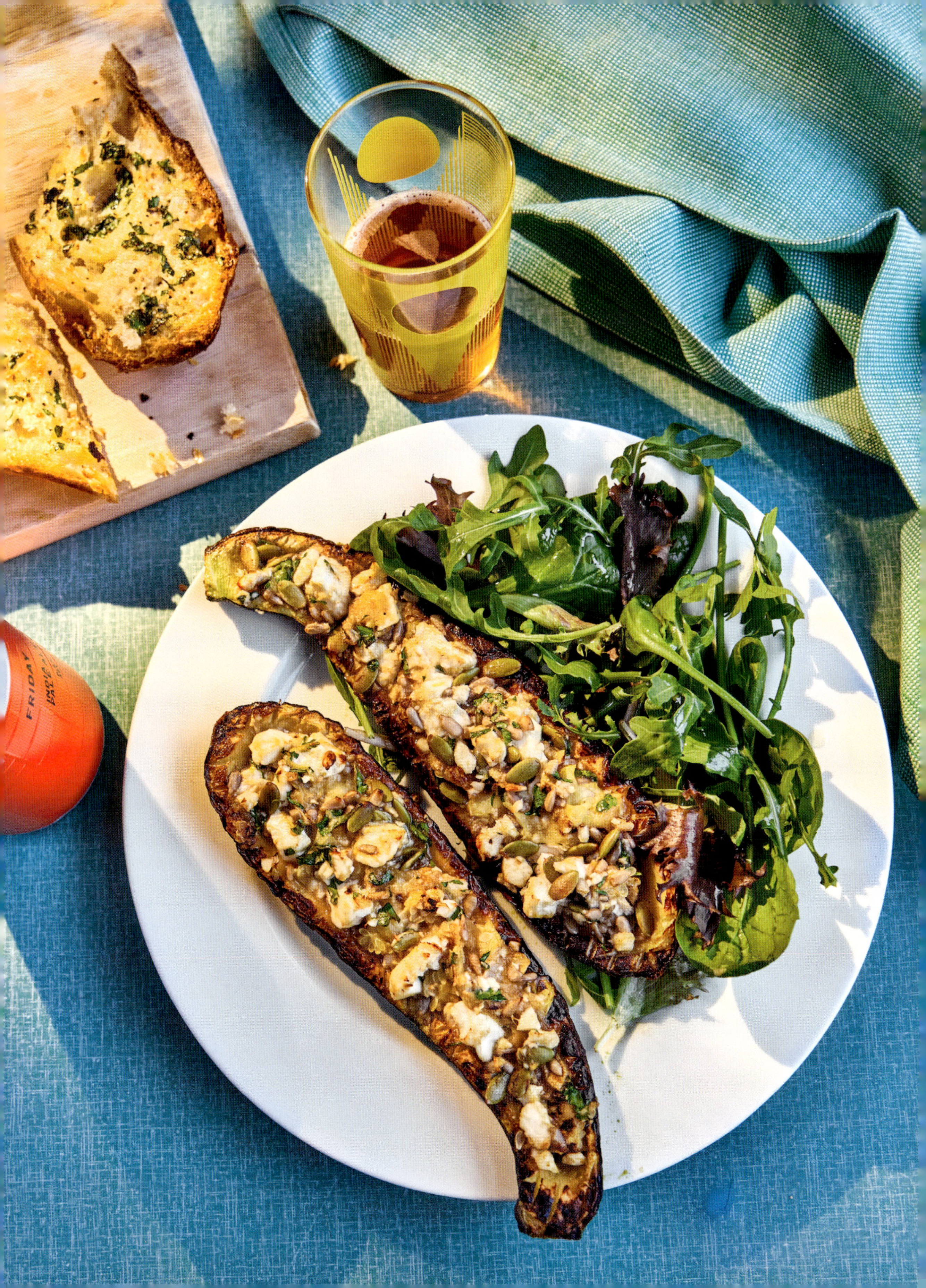
FRIDAY

SERVES. 2 / **PREP TIME.** 10 MINUTES / **COOK TIME.** 30 MINUTES

WHEN DID I LAST EAT A VEGETABLE?

This is a dish so simple that even my brothers can't get it wrong. Full on flavor, low on effort. Put your feet up, grab the remote and relax!

One-Tray Veggie Pasta

① Preheat the oven to 400°F (200°C).

② Roughly chop your bell peppers and onion and lightly crush your garlic, leaving the skins on.

③ Add your bell pepper, onion, garlic and cherry tomatoes to a baking sheet. Drizzle over some olive oil, season with salt, pepper and chilli flakes and give it a mix so the veg is all coated in oil.

④ Roast in the oven for 30 minutes, giving it a mix once or twice.

⑤ Bring a pan of salted water up to the boil and cook your pasta according to the package instructions. Once cooked, reserve a mug of pasta water and drain the pasta through a colander.

⑥ Once the veggies are beautifully caramelized, remove the pan from the oven. Squeeze the cooked garlic out of their skins (and throw away the skin). Mash the garlic with the back of a spoon and add a good splash of pasta water. Mix the water into the veg, crushing some of the tomatoes as you go.

⑦ Add in your cooked pasta and toss it all together. Season to taste and finish with some grated Parmesan and basil.

3 red bell peppers
1 red onion
6 cloves of garlic, unpeeled
14 oz (400 g) cherry tomatoes
Olive oil
Pinch of chilli flakes
7 oz (200 g) penne pasta
Sea salt and black pepper

TO SERVE

Bunch of basil, torn
Parmesan cheese, grated

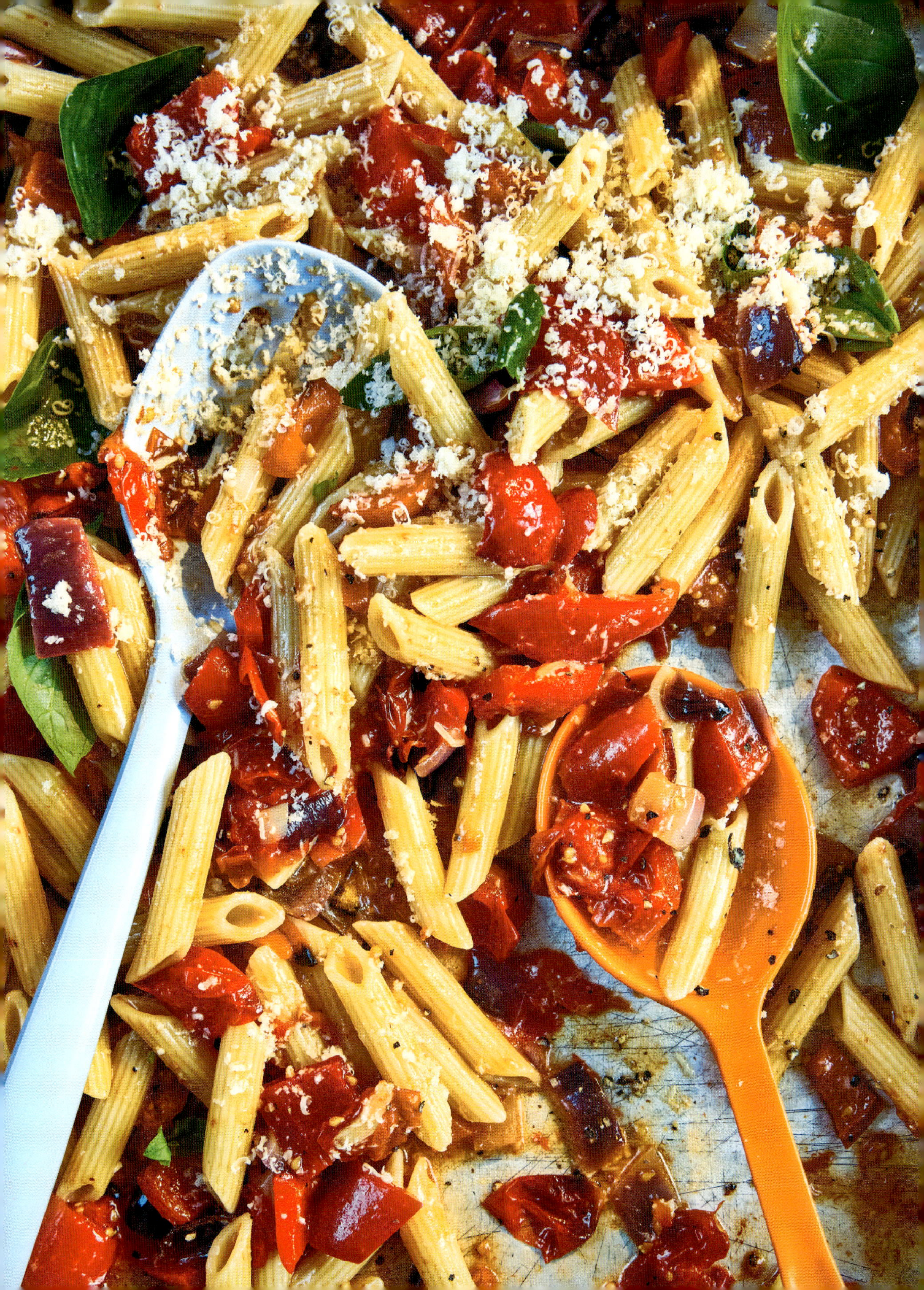

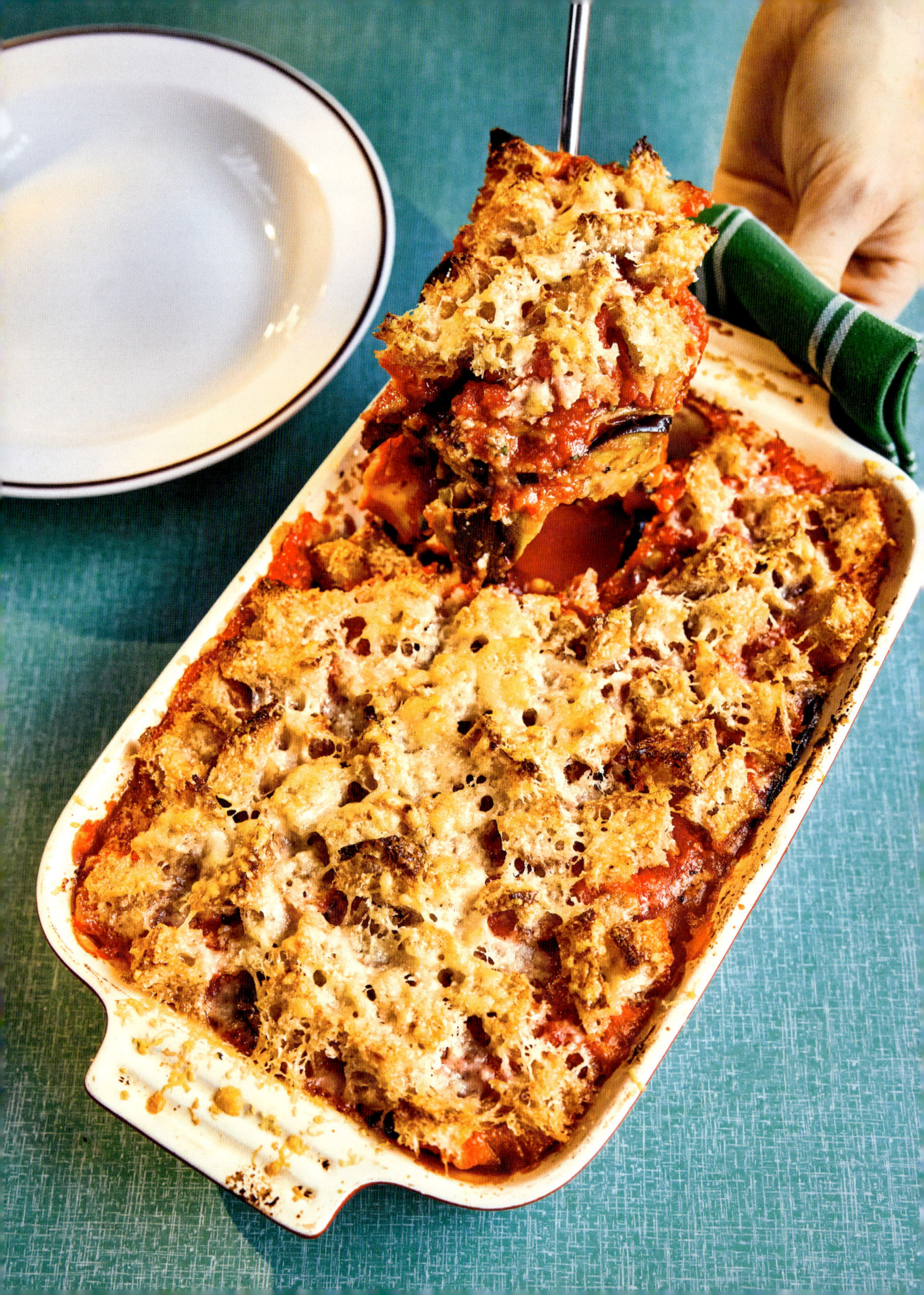

PREP TIME. 15 MINUTES / COOK TIME. 45 MINUTES / SERVES. 4

WHEN DID I LAST EAT A VEGETABLE?

In my eyes, eggplants reign supreme. They are so versatile and can take on so many different flavors. This classic Italian dish is rich, comforting and delicious. Silky eggplants layered with a rich, garlicky tomato sauce and topped with oozy cheese and crunchy croutons. A comfort like no other.

EGGPLANT PARM

① Preheat your oven to the highest it goes.

② With a sharp knife, remove the top and bottom of the eggplants and slice lengthways into thin strips just less than a centimeter (½ inch) thick if you can. Drizzle over a generous amount of olive oil on both sides and season with salt and pepper.

③ Place the slices onto two large baking sheets and bake for 15 minutes.

④ Meanwhile, mince the garlic and cut the bread into small cubes.

⑤ Place the passata into a saucepan, tear the basil and throw in and add the garlic. If you're using homemade tomato sauce, you don't need to add basil and garlic, unless you'd like extra. Bring the sauce up to the boil and let it simmer for 5 minutes.

⑥ Put the cornstarch into a small bowl and add 2 tablespoons of cold water. Mix to combine and add it into the tomato sauce. Stir it in and keep stirring for a minute until it thickens up. Season the sauce with salt, pepper and some sugar.

⑦ Once the eggplants are ready, turn the oven down to 350°F (180°C). Put a third of the eggplants into an ovenproof dish and top with a third of the tomato sauce. Tear a ball of mozzarella into bite-size pieces and scatter on top. Repeat this layering until you have a final layer of eggplant with a thin layer of tomato sauce on top (you should have three layers of eggplant). Scatter over the bread cubes and sprinkle over the Parmesan cheese. Lightly drizzle over some olive oil and bake for 30 minutes.

⑧ Serve with some more bread and a green salad.

Ingredients
2 large or 3 small eggplants
Olive oil
3 cloves of garlic
3 slices of sourdough bread
1 x 24 oz (690 g) jar tomato passata or 1 batch of Sam's Homemade Tomato Sauce (see page 26)
Handful of basil
1 tbsp cornstrarch
2 tsp sugar
2 balls of mozzarella
2 oz (50 g) Parmesan cheese, grated
Sea salt and black pepper

SERVES. 6 / **PREP TIME.** 20 MINUTES / **COOK TIME.** 35 MINUTES

WHEN DID I LAST EAT A VEGETABLE?

A perfect autumnal dish for all that excess of pumpkin that tends to accumulate around Halloween, though butternut squash would work just as well. Massaman is one of my favorite Thai curries, spicy and warming but mellowed with the richness of peanuts. To save you buying additional ingredients, I've used red curry paste here and added peanut butter, to bring this dish to life.

Pumpkin Massaman Curry

① Preheat the oven to 400°F (200°C).

② Cut the pumpkin in half and remove the seeds with a spoon. Use a peeler to remove the skin from the pumpkin halves and then cut into eight wedges. Place in a roasting or baking pan, drizzle over 2 tablespoons of the vegetable oil and season generously with salt and pepper. Bake the pumpkin in the oven for 25–35 minutes, or until the pumpkin is tender and a knife goes into the flesh easily.

③ In the meantime, you can slice your onions and fry them in a large saucepan with the remaining vegetable oil. Season them with salt and cook them over medium heat for 7–8 minutes, or until they are nicely caramelized.

④ Add in the Thai curry paste, mixed spice and cumin and cook for a minute. Pour in the coconut milk and crumble in the vegetable stock cube. Bring up to a boil and then simmer for 10 minutes.

⑤ Add the peanut butter and sugar, then add lime juice and salt to taste. Add in the sliced bell peppers and broccoli and simmer for 5 minutes.

⑥ Take the pumpkin out of the oven, roughly chop up the flesh and add it to the curry. Roughly chop the cilantro, sprinkle over the top and serve the curry up with some jasmine rice.

Ingredients
1 small pumpkin or butternut squash
4 tbsp vegetable oil
2 white onions
7 tbsp Thai red curry paste
1 tsp mixed spice
1 tsp ground cumin
2 x 15.5 oz (439 ml) cans of coconut milk
1 vegetable stock cube
2 tbsp peanut butter
1 tbsp sugar
Juice of 1 lime
2 bell peppers, sliced
10 oz (300 g) broccolini
Handful of cilantro
Sea salt and black pepper
Cooked rice, to serve (see page 22)

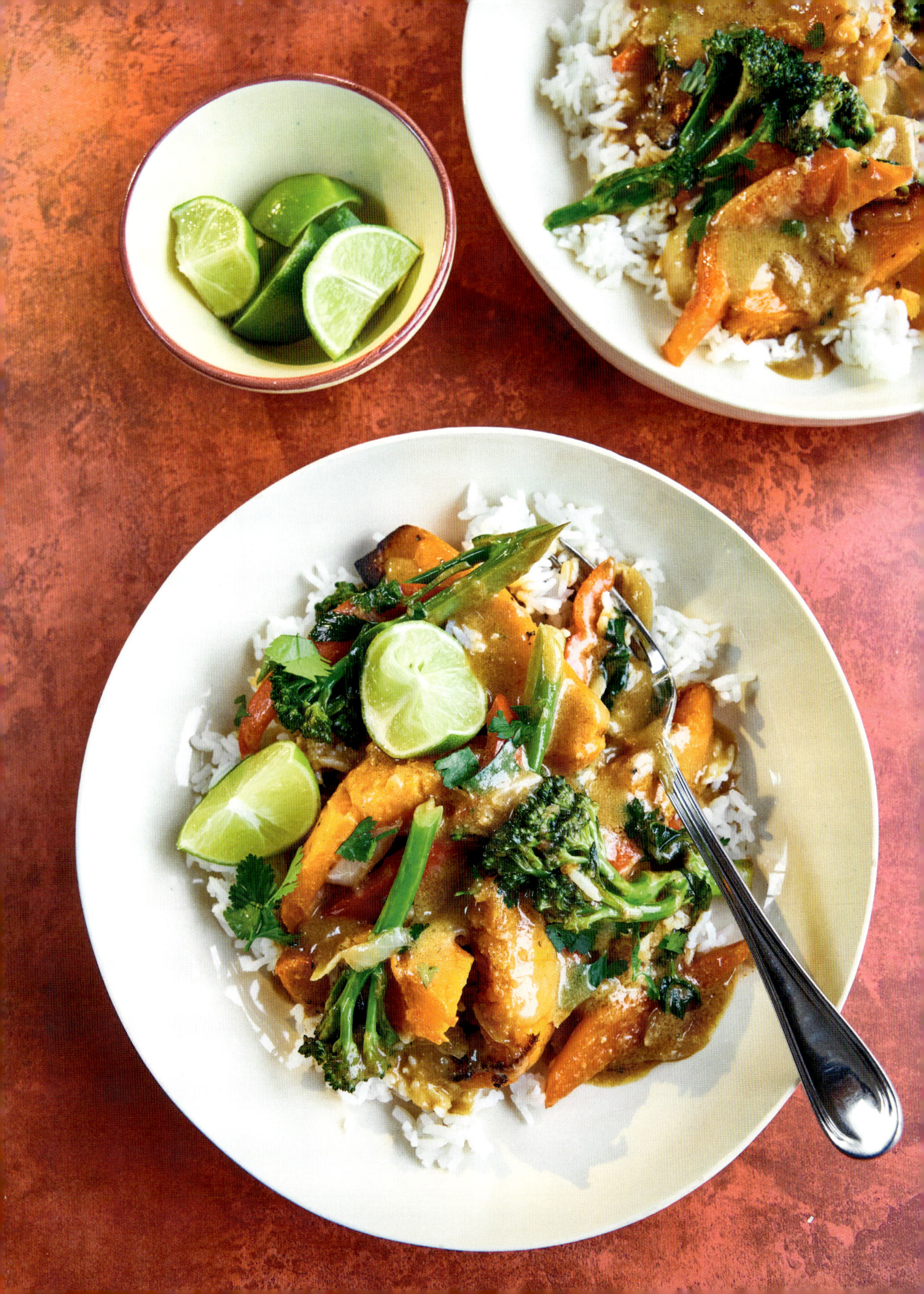

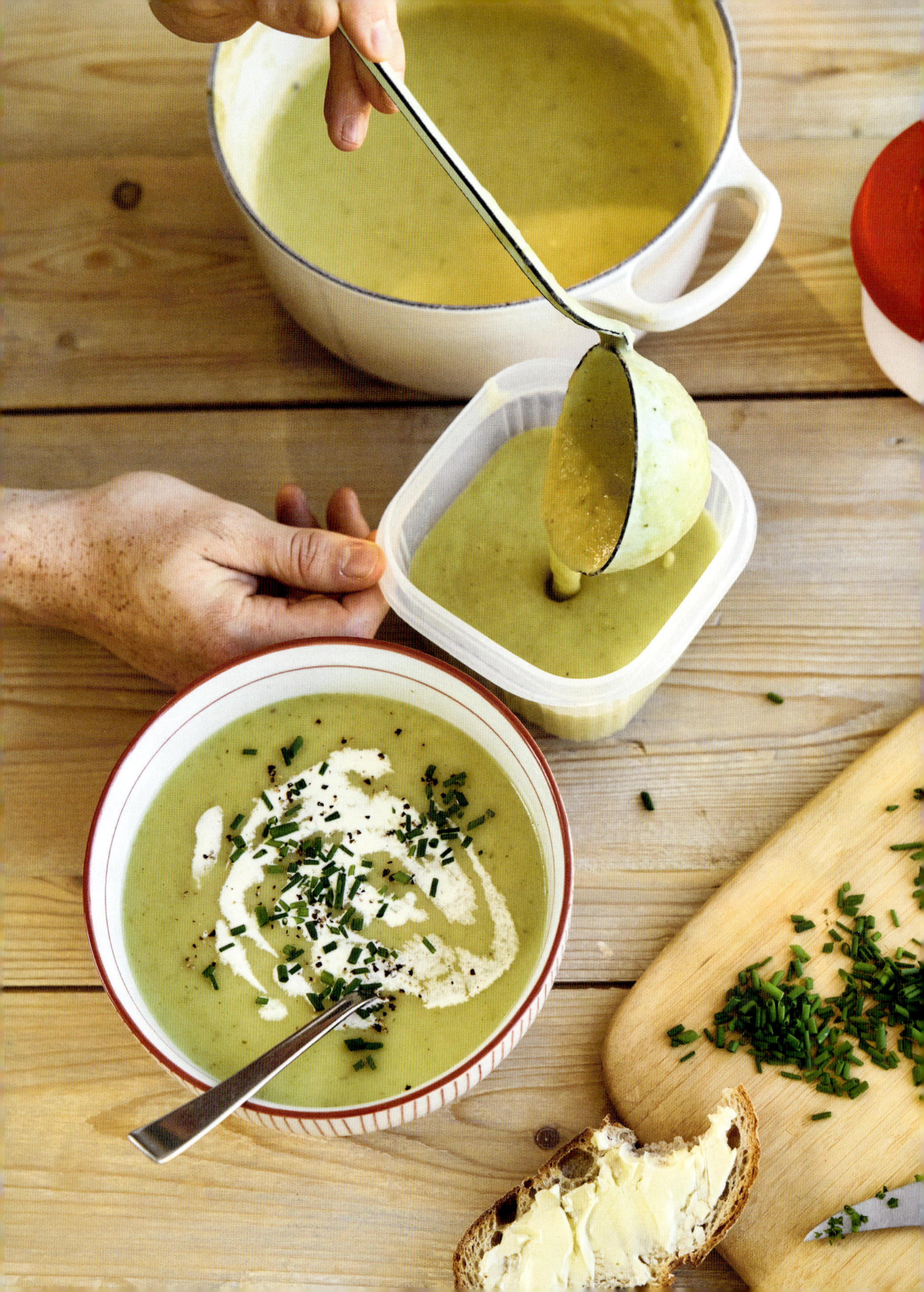

PREP TIME. 15 MINUTES / **COOK TIME.** 30 MINUTES / **SERVES.** 6

WHEN DID I LAST EAT A VEGETABLE?

A bowl of pure comfort that brings me right back to my childhood. It also packs a big bang for its buck as it is made from cheap, readily available ingredients and takes less than 30 minutes to prepare. You will need a blender for this (a small handheld one is fine) to get the silky smooth consistency that you're after.

POTATO & LEEK SOUP

① Cut off the woody ends of the leeks and slice them in half lengthways. Remove the outer layer and rinse the leeks under running water to clean away any soil. Thinly slice the leeks and onion.

② Place a large saucepan over medium to low heat and pour in the vegetable oil. Add in the leeks and onion, season generously with salt and sweat down for 7–10 minutes.

③ In the meantime, peel and roughly chop your potatoes into ¾-inch (2 cm) chunks.

④ Once the leeks and onion are soft, add in the potatoes and cover them with the stock. Bring it up to the boil and then simmer for 15 minutes.

⑤ Once the potatoes are nice and soft, use a stick blender to blitz them to a smooth soup. Stir in the butter until melted along with half the cream and season to taste.

⑥ Serve up, garnished with the leftover cream and the chopped chives.

3 leeks
1 white onion
3 tbsp vegetable oil
3 medium potatoes (around 1 lb [454g])
24 fl oz (1.1 liters vegetable stock)
3½ tbsp butter
½ cup heavy cream
Bunch of chives, chopped
Sea salt and black pepper

SERVES. 4 **PREP TIME.** 15 MINUTES / **COOK TIME.** 30 MINUTES

WHEN DID I LAST EAT A VEGETABLE?

Minestrone is the perfect vehicle for getting loads of veg into your diet. This recipe is brilliant, but feel free to chuck in whatever other veg you have lying around. Serve this with some crusty bread on the side and you've got a hearty, healthy winter meal.

Minestrone

1. Start by dicing the onion, carrot, celery and bell pepper into bite-sized chunks. Put them into a large saucepan with the vegetable oil, season generously with salt and cook over medium to low heat for 10 minutes.
2. Add the minced garlic and tomato paste and cook for 1 minute.
3. Add the chopped tomatoes, drained butter beans, vegetable stock cube, 2½ cups of water and the mixed herbs and bring up to the boil. Lower the heat to a simmer and cook for another 5 minutes.
4. Add the pasta and cook for 10 minutes before adding the kale and basil and cooking for a final 3 minutes.
5. Taste and season with salt and pepper. Serve up with a generous grating of Parmesan and a slice of fresh bread.

½ white onion
1 carrot
1 celery stalk
1 red or yellow bell pepper
2 tbsp vegetable oil
3 cloves of garlic, minced
1 tbsp tomato paste
1 x 15.5 oz (439 g) can of chopped tomatoes
1 x 15.5 oz (439 g) can of butter beans, drained
1 vegetable stock cube
1 tbsp mixed herbs
1½ oz (50 g) penne pasta
1½ oz (50 g) kale
Handful of basil
Sea salt and black pepper

TO SERVE
Parmesan cheese, grated
Bread

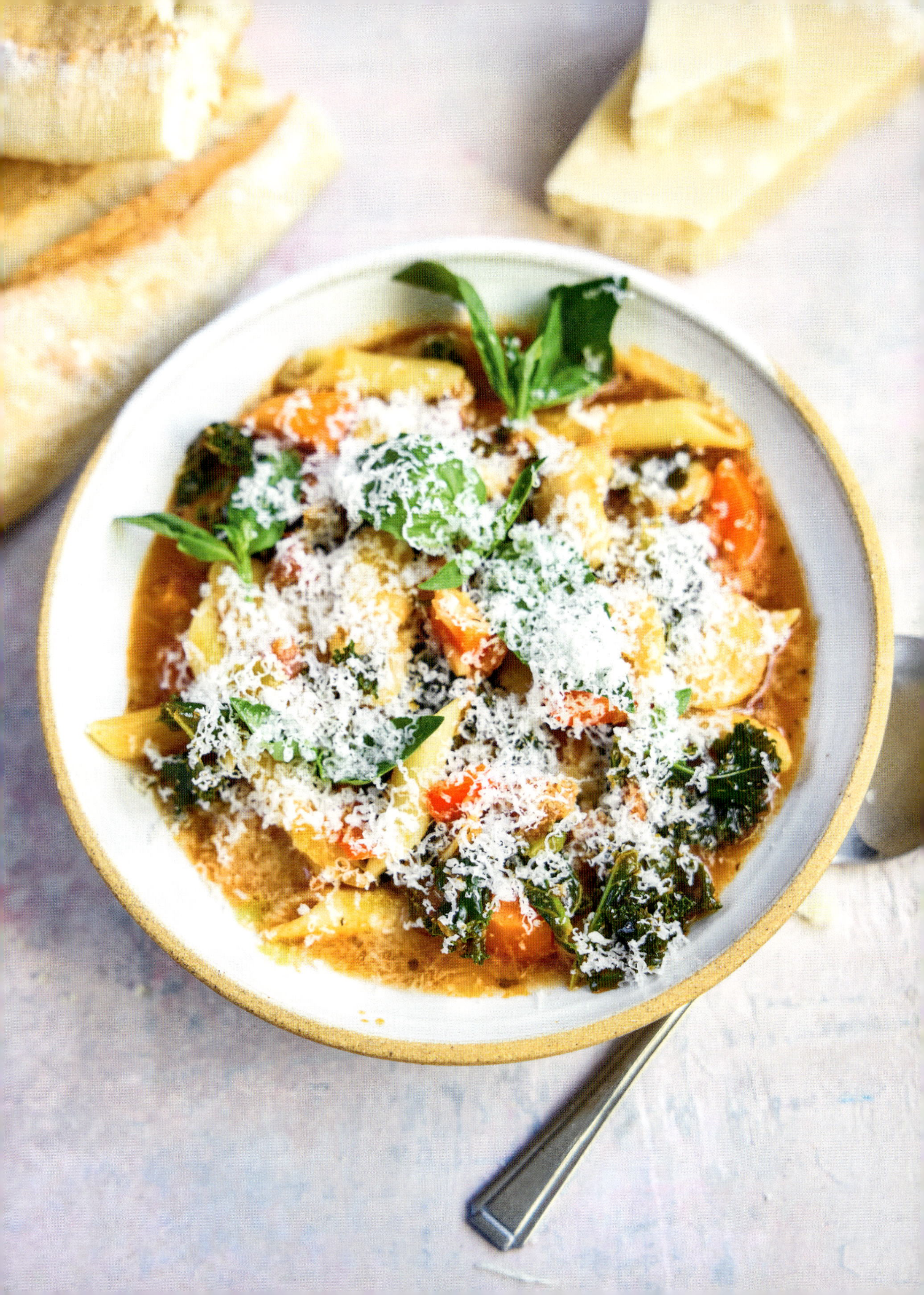

SERVES. 4 / **PREP TIME.** 15 MINUTES / **COOK TIME.** 40 MINUTES

WHEN DID I LAST EAT A VEGETABLE?

Warm, spicy and a bit of a dish... but enough about me. This absolute people pleaser combines two of my favorite Indian takeaway dishes: saag aloo and dhal. Potatoes, spinach and silky lentils all coated in a rich, spiced tomato sauce that is just begging for a naan to be dunked in it, this is a side dish with main character energy. Have it with a curry. Have it on its own. Honestly, just have it.

SAAG ALOO DHAL

① Slice the onion and put it into a large saucepan with 2 tablespoons of the vegetable oil over medium heat. Cook for around 7 minutes until it's nice and caramelized. Don't forget to season it with a pinch of salt.

② While the onion cooks down, thinly slice the chilli and grate the ginger and garlic.

③ Add the chilli, ginger and garlic in with the onions and fry that for a minute.

④ Add in all the spices, the tomato paste and perhaps an additional tablespoon of vegetable oil, if the pan is too dry, and cook this for a minute.

⑤ Finally, add the lentils, chopped tomatoes, 1½ cups of water and the diced potatoes. Bring it to a boil, place a lid on and simmer for 20–30 minutes, or until the potatoes are cooked.

⑥ Remove the lid, add all the spinach, then place the lid back on and simmer for 2 more minutes.

⑦ Once the spinach has wilted, season with salt and pepper, add the butter and serve with naan on the side.

1 white onion
3 tbsp vegetable oil
1 red chilli
1 thumb-sized piece of fresh ginger
3 cloves of garlic
1 tbsp ground cumin
1 tbsp ground coriander
1 tbsp ground turmeric
1 tsp chilli powder
1 tbsp tomato paste
4 oz (120 g) red split lentils
1 x 15.5 oz (439 g) can of chopped tomatoes
4 medium potatoes, peeled and diced into roughly 2 in (4 cm) chunks (like roast potatoes)
10 oz (300 g) spinach
2 tbsp butter
Sea salt and black pepper
Naan, to serve

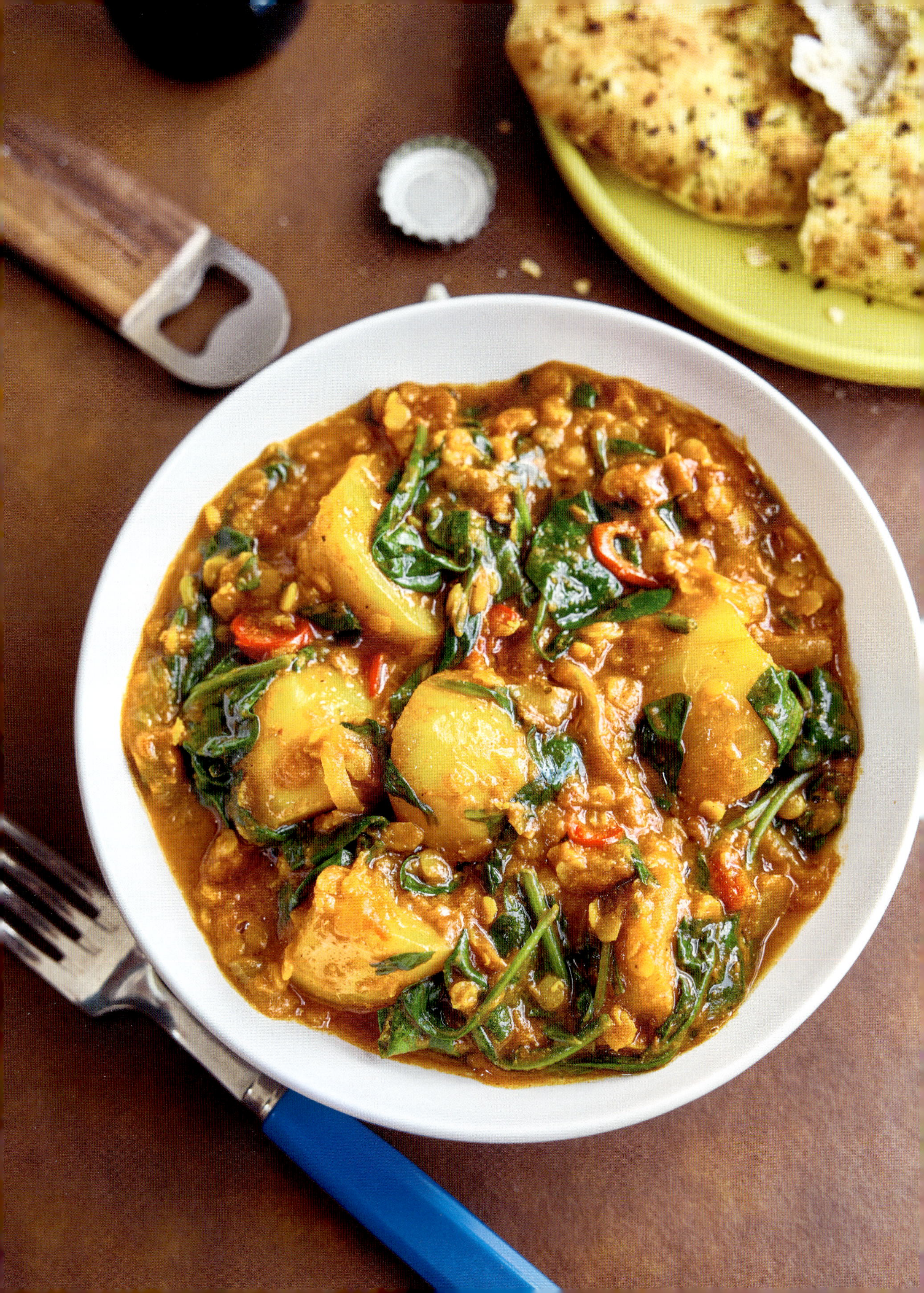

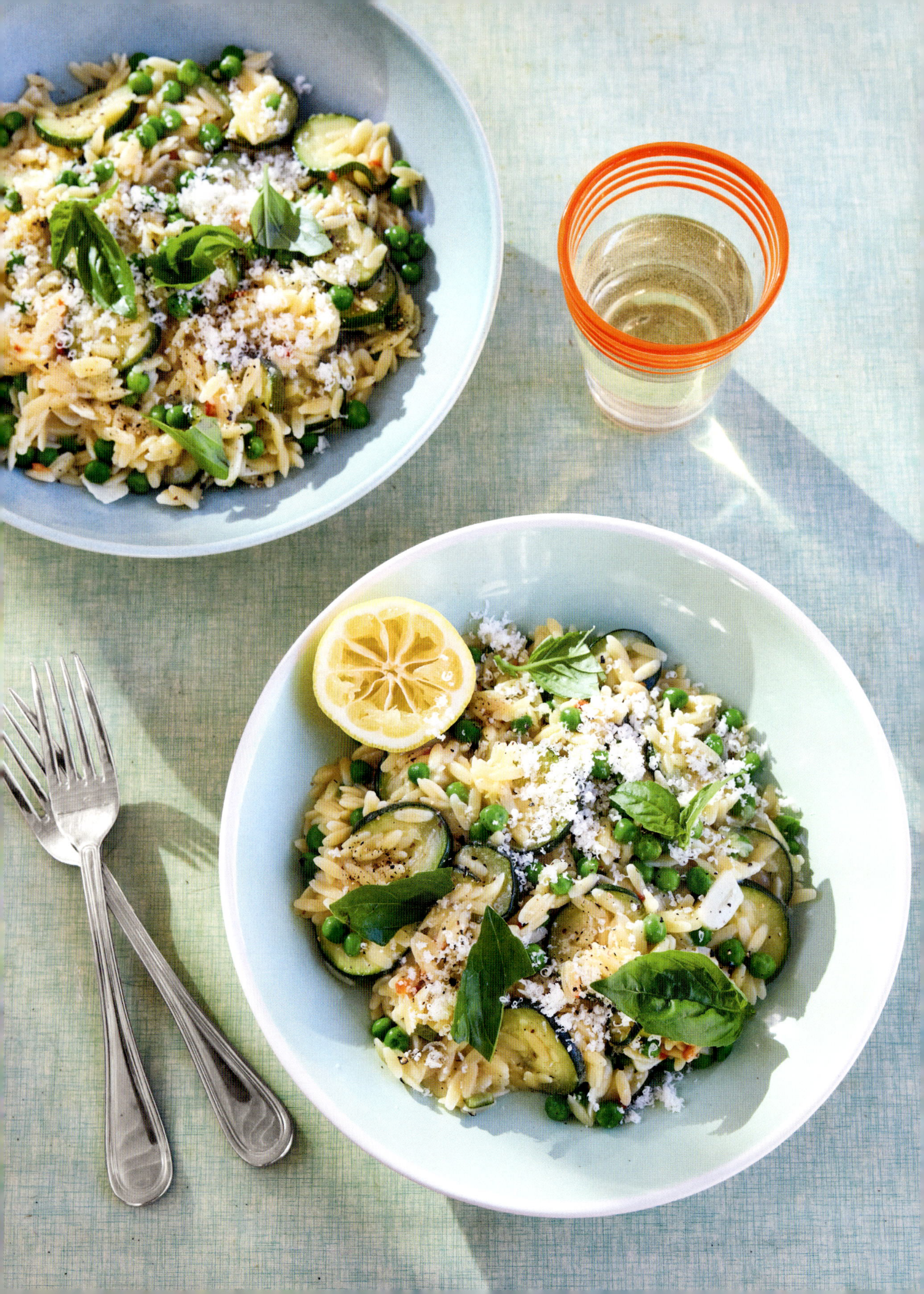

PREP TIME. 10 MINUTES / **COOK TIME.** 20 MINUTES / **SERVES.** 4

WHEN DID I LAST EAT A VEGETABLE?

Easy, fresh and delicious, this dish is one-pot perfection. Orzo is such a brilliant ingredient, offering all the silky goodness of a risotto but ready in a fraction of the time. Peas are a real kitchen hero, always on hand in the freezer for when you're craving veg but the fridge is bare.

Zucchini & Pea Orzo

① Start off by thinly slicing the zucchini and frying them with the olive oil in a large deep pan over medium heat for 3 minutes, stirring regularly, and don't forget to season them with salt and pepper.

② In the meantime, you can thinly slice the garlic and dice the red chilli. Add the garlic and chilli into the pan and fry them for a minute.

③ Add in the orzo and the vegetable stock, stir everything together and bring to the boil. Place a lid on top, lower the heat slightly and simmer for 8 minutes.

④ Take the lid off, add the peas and mix them. Place the lid back on and cook for another 2 minutes.

⑤ Finally, take the pan off the heat and stir in the Parmesan. Season with lemon zest, a squeeze of lemon juice and salt and pepper, to taste.

⑥ Garnish it with the basil and serve with extra Parmesan and a squeeze more lemon juice.

2 zucchini
5 tbsp olive oil
3 cloves of garlic
½ red chilli
8 oz (225 g) orzo
2 cups vegetable stock
1 cup peas
1½ oz (40g) Parmesan cheese, grated, plus extra to serve
Zest of 1 lemon and a squeeze of juice
Sea salt and black pepper
Handful of basil, to serve (optional)

SERVES. 4 / **PREP TIME.** 10 MINUTES / **COOK TIME.** 40 MINUTES

WHEN DID I LAST EAT A VEGETABLE?

In this recipe, we're bringing you all the big flavors from Mexico and whacking them into a luscious quesadilla. Perfect for a Friday night feast for you and your friends. Crack open a few cold ones or pour yourself a cheeky glass of wine and enjoy some lovely food.

veggie quesadillas

① Preheat the oven to 350°F (180°C).

② Start off by thinly slicing the red onion and bell peppers.

③ Pour 2 tablespoons of the vegetable oil into a hot frying pan and add the onion and bell peppers. Season with salt and pepper and cook these for around 3–4 minutes.

④ In the meantime, finely chop the garlic and drain the beans and corn.

⑤ Once the bell peppers have softened, add the garlic and spices and cook for a further minute. You might need to add an additional tablespoon of oil if the pan looks dry.

⑥ Finally, add the beans and corn to warm through before tipping everything into a bowl. Stir in the Mexican sauce and give it one final mix, then taste and season.

⑦ Place the frying pan back over medium heat with a teaspoon of vegetable oil and add a tortilla. On one half of the tortilla, sprinkle over some mozzarella and top it with a couple of spoonfuls of the black bean stew. Add a touch more mozzarella before folding the other half of the tortilla onto itself and pressing down gently for a few seconds to help the cheese stick.

⑧ Once it's golden brown on one side (usually this takes a minute or two), use a spatula to carefully flip it over and wait for the other side to turn golden brown. Keep an eye on the heat and lower it If it browns too quickly.

⑨ Repeat this process for the rest of the tortillas. Place them all onto a baking sheet and bake in the oven for 4–5 minutes to warm them through.

⑩ Cut each quesadilla into three and serve with some guacamole and sour cream ... BOSH!

1 red onion
2 red and yellow bell peppers
4 tbsp vegetable oil
3 cloves of garlic
1 x 15.5 oz (439 g) can of black beans
1 x 15.25 (432 g) can of corn
1 tsp ground cumin
1 tsp smoked paprika
1 tsp ground coriander
3½ oz (100 g) Mexican spicy sauce
8 flour tortillas
1 lb (454 g) mozzarella, grated
Sea salt and black pepper

TO SERVE

Guacamole (see page 128 or store-bought)
Sour cream

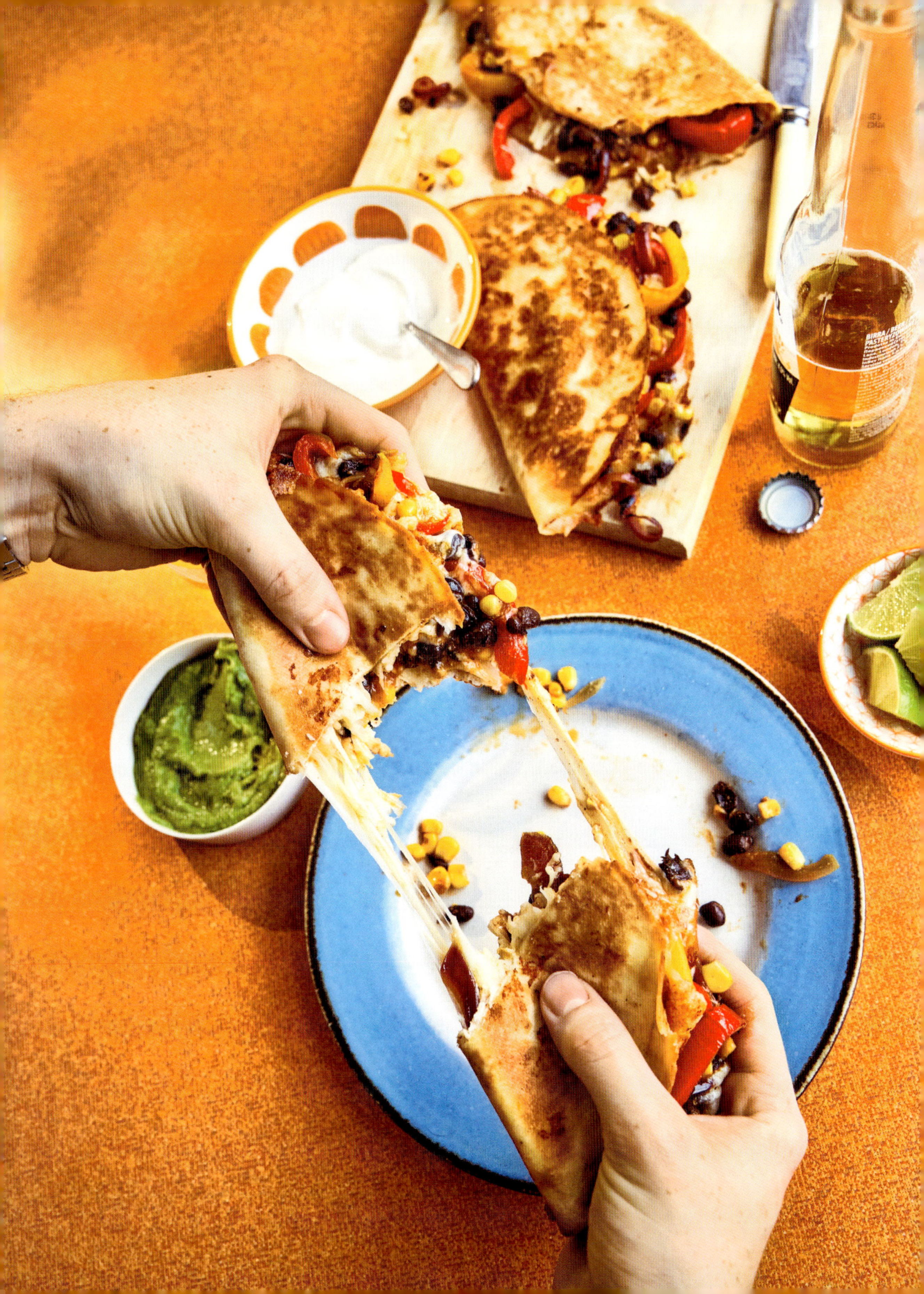

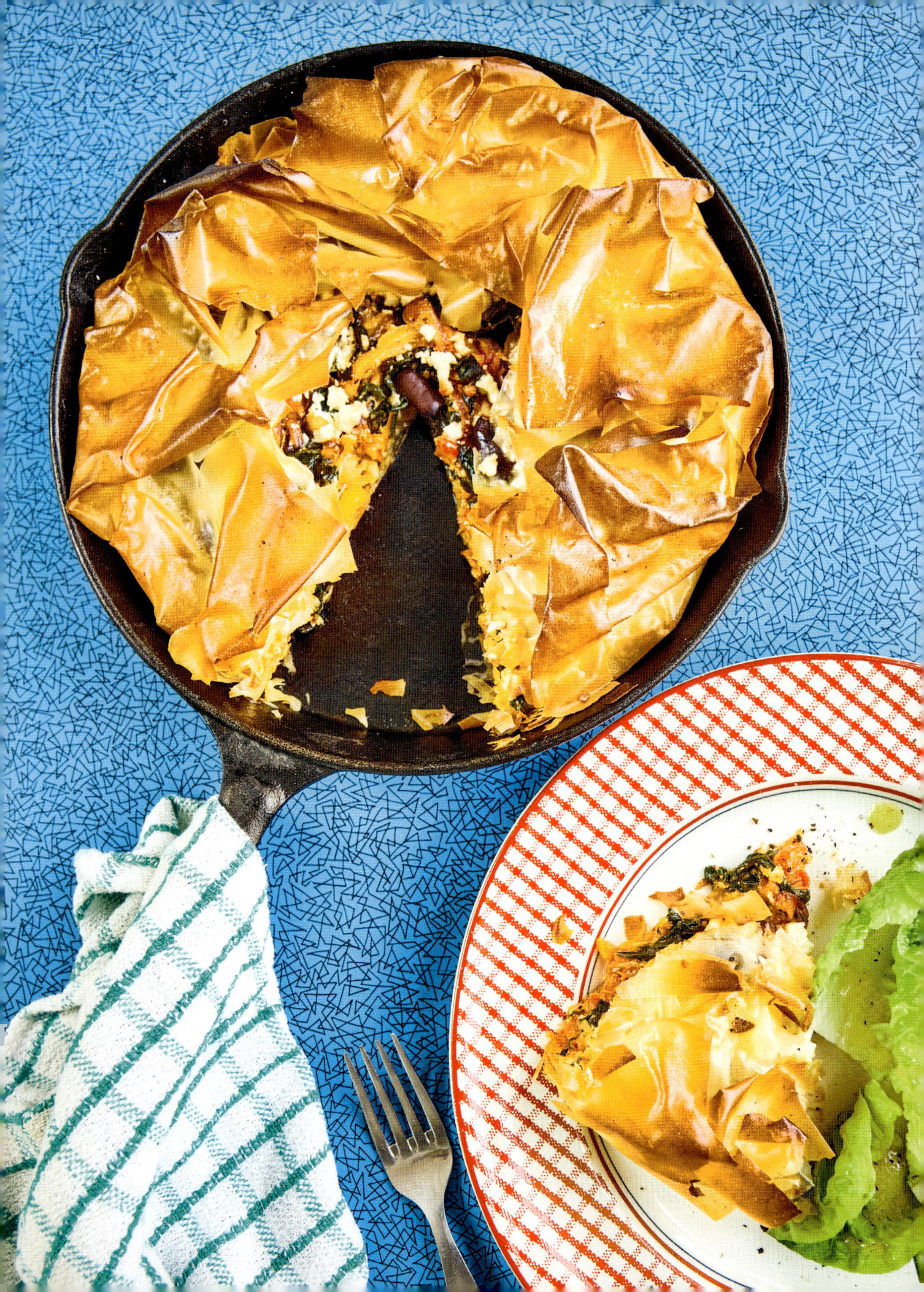

PREP TIME. 10 MINUTES / COOK TIME. 35 MINUTES / SERVES. 4

WHEN DID I LAST EAT A VEGETABLE?

For the little effort that this dish requires, this looks mightily impressive! A middle-of-the-table showstopper that is sure to deliver big flavors and even bigger smiles.

Mediterranean Filo Pie

① Preheat your oven to 400°F (200°C).

② Thinly slice your bell peppers and onion and fry them in a hot frying pan with the vegetable oil for 5 minutes. Make sure you season with salt and pepper.

③ While that's cooking, you can mince your garlic and dice the chilli. Add the garlic and chilli into the pan along with the paprika and cook for a further minute.

④ Add the tomato paste, spinach and crème fraîche and cook it down for around 3 minutes until the spinach has wilted. Zest in half the lemon, season with salt and pepper and set aside.

⑤ Melt the butter in a microwave or small pan and brush onto a single sheet of filo pastry. Lay this in a 8 x 8 inch (20 x 20 cm) ovenproof dish or cake pan roughly 8 inch (20 cm) in diameter, butter side down. You will have pastry hanging over the sides but don't worry, this will become the top of the pie. Repeat this process with six or seven more pieces of filo, placing the pastry down at different angles to make sure the base and sides are all properly covered.

⑥ Spoon in the filling and tear in the fresh basil leaves. Crumble over the feta, top with the olives and fold in the excess pastry hanging over the sides to completely cover the filling. Pour the remaining butter over the top of the pastry and bake for 20–25 minutes until golden brown and crispy. Serve with a green salad.

Ingredients
2 bell peppers (1 yellow, 1 red)
1 red onion
2 tbsp vegetable oil
3 cloves of garlic
½ red chilli
1 tsp paprika
1 tbsp tomato paste
3½ oz (100 g) spinach
½ cup crème fraîche
½ lemon
5 tbsp butter
1 x 10 oz (270 g) package of filo pastry
Handful of basil
3½ oz (100 g) feta cheese
10 black olives, sliced
Sea salt and black pepper
Salad leaves, to serve

MAKES. 6 — **PREP TIME. 40 MINUTES** / **COOK TIME. 15 MINUTES**

WHEN DID I LAST EAT A VEGETABLE?

Making your own flatbreads might seem like a faff, but these are super simple, only use a handful of ingredients and far cheaper than buying ready-made. You can also freeze portions of the dough to defrost and bake off as needed. I've given you two filling options here, but feel free to go wild and come up with your own if you prefer!

SUN-DRIED TOMATO & PESTO-STUFFED FLATBREADS

1. Preheat the oven to 325°F (160°C).
2. Add the flour to a large bowl and add the salt. Pour in the olive oil and Greek yogurt and use a wooden spoon to bring the dough together (the dough might need a few tablespoons of water to help bring it all together).
3. Knead on a lightly-floured chopping board for a couple of minutes and then cut into six even pieces.
4. Take one ball of dough and use a rolling pin to roll it out to a circle roughly 4.5–5 inches (12–13 cm) across.
5. Add 1 teaspoon of pesto into the middle of the dough and top with 2 chopped sun-dried tomatoes and a heaped tablespoon of mozzarella.
6. Fold the outside of the dough into the middle and pinch it together to make a seal. Make sure it is really well sealed, so the filling doesn't leak during cooking. Gently press the bread to flatten slightly to a 4 inch (10 cm) round. Repeat the process with the remaining ingredients.
7. Place the flatbreads into a frying pan over a medium heat and cook them for 3 minutes on each side. Keep an eye on them and lower the heat if they are coloring too quickly.
8. Place the flatbreads into the oven for 8 minutes and serve them nice and hot for your guests.

FOR THE DOUGH

| 2 ⅓ cup self-rising flour |
| 1 tsp salt |
| 2 tbsp olive oil |
| ⅔ cup Greek yogurt |

FOR THE SUN-DRIED TOMATO AND PESTO FILLING

| 6 tsp basil pesto |
| 12 sun-dried tomatoes, roughly chopped |
| 6 heaped tbsp grated mozzarella |

Garlic butter filling

For an alternative filling, mix ¼ cup softened butter with 1 teaspoon of minced garlic and 1 teaspoon of mixed herbs. Put 1 teaspoon of garlic butter into the middle of each dough piece and top with 1 teaspoon of caramelized onion chutney and a heaped tablespoon of grated mozzarella before folding.

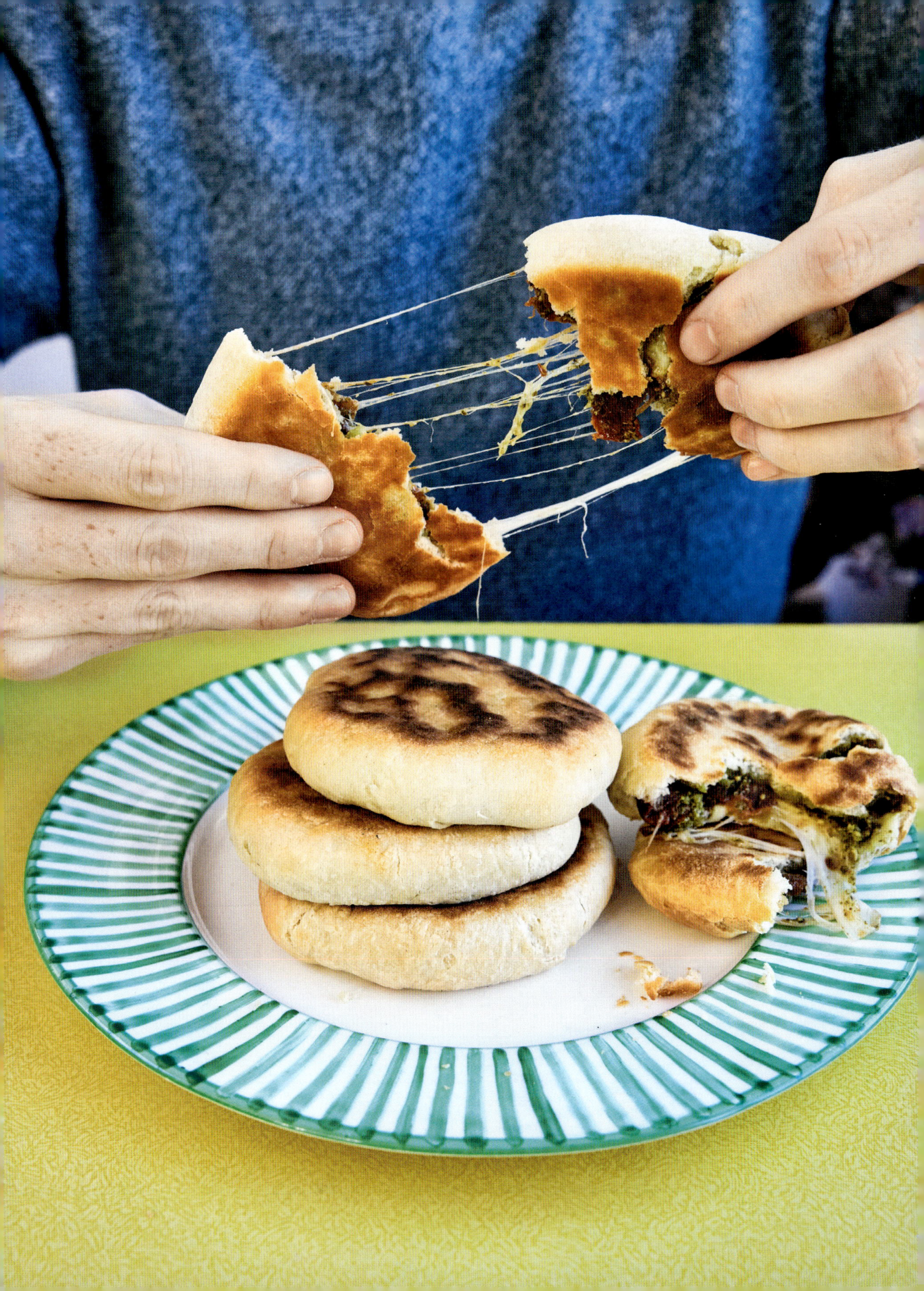

monday meal

PReP

You might think meal prep is just for gym bros looking to fill their fridge with as much protein as possible, but doing a bit of work on a Monday (or any other day that takes your fancy!) will leave you with easy, ready-to-go meals that will save you time and money for the rest of the week. This chapter includes warming soups, tasty sandwich fillings, meaty mains and even the odd sweet treat to keep you smiling all week long.

MONDAY MEAL PREP

SERVES. 6 / **PREP TIME.** 10 MINUTES / **COOK TIME.** 1 HOUR 15 MINUTES

This is a brilliantly versatile recipe that begins as a wonderful spaghetti Bolognese and, with a few simple additions, can be transformed into a showstopping chili con carne (see page 167). Leftovers that keep on giving throughout the week!

Big Batch Bolognese

① Start by finely dicing the onion, carrot and celery. Place a large saucepan over medium heat with the vegetable oil. Add in the veg, season with salt and sweat for 5–7 minutes.

② Season the beef with some salt and turn the heat up in the pan. Add the meat and brown it off for 2–3 minutes.

③ Add in the flour and tomato paste and cook for 1 minute.

④ Finally, pour in the red wine, add the chopped tomatoes, ¾ cup of water and the beef stock cube. Bring it up to the boil, then place a lid on. Lower the heat and simmer for 1 hour, stirring occasionally.

⑤ Finally, taste and season with some more salt and pepper.

1 white onion
1 carrot
2 celery sticks
2 tbsp vegetable oil
1 lb (500 g) ground beef
2 tbsp plain flour
1 tbsp tomato paste
⅔ cup red wine
2 x 15.5 oz (429 g) cans of chopped tomatoes
1 beef stock cube
Sea salt and black pepper

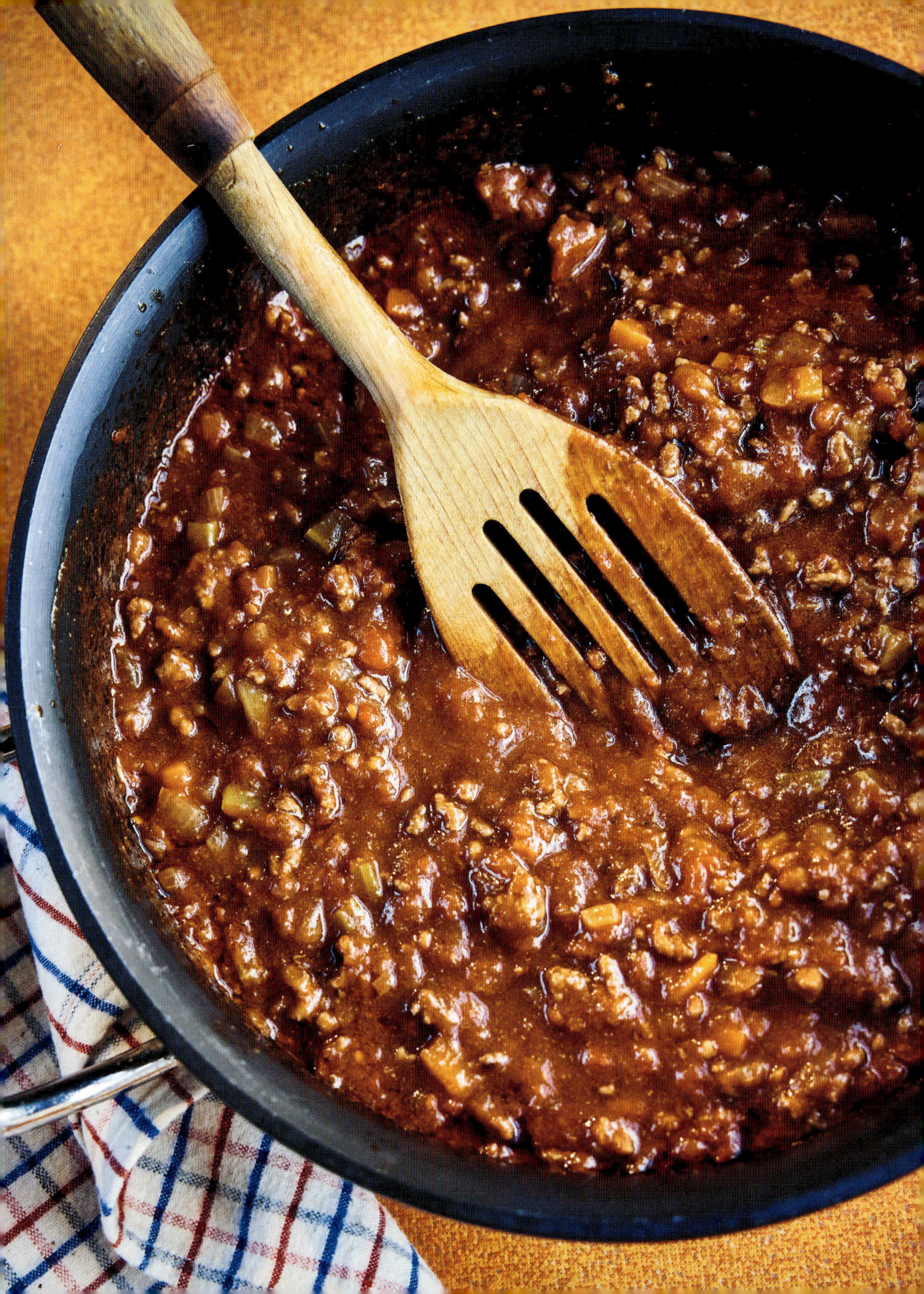

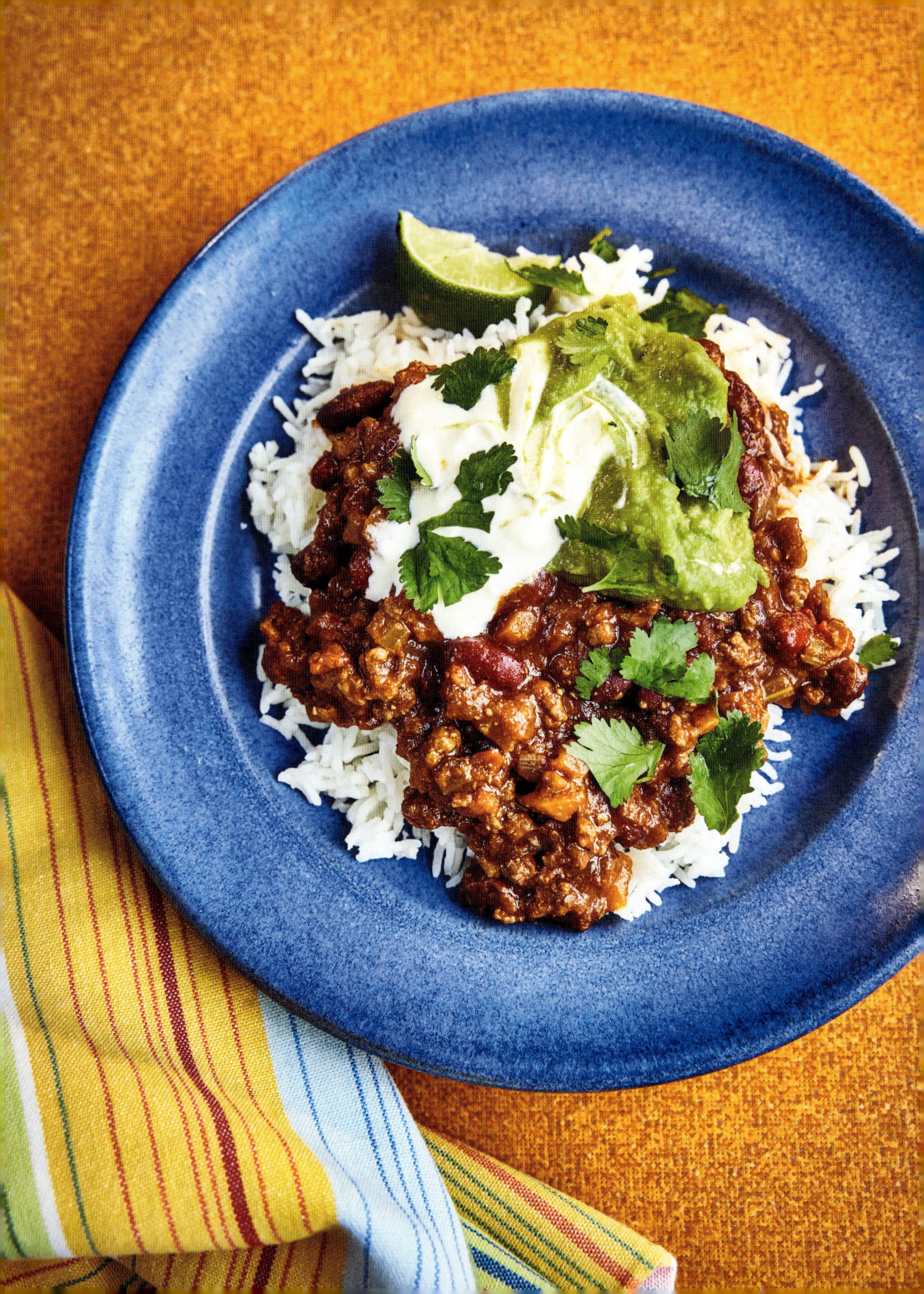

PREP TIME. 5 MINUTES / **COOK TIME.** 15 MINUTES / **SERVES.** 4

MONDAY MEAL PREP

Transform your leftover Bolognese (see page 164) into this warming chili, full of flavor and rich with mellow spice. This is delicious served with rice and topped with creamy guac, but also makes a banging filling for a jacket potato.

ROLLOVER CHILI

① Pour the vegetable oil into a large saucepan over medium heat. Add the oregano and spices and fry for 1 minute.

② Add the Bolognese with the drained kidney beans and simmer for 10 minutes.

③ Taste and season with some salt and pepper and serve with rice, sour cream, guacamole, lime wedges and cilantro.

2 tbsp vegetable oil
1 tbsp dried oregano
1 tbsp ground cumin
1 tbsp ground coriander
½ tsp ground cinnamon
1 tsp chilli powder
3 cups Big Batch Bolognese (see page 164)
1 x 15.5 oz (439 g) can of red kidney beans
Sea salt and black pepper

TO SERVE

Cooked rice (see page 22)
Sour cream
Guacamole (see page 128 or store-bought)
Lime wedges
Cilantro leaves

MONDAY MEAL PREP

MAKES. 5 LUNCHES / **PREP TIME.** 15 MINUTES / **COOK TIME.** 35 MINUTES

This is a brilliant meal-prep option that will keep you in healthy, tasty lunches all week long. If you are making this ahead to box up for the fridge, make sure to let the chicken cool to room temperature before transferring to your meal-prep boxes. This will keep for up to five days in the fridge.

Middle-Eastern Chicken Couscous Boxes

1. Preheat the oven to 350°F (180°C).
2. Put the spices into a bowl along with vegetable oil and lemon zest. Mix them together until they're nicely combined.
3. Place the chicken breasts into a roasting pan and cover with the marinade. Season with salt and pepper and use your hands to make sure the chicken is nicely coated.
4. Bake in the oven for 25–35 minutes, or until there is no pink in the middle of the chicken breasts.
5. Meanwhile, put the couscous into a bowl and cover with 1 cup boiling water. Wrap in cling film and leave on the side for 10 minutes.
6. In the meantime, you can finely chop your tomatoes, red onion and cucumber.
7. Remove the cling film and use a fork to fluff up the couscous. Then add the tomato, onion, cucumber, harissa paste and a generous squeeze of lemon juice. Season with salt and pepper and mix everything together.
8. Chop the chicken up and add it back into the roasting pan to mop up all the remaining flavor left in the tray. Add a squeeze of lemon juice and give it one last seasoning with salt and pepper.
9. Serve up the chicken and couscous with some tzatziki and hummus. Box it up and enjoy it for the rest of the week for lunch.

1 tbsp ground cumin
1 tbsp ground coriander
1 tbsp smoked paprika
3 tbsp vegetable oil
Zest and juice of 1 lemon
4 chicken breasts
1 ⅓ cup couscous
15 cherry tomatoes
1 red onion
½ cucumber
1 heaped tbsp harissa paste
Sea salt and black pepper

TO SERVE
Tzatziki (see page 185)
Hummus (see page 185)

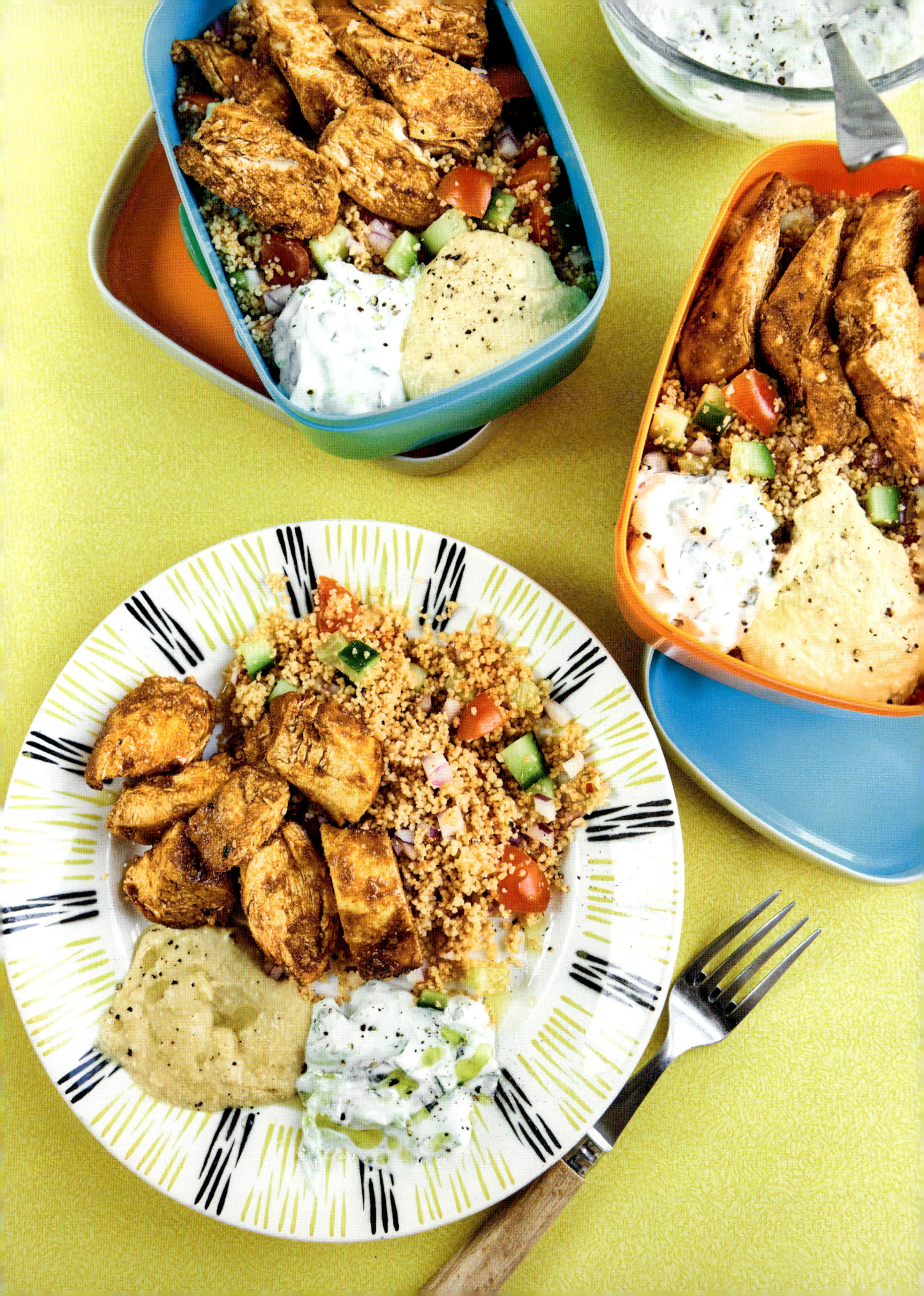

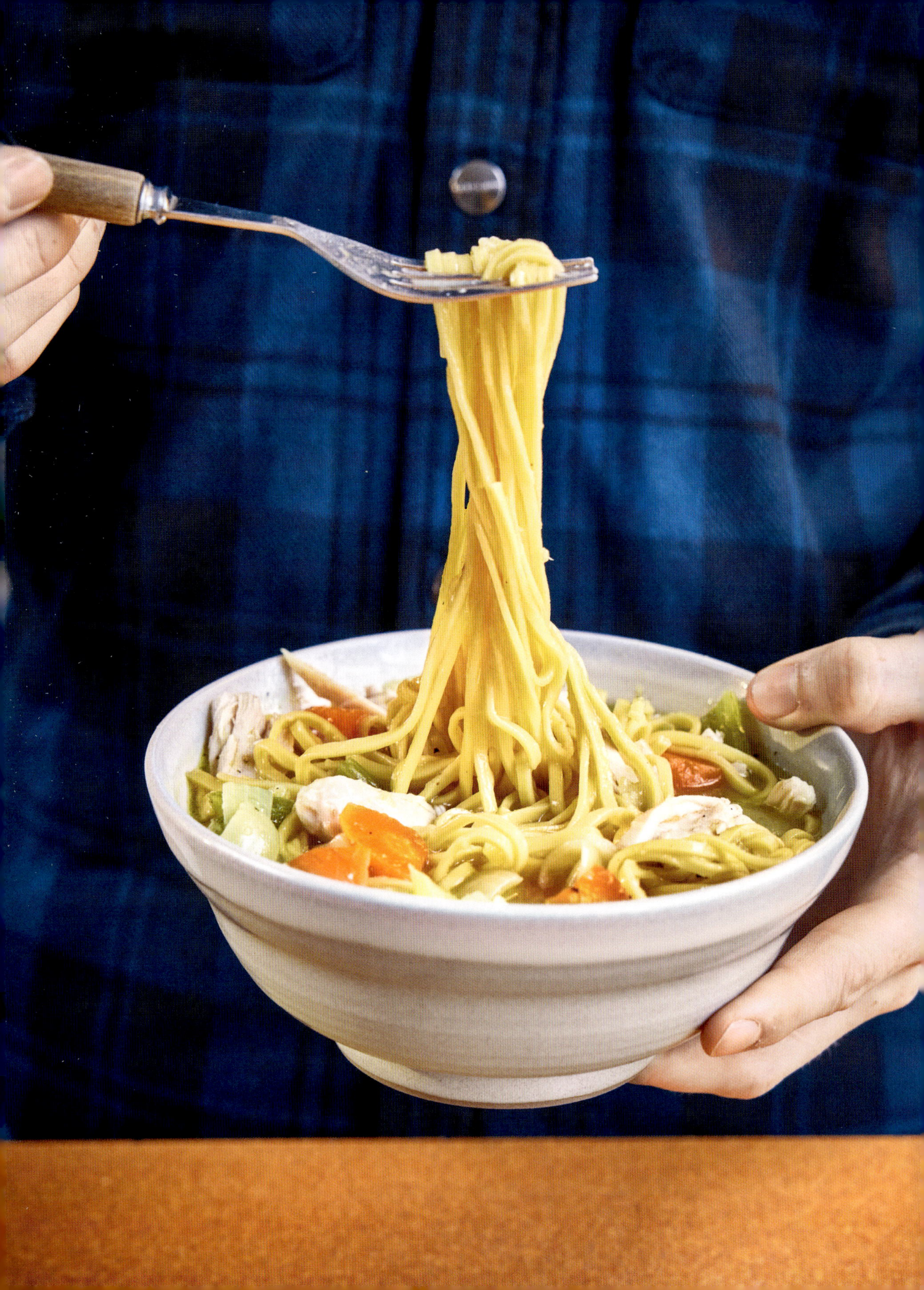

PREP TIME. 10 MINUTES / **COOK TIME.** 25 MINUTES / **SERVES.** 4

MONDAY MEAL PREP

Wholesome, nourishing and perfect as a pick-me-up, this is my take on an instant noodle pot, but with more flavor and fewer additives. Keep it in the fridge and reheat for an easy, warming lunch throughout the week.

Feel-Better Chicken Noodle Soup

① Roughly chop the onions, carrots and celery into bite-size pieces. Place a large saucepan over medium heat with the vegetable oil and add the veggies. Season with salt and cook over medium to low heat for 10 minutes.

② Grate the garlic and ginger, add them to the pot and cook for 1 minute.

③ Add the stock cubes and 1.5 litres of water and bring to the boil.

④ Season the chicken with salt and pepper and add to the broth. Reduce to a simmer and poach the chicken for 8 minutes.

⑤ Take off the heat and remove the chicken from the broth. Use two forks to shred the chicken into bite-sized pieces.

⑥ If you are meal prepping this and not eating it straight away, now is a great time to split the soup into individual portions, so all you need to do is reheat the soup and cook one portion of noodles when you are ready for it.

⑦ Add the noodles into the broth and cook as per the packet instructions. Give it one final taste, season and enjoy.

2 white onions
2 carrots
2 celery sticks
2 tbsp vegetable oil
5 cloves of garlic
2 thumb-sized pieces of fresh ginger
2 chicken stock cubes
22 oz (650 g) chicken thighs, skinless and boneless
7 oz (200 g) egg noodles
Sea salt and black pepper

MONDAY MEAL PREP

SERVES. 4 / PREP TIME. 10 MINUTES / COOK TIME. 30 MINUTES

This beautiful, spiced soup is perfect for cold winter days. A comforting classic that is perfect for using up excess vegetables. Make a big batch to last throughout the week as a lunchtime staple or light evening dinner. You can even freeze it, making it super versatile, available and always on point.

CURRIED CARROT SOUP

① Peel and finely slice the carrots and onion.

② Preheat a large pot with 2 tablespoons of the vegetable oil. Once hot, add in the veggies, season generously with salt and cook for 5 minutes.

③ Peel and grate the ginger and garlic and add them, along with the spices, to the carrots. Cook this down for a minute. You might need to add the remaining tablespoon of vegetable oil if it looks too dry.

④ Pour in the coconut milk and vegetable stock and simmer for 20 minutes, or until the carrots are completely soft.

⑤ Use a hand blender to blitz it until smooth. Season with salt and pepper and adjust the consistency with more water if necessary.

⑥ Serve up garnished with a touch of cream in each bowl.

5-6 carrots (around 1 lb [450 g])
1 onion
3 tbsp vegetable oil
1 thumb-sized piece of fresh ginger
3 cloves of garlic
1 tbsp mild curry powder
2 tsp ground turmeric
1 x 15.5 oz (400 ml) can of coconut milk
4½ cups vegetable stock
Sea salt and black pepper
4 tsp heavy cream, to serve

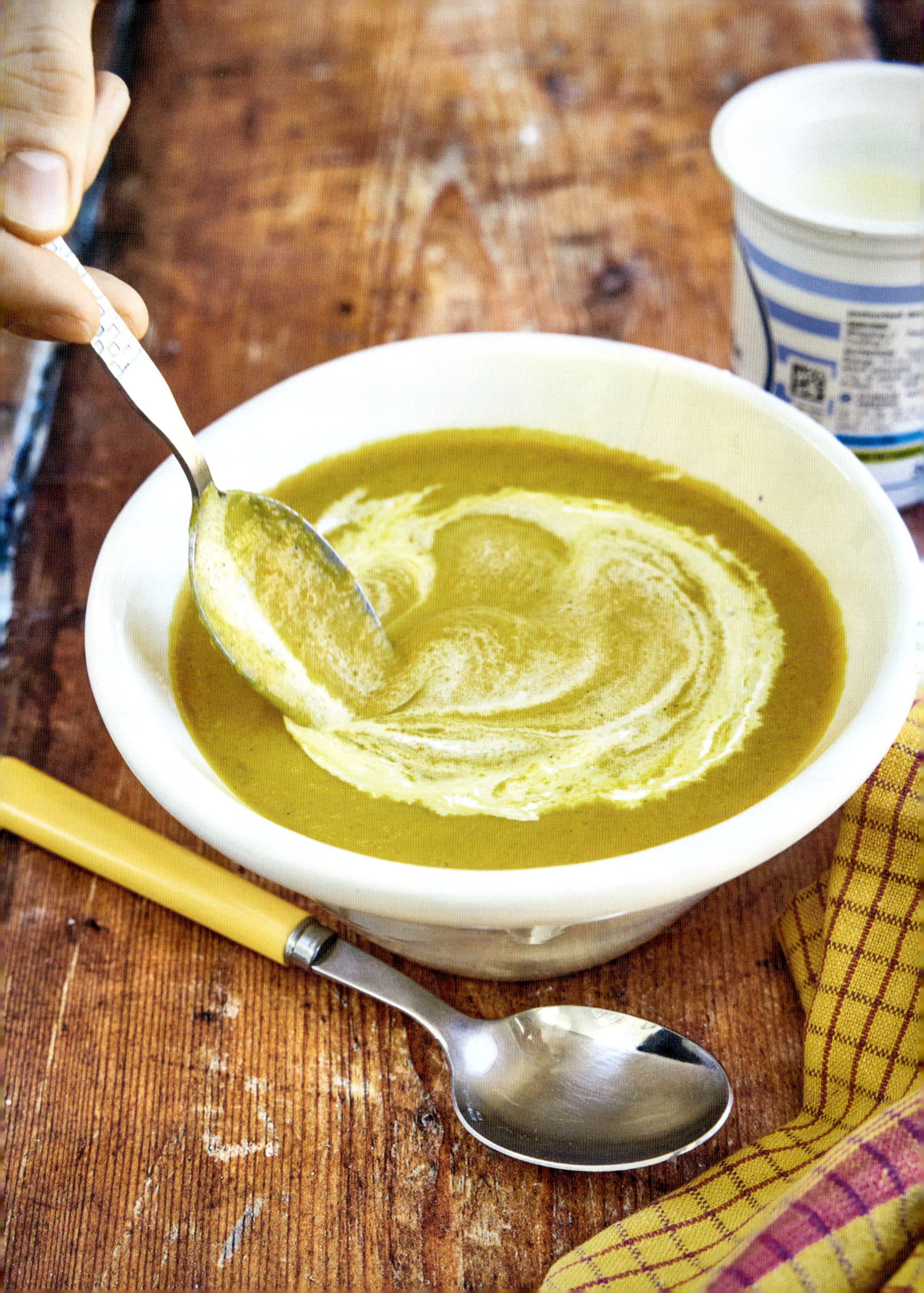

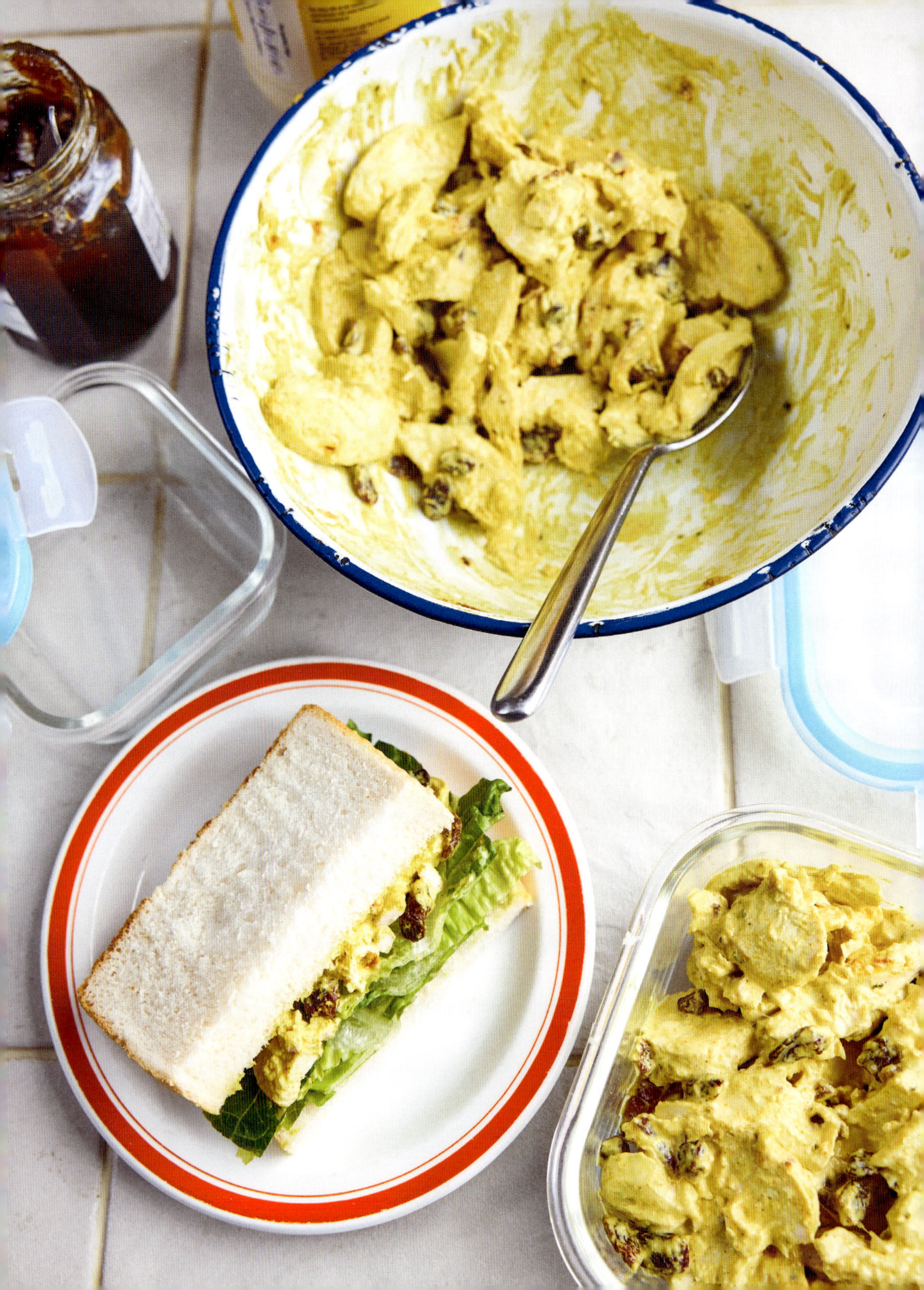

PREP TIME. 15 MINUTES + 1 HOUR MARINATING / **COOK TIME.** 30 MINUTES / **SERVES.** 4

MONDAY MEAL PREP

A dish fit for royalty. Invented in 1953 for the Coronation of Queen Elizabeth II, this has been a British staple ever since. Make a big batch on Monday and your work is done. Ideal as a sandwich filler, a potato topper or to make a salad sing.

Coronation Chicken

1 cup Greek yogurt
1 tbsp curry powder
1½ tbsp ground turmeric
4 chicken breasts
⅓ cup golden raisins
½ cup mayonnaise
1½ tbsp caramelized onion chutney or mango chutney
Sea salt and black pepper

① Put ¾ cup of the yogurt into a bowl, add the curry powder and turmeric and season with salt and pepper. Add the chicken and leave to marinate for 30 minutes to an hour.

② Preheat your oven to 350°F (180°C).

③ Lift the chicken out of the marinade bowl and place it on a baking sheet. Cook your chicken for 25–30 minutes, or until the chicken is piping hot all the way through.

④ Once the chicken is cooked, slice it thinly, place it into a big mixing bowl and leave to cool to room temperature.

⑤ Add in the golden raisins, mayonnaise, the rest of the yogurt and the chutney and mix till it's nicely combined. Taste and season with salt and pepper.

⑥ Place it into your meal prep boxes and job done.

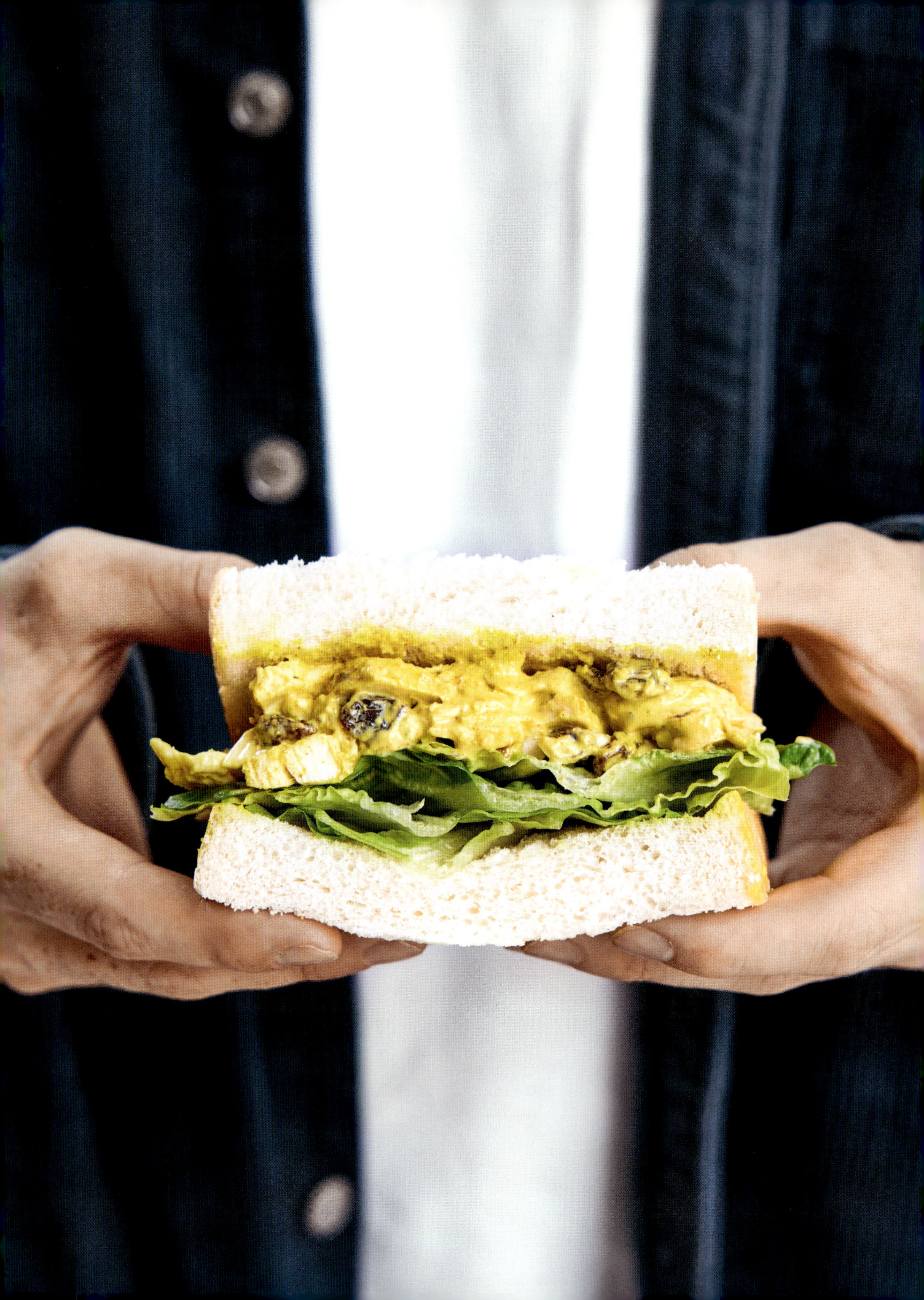

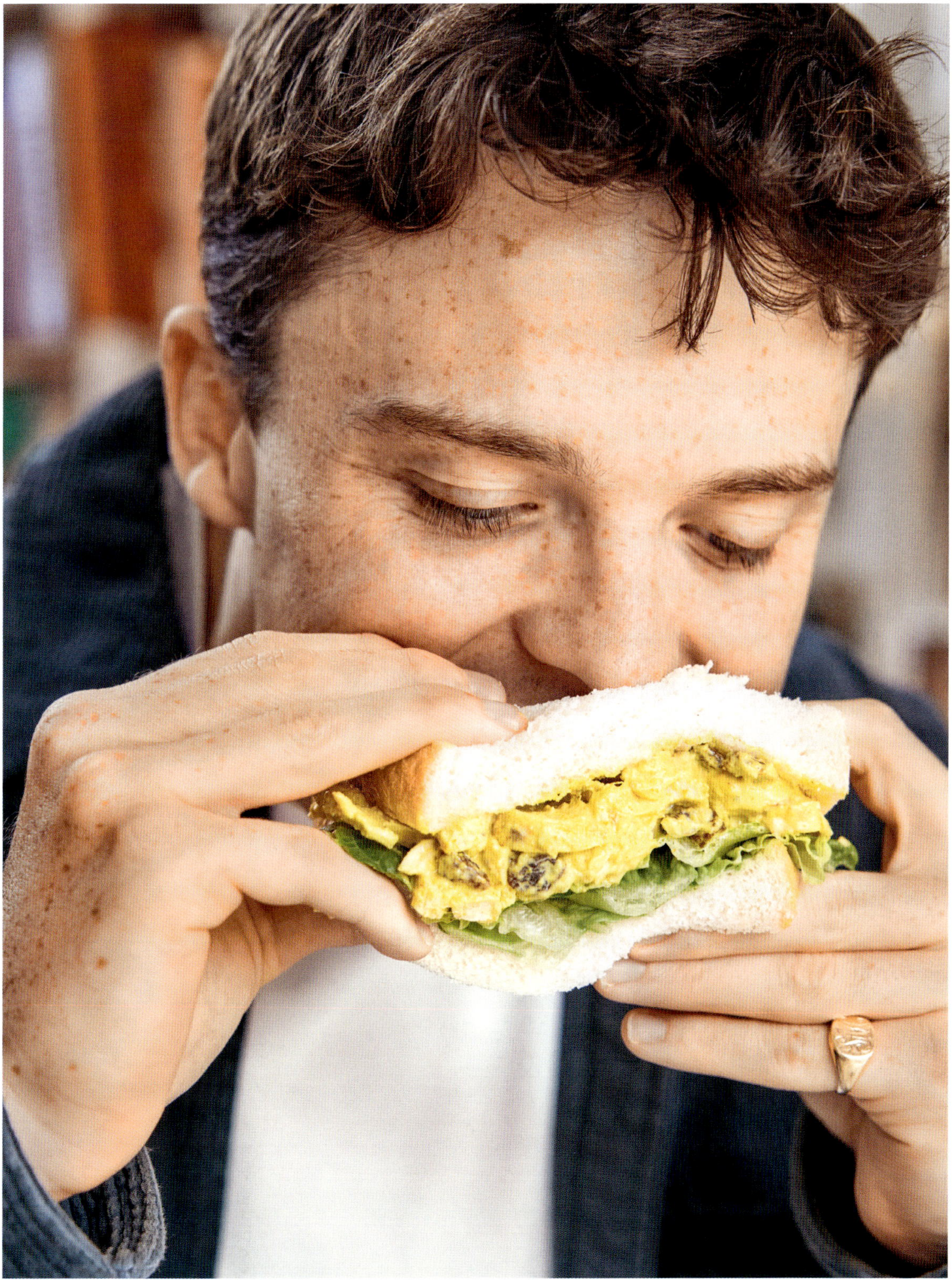

MONDAY MEAL PREP

SERVES. 6 / **PREP TIME.** 10 MINUTES / **COOK TIME.** 30 MINUTES

There is nothing more comforting than a chicken pie on a chilly day. But people often don't know how versatile it is. Sure, it goes brilliantly with pastry and mash. But it's also delicious with some pasta, rice, chips, or just sling it on top of a jacket potato and you're onto a winner. Win, win, win!

Chicken Pie Filling

① Chop the woody ends off the leeks and slice them in half lengthwise. Remove the outer layer and rinse the leeks under running water to clean away any soil. Thinly slice the leeks, grate the carrot, slice the mushrooms and place into a big bowl.

② Season the chicken thighs with salt and pepper on both sides. Fry them in a big saucepan over a high heat with 2 tablespoons of the oil for around 2 minutes on each side or until they are nice and golden brown. You might have to fry them in batches if they don't fit in one pan. Once they're nicely browned, put them in a bowl and set aside for later.

③ Add all the vegetables to the same pan (I know it looks like a lot but trust me it'll cook down). Season generously with salt and add the remaining oil. Cook these down for around 7–8 minutes until they are nice and soft.

④ Add the flour into the pan and mix to incorporate, then cook for a minute. Slowly pour in the wine and chicken stock while stirring continuously to avoid any lumps.

⑤ Bring to the boil and add the chicken back into the pan along with the cream, mixed herbs and mustard. Reduce to a simmer and cook for 10 minutes.

⑥ Once the chicken is cooked, use two forks to shred it into large chunks. Taste and season with more salt, pepper and mustard, if necessary, and enjoy.

Chicken pie pastry tops:

Cut a sheet of ready-rolled puff pastry into six squares. Place on a baking sheet lined with the paper the pastry came on, brush with beaten egg and bake for 16–18 minutes in an oven preheated to 400°F (200°C).

Ingredients
2 large leeks or 3 small ones
2 carrots
8 oz (227 g) mushrooms
2 lbs (1kg) chicken thighs, skinless and boneless
4 tbsp vegetable oil
⅓ cup all-purpose flour
½ cup white wine
1½ cups chicken stock
3½ tbsp cream
1 tbsp mixed herbs
2 heaped tsp English mustard
Sea salt and black pepper

Chicken bakes:

Unroll a sheet of ready-rolled puff pastry. Cut it into eight equal rectangular pieces. Brush four of the rectangles with a little beaten egg around the edges. Spoon 2 tablespoons of chicken pie filling into the center of each rectangle, making sure to leave at least a ½ inch (1 cm) around the edge. Place the other rectangles on top and seal around the edges by pressing down gently with your fingers, then using a floured fork to seal. Place on a baking sheet lined with the paper the pastry came on, brush with beaten egg and bake for 20-25 minutes until golden. Check they are cooked by carefully lifting up a chicken bake to check that the underside of the pastry is golden.

MONDAY MEAL PREP

PREP TIME. 5 MINUTES

SALAD DRESSINGS

These three dressings will bring even the saddest salads to life. They will keep in a jam jar in the fridge for a week or two to be used as needed, and just need a quick shake to bring them back together before using.

FRENCH VINAIGRETTE

6 tbsp olive oil
1½ tsp Dijon mustard
2 tbsp white wine vinegar
1 tsp sugar
Pinch of sea salt

❶ Place everything into a bowl and mix it up.

HONEY MUSTARD DRESSING

1 tbsp honey
1 heaped tbsp wholegrain mustard
3 tbsp olive oil
Juice of ½ lemon
1 tbsp water
Pinch of sea salt

❶ Place everything into a bowl and mix it up.

SOY & SESAME DRESSING

2 cloves of garlic
2 tsp fresh ginger, grated
4 tbsp sesame oil
2 tbsp light soy sauce
1 tbsp honey
Juice of 1 lime

❶ Mince the garlic, then place everything into a bowl and mix it up.

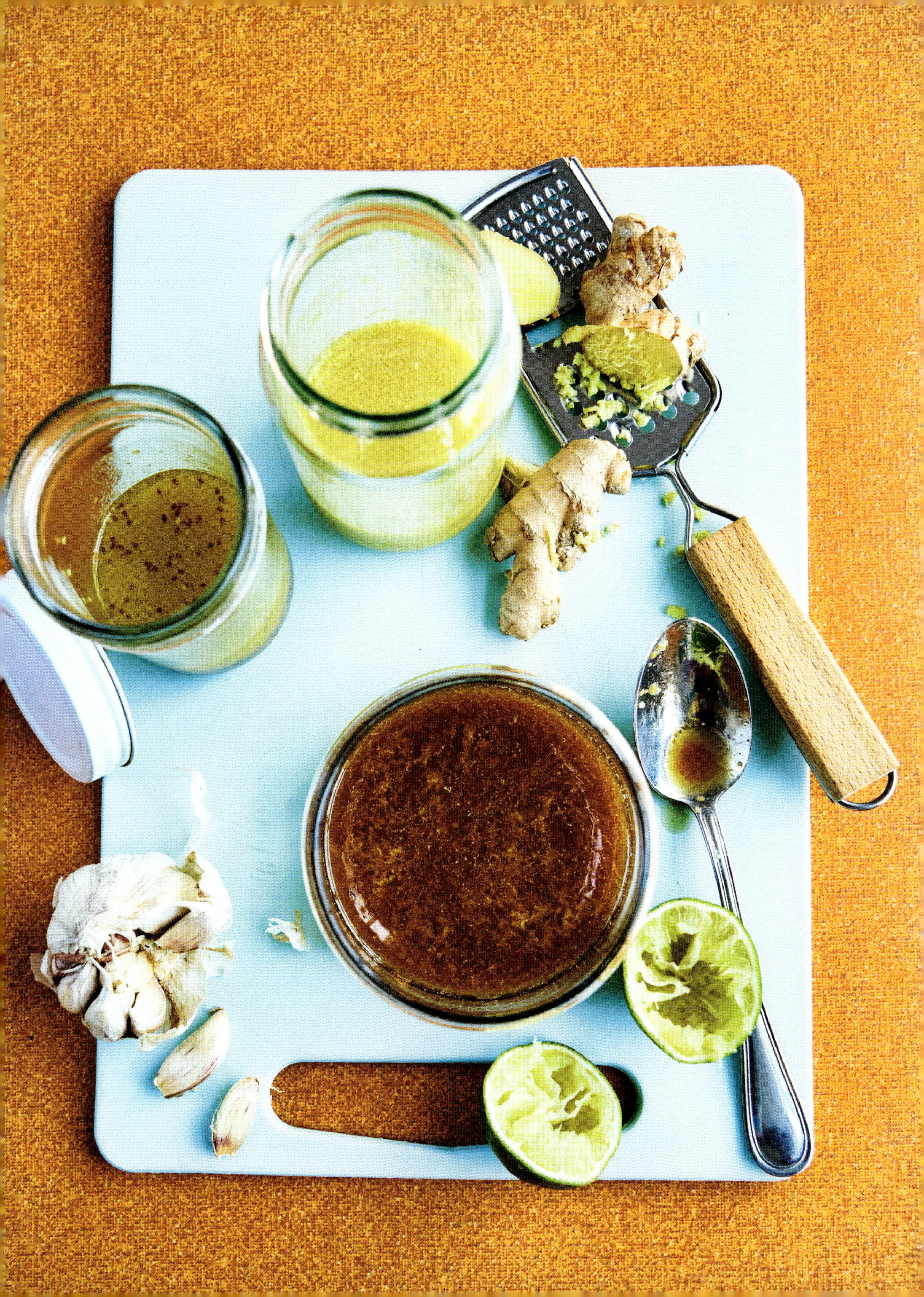

DIPS & SAUCES

Dips for days! I've given you a trio of Hummus recipes here, as well as a classic Tzatziki and a fresh and flavorful Pea & Mint Sauce. These will all keep in the fridge for a few days and are great to pull out with a few crisps, pita or crunchy veg to enjoy with friends alongside some beers. Just remember, double dipping will not be tolerated!

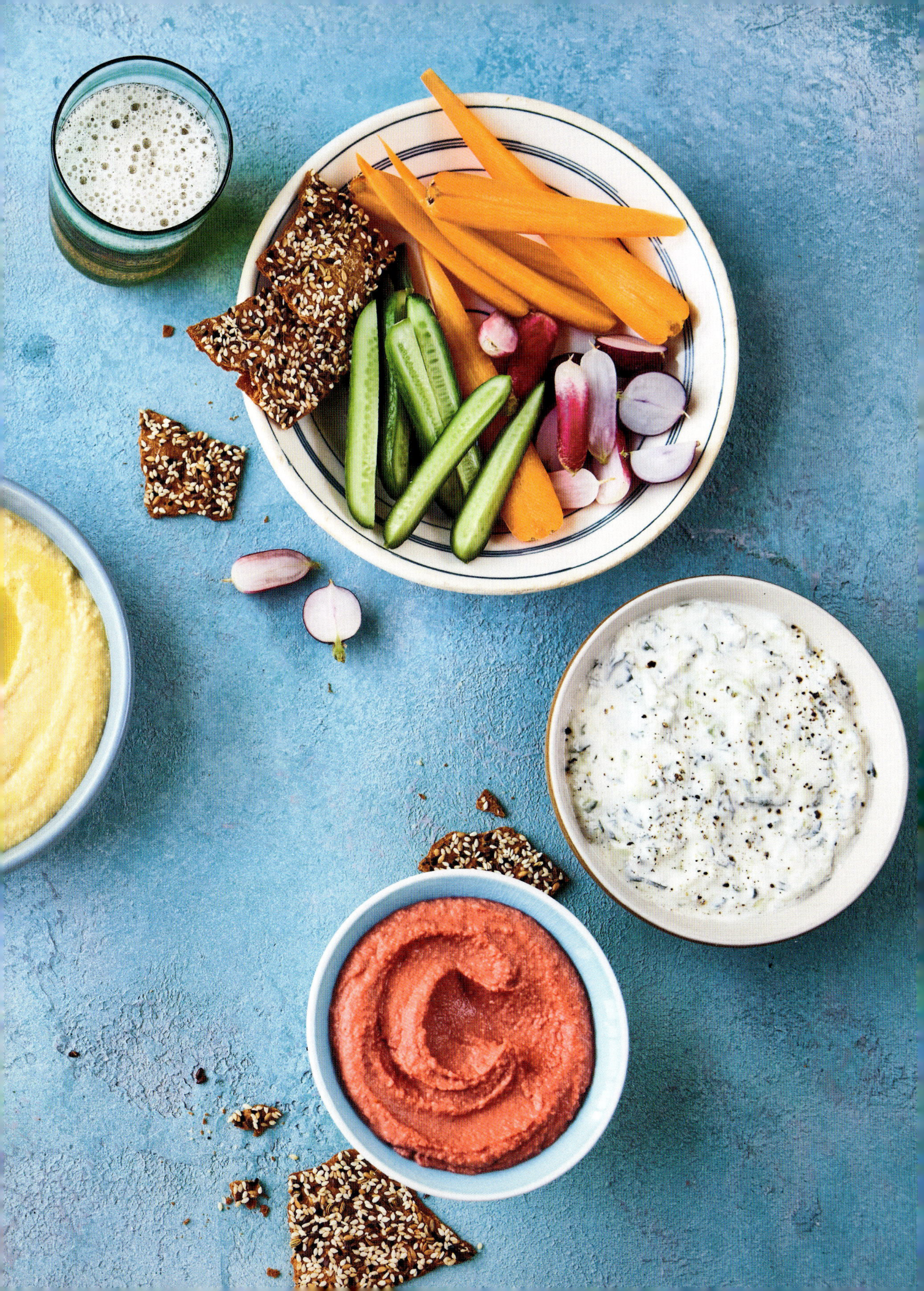

MONDAY MEAL PREP

ALL RECIPES SERVE. 4 WITH PITA BREADS, CHIPS OR CRUDITÉS

ROASTED RED PEPPER HUMMUS

Roasted red peppers give an instant punch of flavor and are a great thing to have in the back of the fridge. I use them here and in the Piri Piri Chicken recipe on page 127, so buy a jar and get cooking!

1 x 15.5 oz (439 g) can of chickpeas
1 clove of garlic
2 roasted red peppers (from a jar)
1 heaped tsp harissa paste
2 tbsp tahini
Juice of 1 large lemon
1 tsp ground cumin
Sea salt and black pepper

❶ Drain the chickpeas, place in a blender with the minced garlic and all the other ingredients and blitz to a smooth purée. Taste, season and enjoy!

PEA & MINT SAUCE

COOK TIME. 2 MINUTES

This is a wonderful dip, but also makes for a really tasty pasta sauce. Just stir through cooked pasta with a ladleful of pasta water (see page 23), grate over some Parmesan and dig in!

Handful of mint
8 oz (100 g) cream cheese
1½ cups frozen peas
Zest of 1 lemon
Pinch of chilli flakes
1 tbsp olive oil
Sea salt and black pepper

❶ Place a pan of water over a high heat.

❷ While we wait for the water to boil, place the mint and cream cheese into a blender.

❸ Once the water is boiling, add the frozen peas and cook for 2 minutes.

❹ Drain the peas and run them under cold water for a minute until they are cold, then add them to the blender and blitz till smooth.

❺ Season with salt and pepper and place in a bowl. Zest a lemon over the top, sprinkle on the chilli flakes, drizzle over the olive oil and enjoy!

BOG-STANDARD HUMMUS

1 x 15.5 oz (439 g) can of chickpeas
2 tbsp tahini
1 clove of garlic
5 tbsp olive oil
1 tsp ground cumin
Juice of 1 large lemon
Sea salt and black pepper

1. Drain the chickpeas and put them into a blender along with the tahini, minced garlic, olive oil, cumin, 3–4 tablespoons water and the juice of a lemon. Season with salt and pepper and blitz to a smooth purée.

2. Taste, season with salt and pepper and you're done! It's as simple as that.

TZATZIKI

½ cucumber
¾ cup Greek yogurt
Squeeze of lemon juice
1 clove of garlic
Handful of mint
Sea salt and black pepper

1. Grate the cucumber, then pick it up in your hands and squeeze out all the liquid.

2. Place the drained cucumber into a bowl, add the yogurt and lemon juice and season with salt and pepper.

3. Finally, mince your garlic and finely chop the mint, then add into the yogurt and mix to combine. Taste, season and your dip is ready.

BEET HUMMUS

Make sure to use the ready-cooked, vacuum-packed beets here, not the pickled kind that come in jars.

1 x 15.5 oz (439 g) can of chickpeas
2 cooked beets (store-bought)
1 clove of garlic
2 tbsp tahini
Juice of 1 large lemon
3 tbsp olive oil
1 tsp ground cumin
Sea salt and black pepper

1. Drain the chickpeas, roughly chop the beets and place both into a blender with the minced garlic, all the other ingredients and 1½–2 tablespoons of water. Blitz to a smooth purée. Taste, season and enjoy!

MONDAY MEAL PREP

MONDAY MEAL PREP

MAKES. 14 **PREP TIME.** 30 MINUTES **COOK TIME.** 20 MINUTES

Don't be wasting your money on a takeaway sausage roll, they're so easy to make and much nicer. Whether you enjoy them warm straight out the oven or decide to eat them cold the next day, this recipe has got you covered. You can freeze them before they're baked and add an additional 10 minutes of cooking time or freeze them after they're baked. Just defrost them the night before and bake for 10 minutes to bring them back to life.

Sausage Rolls

① Preheat the oven to 400°F (200°C).

② Using a small knife, score down the length of the sausages, remove the skins and put the sausage meat into a bowl. Add in the sage, mustard and onion chutney and season with salt and pepper. Use a spoon, or your hands, to mix it up until everything is nicely combined.

③ Cut the puff pastry in half lengthwise and, with wet hands, shape the sausage meat into two long cylinders. Place in the middle of each length of pastry.

④ Brush a little beaten egg along the pastry on one side of the sausage meat and fold the other half over to form your sausage-roll shape. Press down lightly to seal the pastry together.

⑤ Dip the fork in the flour and press the two pieces of pastry together to seal them, then, using a sharp knife, trim away the excess pastry along the seal, leaving a finger's width.

⑥ Use a serrated knife to cut each of the sausage rolls into seven and place them onto a baking sheet lined with the paper the pastry came on. Brush over more beaten egg and bake for 20 minutes.

⑦ Once they're risen and golden, they can be enjoyed warm or cold.

6 sausages of choice
1 tbsp dried sage
1 tsp Dijon mustard
3½ tbsp caramelized onion chutney
1 x 14 oz (396 g) package of ready-rolled puff pastry
1 egg
1 tbsp all-purpose flour
Sea salt and black pepper

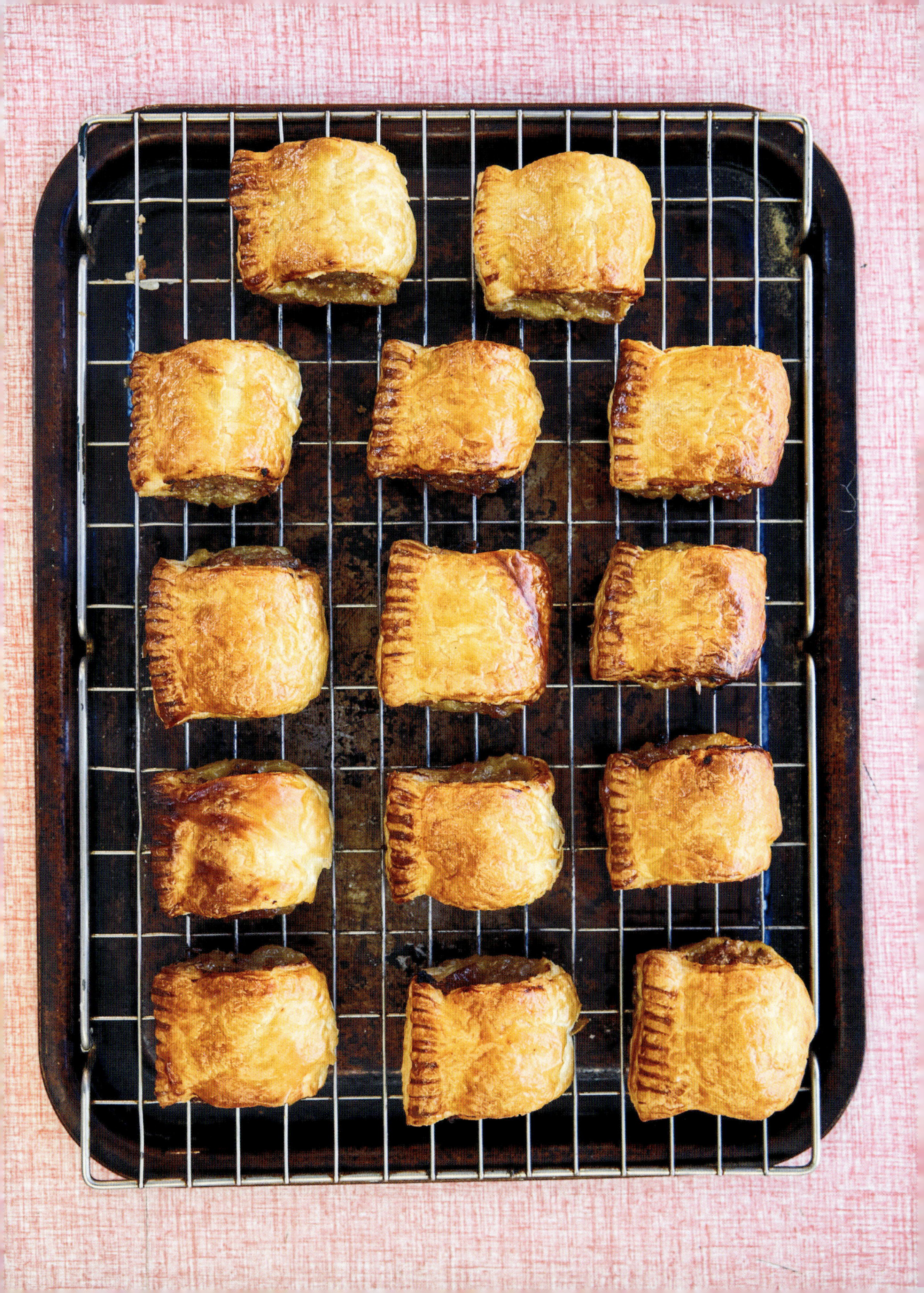

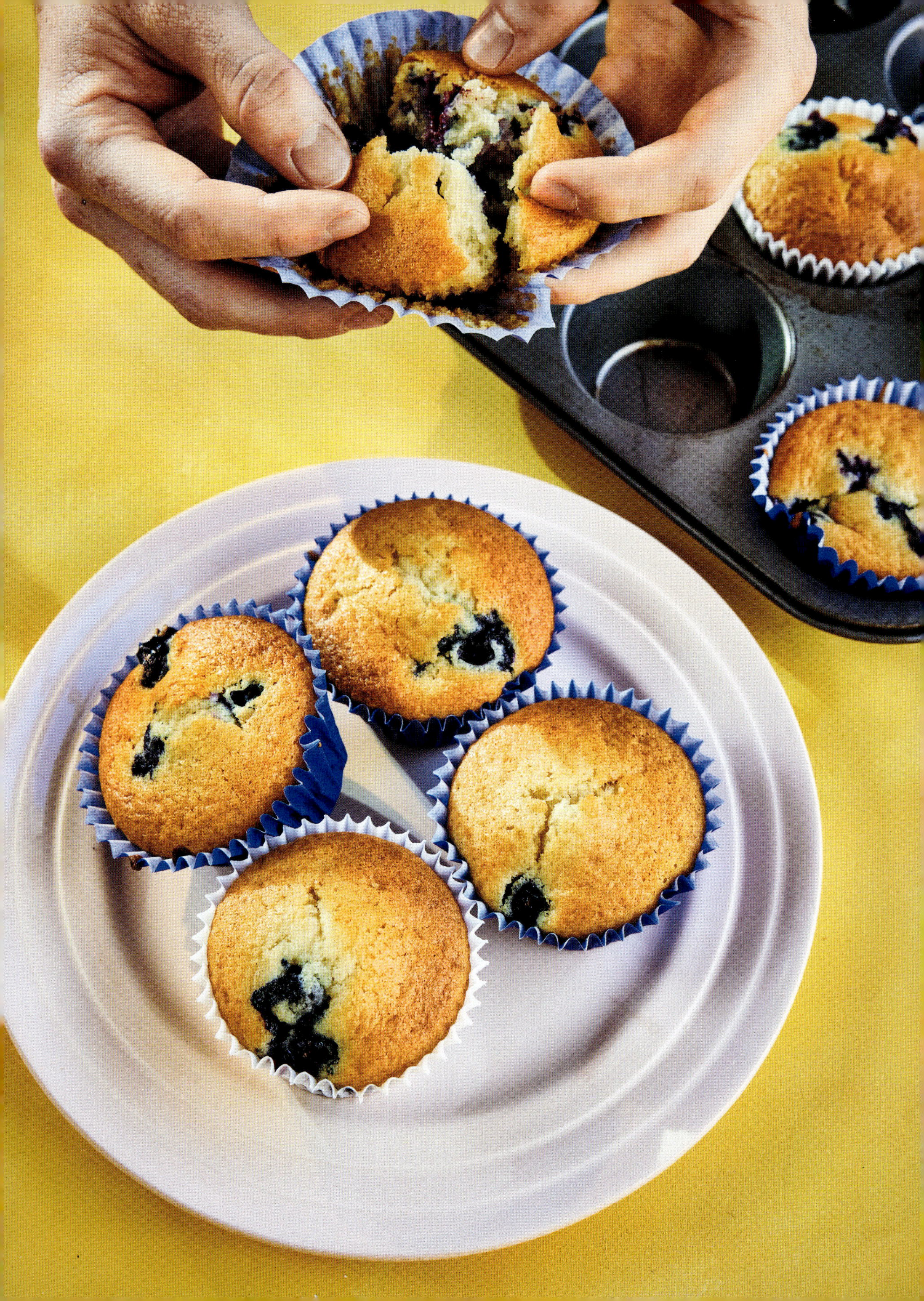

PREP TIME. 15 MINUTES / **COOK TIME.** 20 MINUTES / **MAKES.** 7

MONDAY MEAL PREP

Easy to make and easy to save some serious dosh, these muffins keep really well in a sealed container and brighten up any breakfast.

BLUEBERRY MUFFINS

① Preheat your oven to 350°F (180°C).

② Put the flour, baking powder, sugar and salt into a large mixing bowl.

③ Put the milk, oil, vanilla and egg into a separate bowl and use a fork to whisk them together.

④ Add the wet ingredients in with the dry ingredients and whisk to combine until smooth. Add three-quarters of the blueberries and fold them into the batter.

⑤ Pour the batter into a muffin tray lined with muffin cases and fill about two-thirds of the way up. Top with the remaining blueberries and bake in the oven for 20 minutes.

1 ¼ cups self-rising flour
1 tsp baking powder
⅔ cup superfine sugar
Pinch of salt
½ cup milk
3 ½ tbsp oil
Dash of vanilla extract
1 egg
⅔ cup blueberries

MONDAY MEAL PREP

SERVES. 6 / PREP TIME. 10 MINUTES / COOK TIME. 30 MINUTES

Homemade granola is a jar full of loveliness. Layer it up with yogurt and a fresh berry compote and it's hard to imagine a better way to start anyone's day.

GRANOLA + BERRY COMPOTE

① Preheat your oven to 325°F (160°C).

② Put the oats, almonds, pecans, pumpkin seeds, sunflower seeds, maple syrup, olive oil, cinnamon, vanilla extract and a pinch of salt into a large bowl. Mix until they are nicely combined and the maple syrup has coated everything evenly.

③ Place on a large baking sheet lined with baking paper and bake for 20 minutes.

④ Meanwhile, put the frozen berries into a saucepan and add the sugar. Bring it to a boil and simmer for 5 minutes. Mix the cornstarch with 2 tablespoons cold water until smooth, then stir it into the compote. Simmer for another minute until the compote has just thickened up before leaving it to cool at room temperature.

⑤ Take the granola out of the oven and add in the golden raisins. Give the granola a gentle stir to mix them in (don't go mad as you'll break up the lovely clumps) and bake for a further 10 minutes until it is nice and golden.

⑥ Once everything has cooled down to room temperature, serve with the berry compote and Greek yogurt.

2½ cups jumbo rolled oats

¼ cup flaked almonds

¼ cup pecans

¼ cup pumpkin seeds

⅓ cup sunflower seeds

⅔ cup maple syrup

2 tbsp olive oil

1 tbsp ground cinnamon

1 tsp vanilla extract

Pinch of salt

½ cup golden raisins

Greek yogurt, to serve

FOR THE BERRY COMPOTE

2¾ cups frozen berries

⅔ cup superfine sugar

1 tsp cornstarch

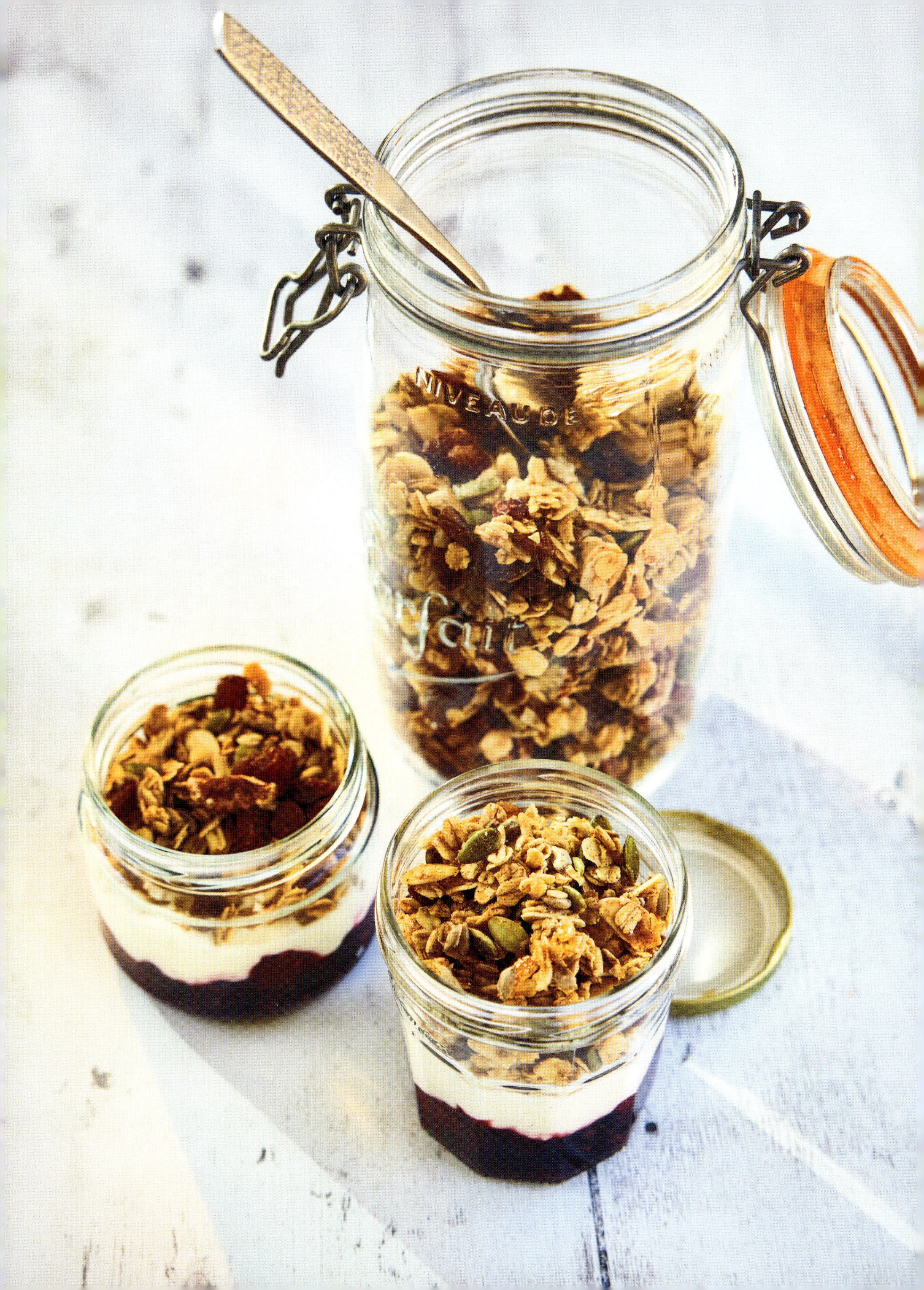
NIVEAU DE

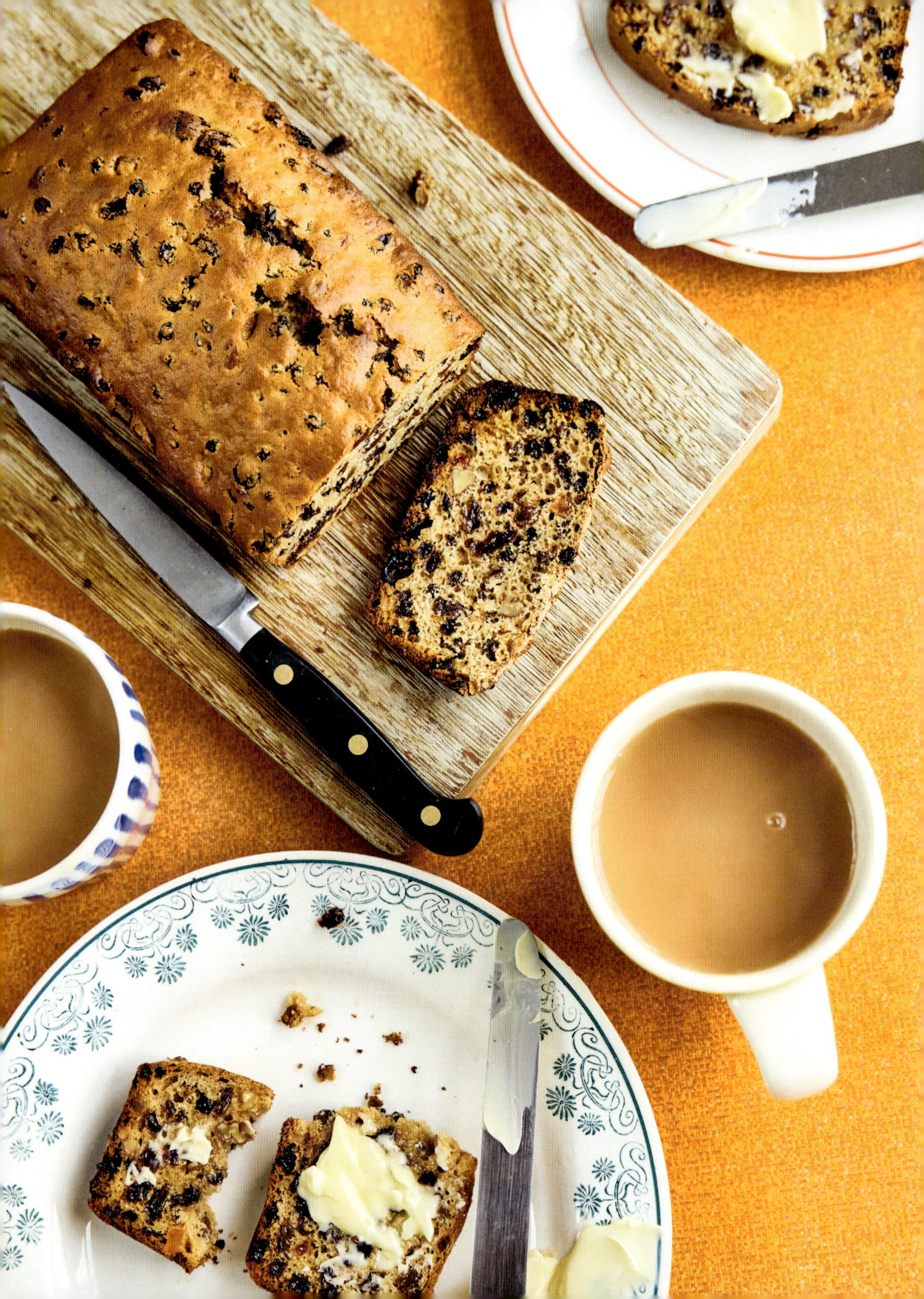

PREP TIME. 15 MINUTES / **COOK TIME.** 45 MINUTES / **MAKES.** 1 LOAF

MONDAY MEAL PREP

My Granny Tess is special. She is funny, super-kind and the matriarch of Team Holland. Oh, and a brilliant home cook. Growing up, she thrilled us with her kitchen wizardry and I'm delighted to share some of her magic with you here. Her Irish fruit loaf is one of my favorites. Enjoyed with a strong cuppa (Brothers Trust mug preferably) and an overdue catch-up, these are memories I cherish. It is so easy to make and is perfect for breakfasts on the run or afternoon tea. Bake this on Monday and it will make you smile all week. Thanks GT.

Granny Tess' Irish Fruit Loaf

1. Preheat your oven to 350°F (180°C).
2. Pour ½ cup of boiling water into a jug, add the Earl Grey tea bag and brown sugar and steep for 4 minutes.
3. Put the currants, golden raisins, raisins and candied peel into a big bowl and pour over the sugary tea mixture.
4. Crush the pecans into small chunks and add into the bowl along with the self-rising flour and beaten egg. Use a spatula to mix it in until there are no visible lumps of flour left.
5. Grease a 2 lb (900 g) loaf tin well with a knob of butter and pour in the mixture, smoothing out the top.
6. Bake for 40–45 minutes, or until you can stick a knife into the center of the cake and it comes out clean. Use a small knife to cut around the edge of the loaf to release it and then turn it out and leave to cool.
7. Serve up, slathered with some butter and enjoy with a good cuppa tea!

1 Earl Grey tea bag
½ cup light brown sugar
¾ cup currants
¾ cup golden raisins
¾ cup raisins
¼ cup candied peel
¼ cup pecans
1¾ cup self-rising flour
1 egg
Knob of butter

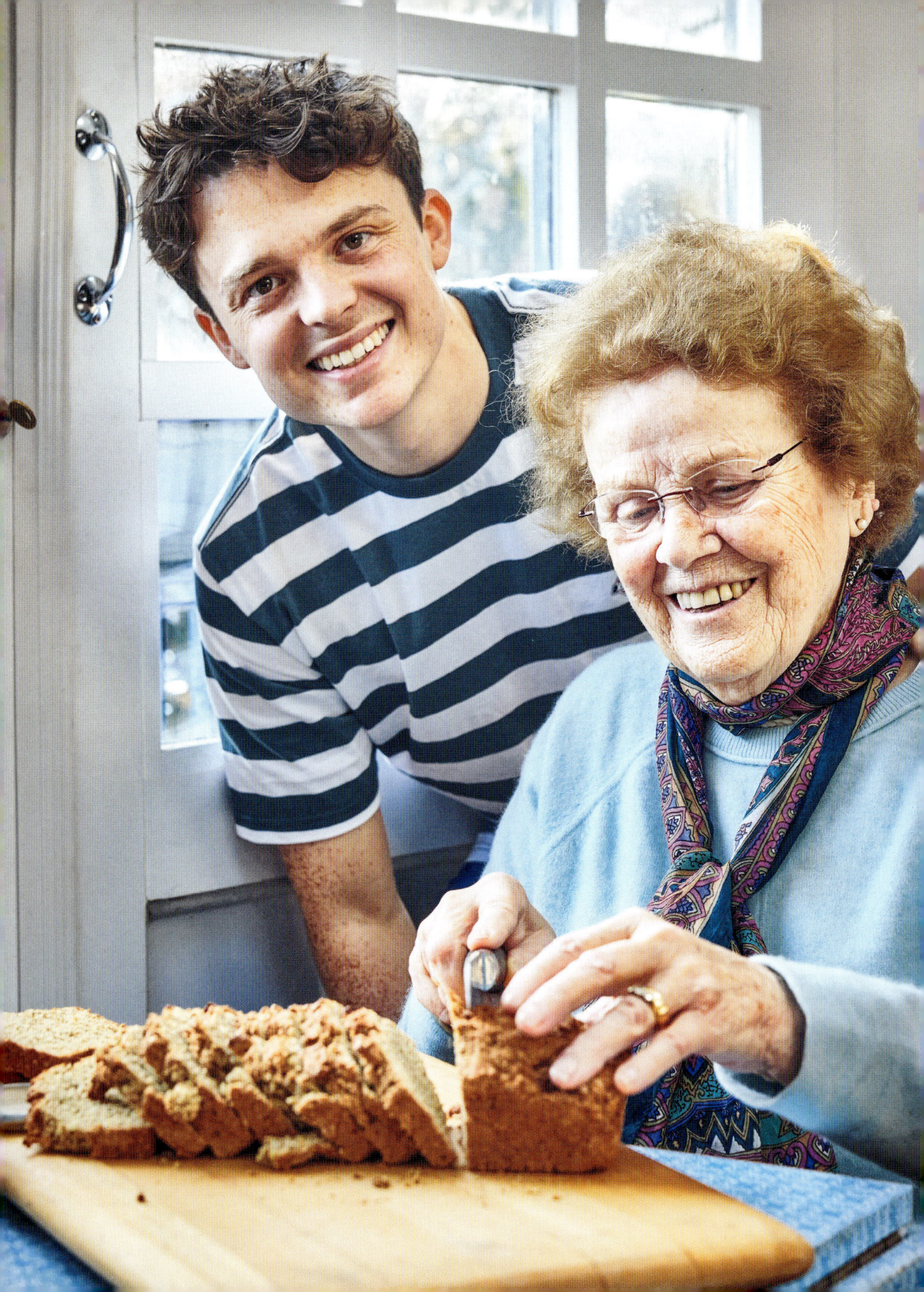

PREP TIME. 15 MINUTES / **COOK TIME.** 30 MINUTES / **MAKES.** 2 LOAVES

MONDAY MEAL PREP

Another Granny Tess classic. To keep this super authentic to Granny's recipe, I've included wheat or oat bran in the ingredients, which you should be able to find in your local health food store. If that's a step too far, just substitute with a bit more wholemeal flour. It won't be **100%** Granny Tess-authentic, but I won't tell her!

GRANNY TESS' SODA BREAD

Ingredients
1 ⅓ cups self-rising flour
2 ⅔ cups whole wheat flour
1 ¼ cups wheat bran or oat bran, plus extra for dusting
1 heaped tsp baking soda
Big pinch of salt
10–11 oz (568–600 ml) buttermilk
3 ½ tbsp vegetable oil, plus another 2 tsp
1 egg
Knob of butter

① Preheat the oven to 350°F (180°C).

② Put the self-rising flour, whole wheat flour, bran, baking soda and salt into a large bowl and mix it together.

③ In a separate bowl, whisk to combine the buttermilk, vegetable oil and the egg.

④ Add the wet ingredients to the dry ingredients and mix with a spoon until nicely combined and there are no dry lumps. Split the dough into two.

⑤ Use the butter to thoroughly grease the inside of two 2 lb (900 g) loaf tins and put half of the bread dough into each tin. Push the dough into the corners and make sure it is nice and flat.

⑥ Drizzle 1 teaspoon vegetable oil over each loaf and dust with bran.

⑦ Place in the oven and bake for 30 minutes.

⑧ Remove from the oven and leave to cool for 10 minutes in the tins before running a butter knife around the edge of the loaves to remove them from the tins, then leave to cool.

THE SWEET SPOT

Dessert doesn't need to be difficult and the recipes in this chapter are my go-to simple showstoppers that will be the crowning glory to any meal. You'll also find cakes, bakes and cookies that will make you the most popular person in the room, as well as a few party drinks that will make the world a better place (for a short time at least!).

MAKES. 9   **PREP TIME.** 20 MINUTES   **COOK TIME.** 35 MINUTES

THE SWEET SPOT

As kids, Harry and I set up our own business, selling baked goods door to door. *The Twin Bakers* were born. Mum fronted us the cash (her returns remain outstanding), Tom designed our logo, I had the baking skills and yet Harry was somehow in charge. We sold brownies and GT bread (see page 195) to our neighbors, but sadly the business disbanded when self-awareness and puberty kicked in. Matching uniforms and selling brownies was not a good look at 13. The Twin Bakers are no longer but the brownie recipe lives on ...

Twin Baker Brownies

Ingredients
7 oz (200 g) dark chocolate (at least 70% cocoa solids)
1 cup butter
4 medium eggs
Dash of vanilla extract
2 ⅓ cups superfine sugar
¾ cup all-purpose flour
Pinch of salt

① Preheat the oven to 350°F (177°C).

② Place the chocolate and butter into a heatproof bowl and melt it over a pan of barely simmering water on a low heat (make sure the water isn't in direct contact with the bowl).

③ Once melted, remove from the heat and leave to cool for 5 minutes. Crack the eggs into a separate bowl and add the vanilla extract and sugar and whisk well. Then slowly add in the melted chocolate and butter mix, whisking continuously.

④ Sieve in the flour and a pinch of salt and fold in until fully incorporated.

⑤ Pour into a 8 x 8 inch (20 x 20 cm) cake pan lined with baking paper. Cook in the center of the oven for 35 minutes.

⑥ Leave to cool completely before cutting.

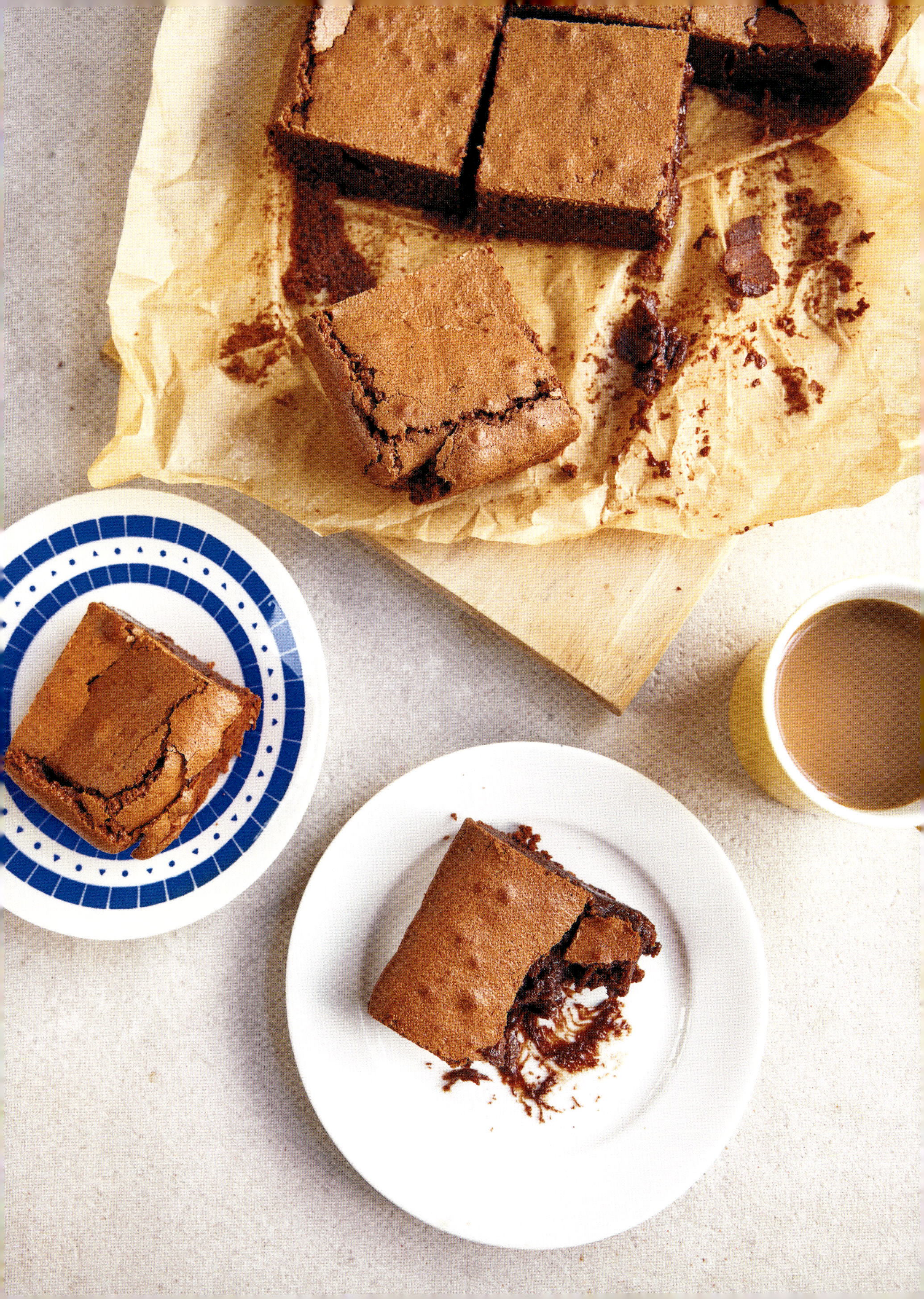

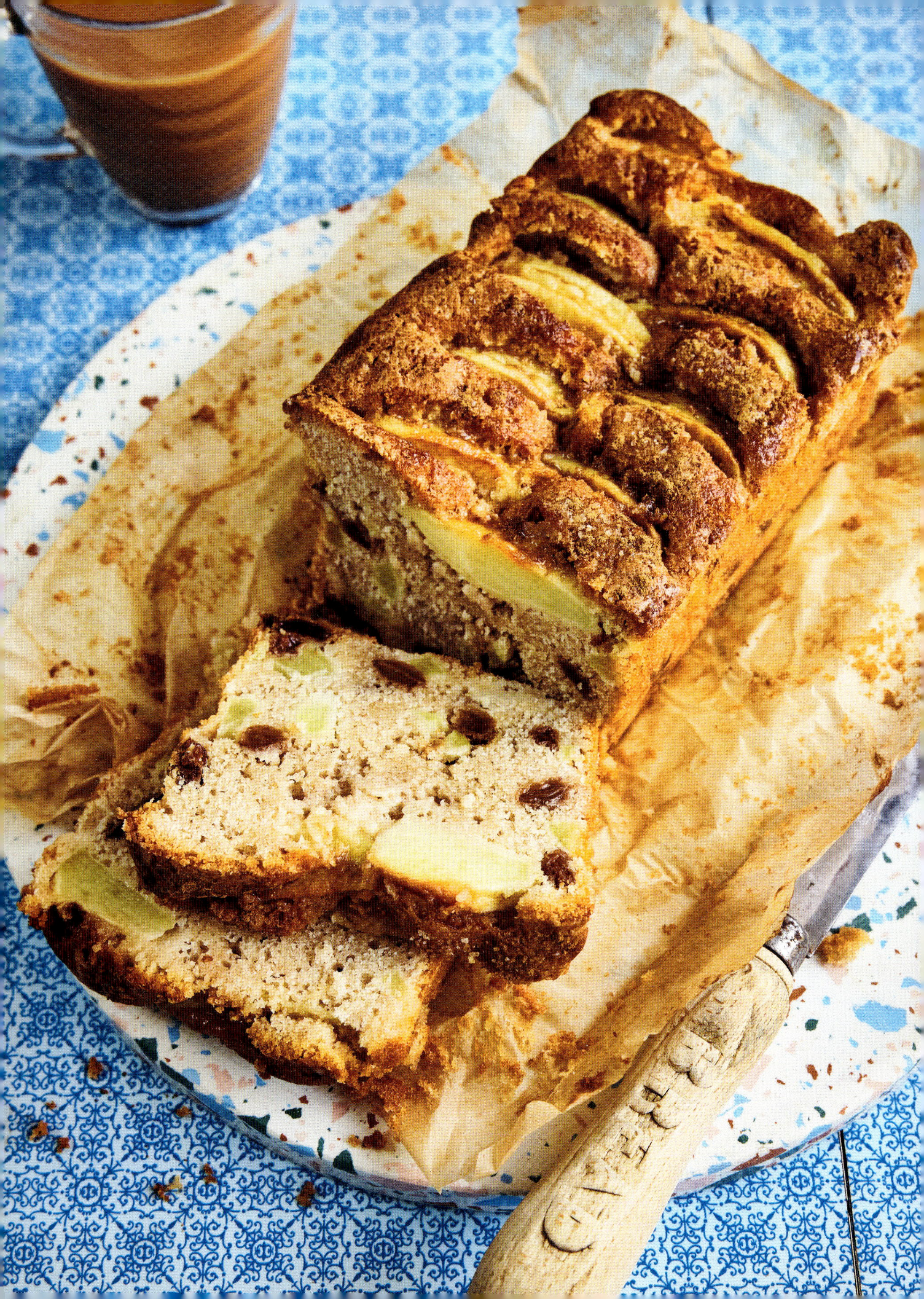

PREP TIME. 20 MINUTES / **COOK TIME.** 45 MINUTES / **MAKES.** 1

THE SWEET SPOT

Germany is known for its excellent engineering, and this is a Mercedes Benz of a dessert. Simply stunning and works every time. Serve with whipped cream or custard, or just have a slice on its own to get you through the afternoon.

German Apple Cake

① Preheat the oven to 325°F (160°C).

② Peel and quarter the apples and remove the core. For 2 of the apples, roughly chop into bite-size pieces and for the other 2, cut each quarter in 2. Keep them in separate bowls.

③ Place the softened butter in a bowl with the sugar and whisk together until light and fluffy.

④ Add in one egg at a time and mix to combine. Add the milk, flour, baking powder, cinnamon, vanilla, golden raisins and roughly chopped apples and fold together until the batter is smooth.

⑤ Line a loaf tin with baking paper, spoon in the cake batter and use a spatula to make sure it is nice and flat.

⑥ Press the rest of the apples into the top of the cake, sprinkle over the demerara sugar and finally, sprinkle over a pinch of cinnamon.

⑦ Bake in the center of the oven for 45 minutes.

⑧ Turn out onto a board and allow to cool, Serve with whipped cream.

4 dessert apples (I used Braeburn)
⅔ cup butter, softened
1 cup superfine sugar
2 large eggs
3½ tbsp milk
1⅔ cups all-purpose flour
2 tsp baking powder
1 tsp ground cinnamon, plus extra for dusting
Dash of vanilla extract
¾ cup golden raisins
1–2 tbsp demerara or brown sugar
Whipped cream, to serve

SERVES. 6-8 / **PREP TIME.** 20 MINUTES / **COOK TIME.** 25 MINUTES

THE SWEET SPOT

We've all been there...when the garage forecourt seems like the only option. This recipe is a bit of a game changer and can turn your fortunes from doghouse to penthouse in **30** minutes flat. You'll be surprised by how many of the ingredients you already have, just make sure to allow some cooling time (maybe to wrap a present?) before icing the cake.

Last-Minute Birthday Cake

① Preheat your oven to 350°F (180°C). Line a small rectangular (roughly 11 x 6½ inch [28 x 17 cm]) cake pan or roasting pan with baking paper.

② Pour the vegetable oil into a bowl, add the eggs and vanilla extract and whisk well until fully combined.

③ Add in the sugar, flour, grated carrot, baking powder, cinnamon, walnuts, golden raisins and a pinch of salt, then use a spatula to mix it in until there are no lumps.

④ Pour the mixture into the prepared pan and smooth the top. Bake in the middle of the oven for 25 minutes, or until you can stick a knife into the center and it comes out clean.

⑤ Take the cake out of the pan and allow it to cool to room temperature, usually around an hour or so.

⑥ For the frosting, put the softened butter into a mixing bowl and beat until smooth. Sieve the powdered sugar into the bowl in a few stages, whisking really well in between each addition until it is all combined and the butter and sugar mix is totally smooth. Add the cream cheese and gently fold it through the butter and sugar using a spatula or wooden spoon. Don't be tempted to whisk the cream cheese in or your frosting will turn runny.

⑦ Slather the frosting on top of the cake and garnish with some chopped walnuts or go mad with sprinkles. Write Happy Birthday with icing and top with sparklers and candles!

Ingredients
½ cup vegetable oil
2 eggs
Dash of vanilla extract
½ cup light brown sugar
½ cup self-rising flour
½ cup carrot, grated
1 tsp baking powder
1 tsp ground cinnamon
1 oz (28 g) chopped walnuts, plus extra for decorating
¼ cup golden raisins
Pinch of salt

FOR THE FROSTING

½ cup butter, softened
¾ cup powdered sugar
¾ cup cream cheese

FOR THE DECORATION

Sprinkles
Writing icing
Sparklers
Candles

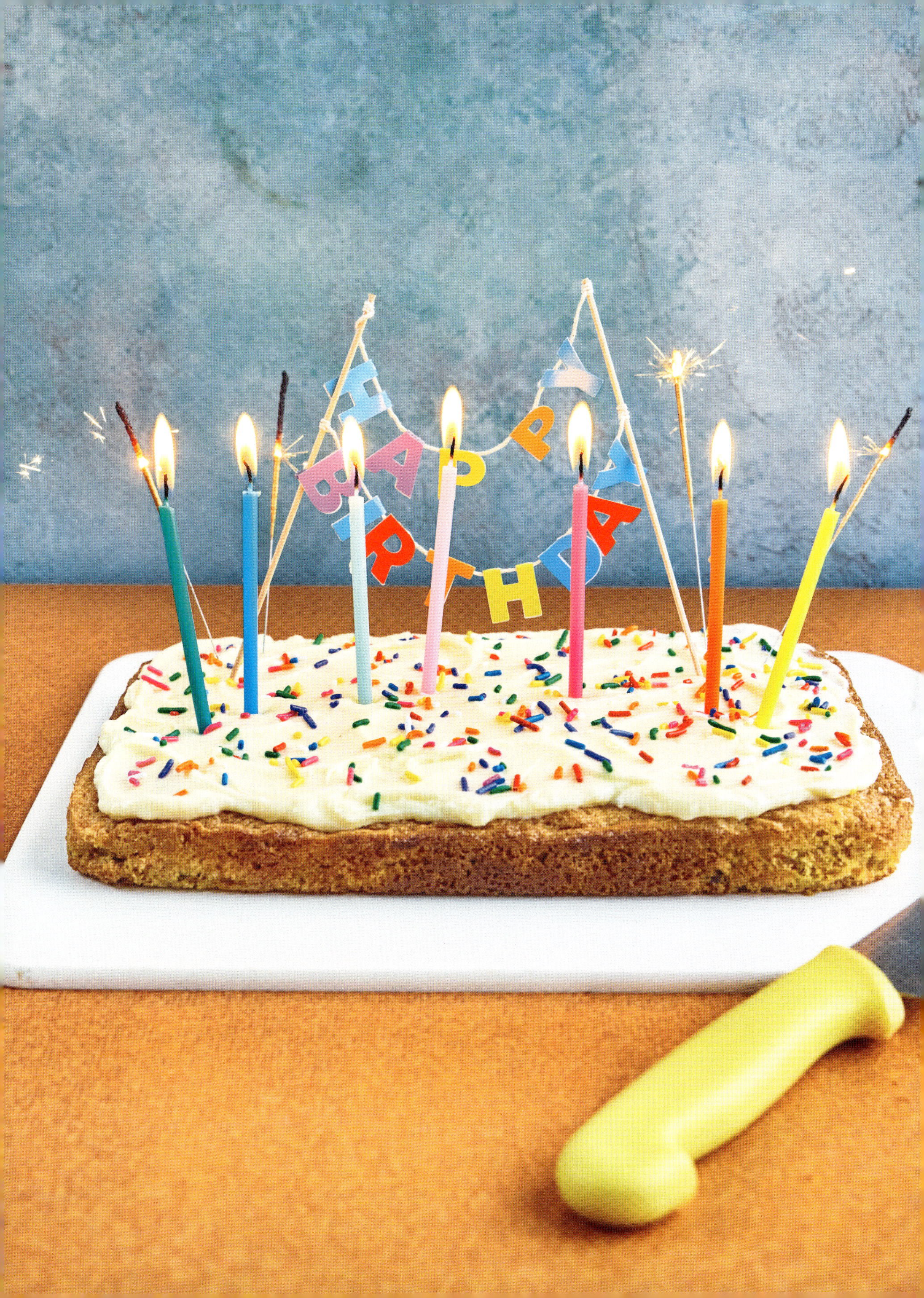
HAPPY
BIRTHDAY

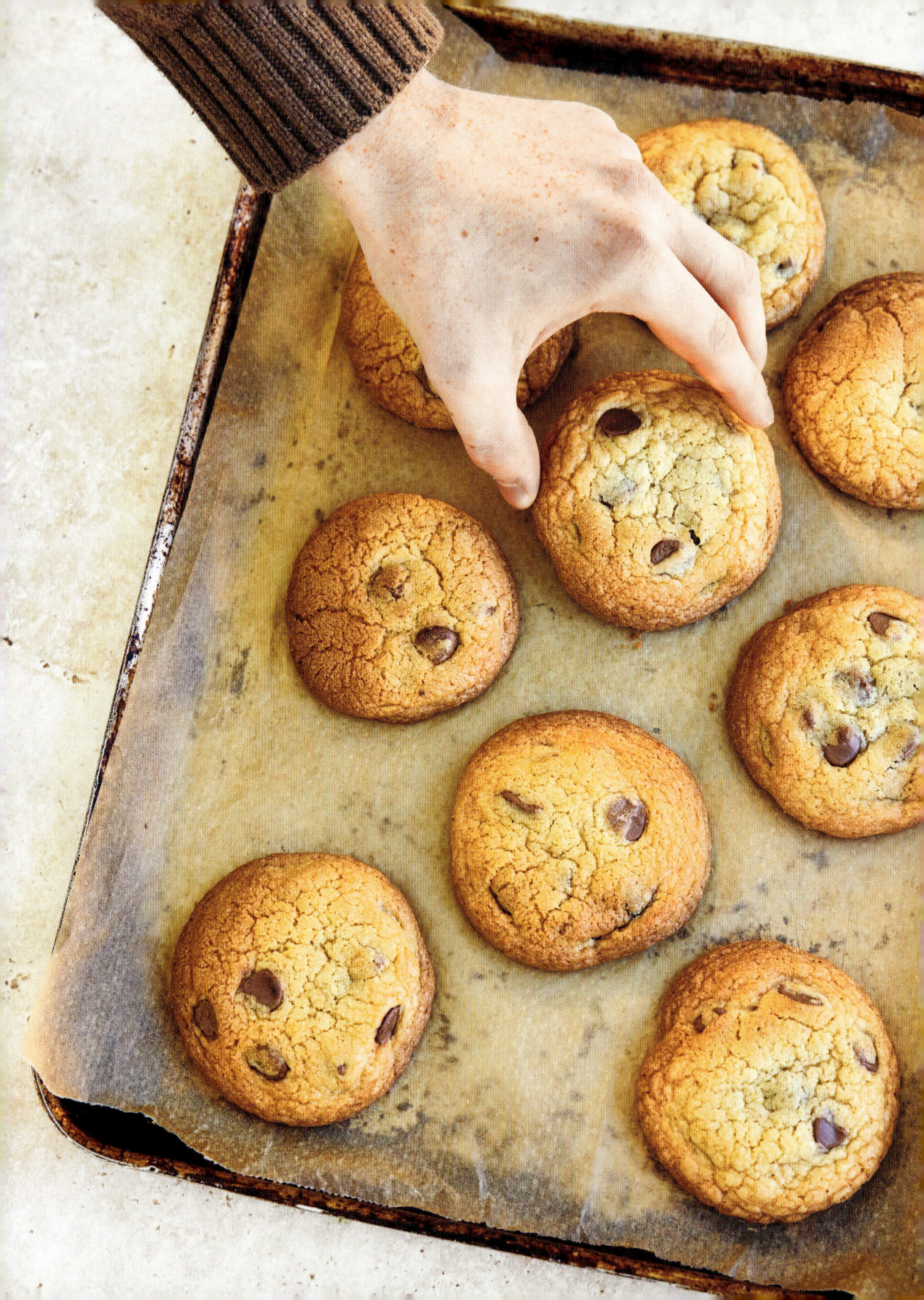

PREP TIME. 20 MINUTES (PLUS RESTING THE DOUGH OVERNIGHT) / **COOK TIME.** 15 MINUTES / **MAKES.** 12

THE SWEET SPOT

Every self-respecting cook needs a great cookie recipe in their arsenal and this IS a great one. It makes 12 cookies, but if you're not baking for a crowd, you can freeze the balls of cookie dough and bake them as needed. Just increase the cooking time by 4-5 minutes. Eat them slightly warm with a scoop of ice cream for the ultimate indulgence.

Chocolate & Orange Cookies

① Melt the butter in the microwave in 20-second intervals (it melts quickly, so keep an eye on it). Pour that into a mixing bowl, add the brown sugar and superfine sugar and mix to combine.

② Crack in the egg and whisk for a few minutes.

③ Zest in the oranges, then add the flour, baking powder, chocolate chips and a pinch of salt. Mix them until they're nicely combined.

④ Wrap in plastic wrap and rest in the fridge for at least 4 hours or best overnight.

⑤ Preheat your oven to 350°F (180°C).

⑥ Roll the cookie dough into 12 balls (each will weigh just over 2 ounces (50 g), if that helps you split the dough evenly).

⑦ Space them out on a baking sheet lined with baking paper at least 4 inches (8 cm) apart (use two trays if you need to) and bake for 12–15 minutes, or until they are just golden.

⑧ Remove from the oven and leave to cool on the tray. The cookies will seem very soft when you take them out of the oven, but they will firm up as they cool.

¾ cup butter
½ cup light brown sugar
½ cup superfine sugar
1 egg
Zest of 2 oranges
2⅓ all-purpose flour
1 tsp baking powder
¾ cup milk chocolate chips
Pinch of salt

THE SWEET SPOT

MAKES. 9 / PREP TIME. 15 MINUTES (PLUS CHILLING OVERNIGHT) / COOK TIME. 10 MINUTES

Melted chocolate, biscuits, fruit and marshmallows. If you're not sold already, then I'm not sure what else will do it. Make this for your mum, make it for your friends or just make it for yourself. You won't want to share anyway.

ROCKY ROAD

- ¾ cup butter
- ¾ cup granulated sugar
- 5 oz (150 g) milk chocolate
- 3½ oz (100 g) dark chocolate (at least 70% cocoa solids)
- 5 oz (150 g) digestive biscuits
- ½ cup mini marshmallows
- ½ cup golden raisins

1. Place the butter, sugar, milk and dark chocolate, broken into squares, into a heatproof bowl over a pan of barely simmering water on a low heat (make sure the water isn't in direct contact with the bowl). Stirring occasionally, allow the chocolate to melt and then set aside. Don't let the water boil or the chocolate will get too hot.

2. Break the biscuits into small, bite-sized pieces and put them in a large mixing bowl along with the marshmallows and golden raisins.

3. Once the chocolate has melted, pour it over the biscuit mix and stir until well combined.

4. Line a 8 x 8 inch (20 x 20 cm) cake pan with plastic wrap and pour in the Rocky Road mix. Push it into the corners, wrap the whole dish in cling film and leave to cool and set in the fridge overnight.

5. Portion it up the next day for you and your friends.

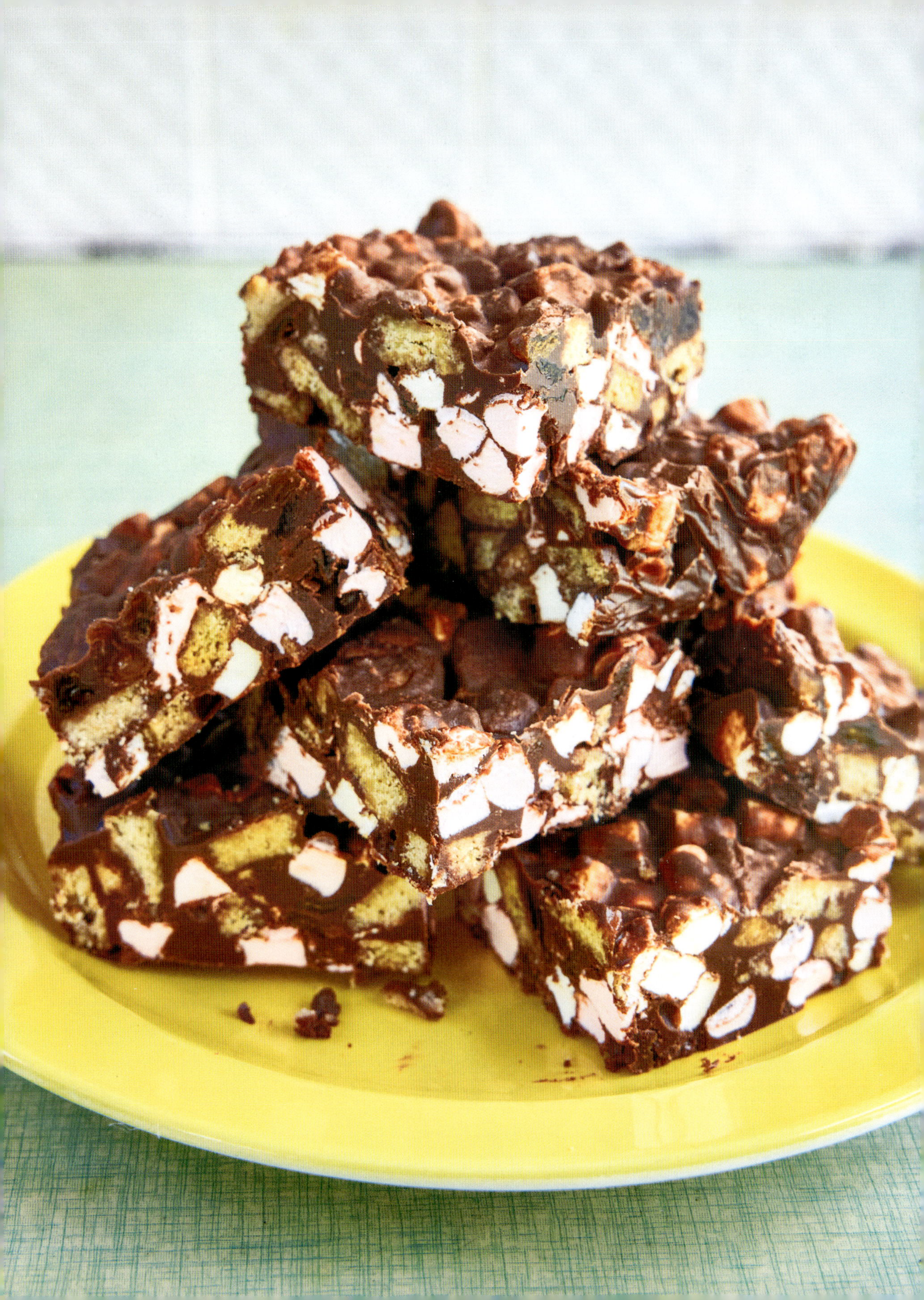

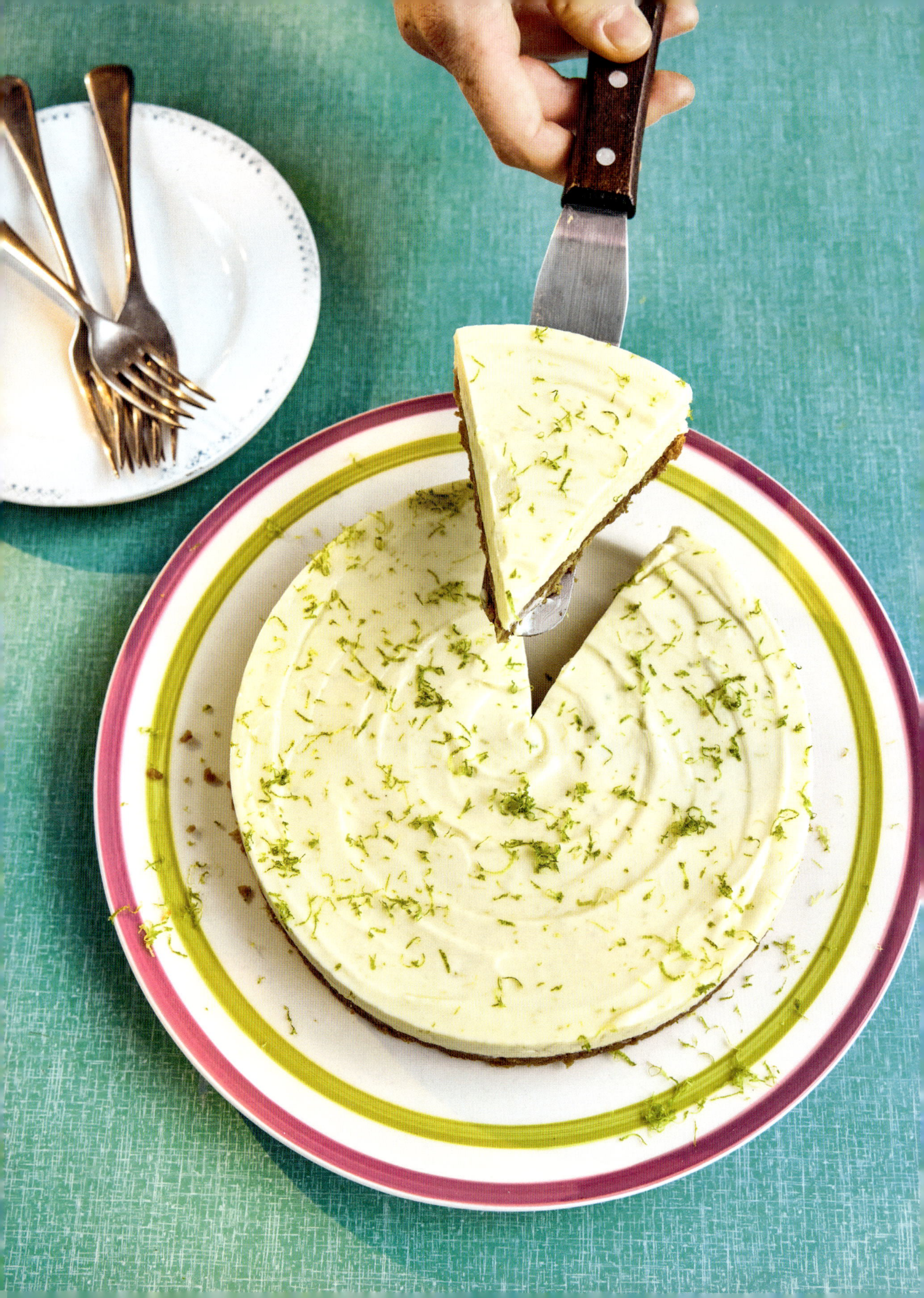

PREP TIME. 25 MINUTES (PLUS REFRIGERATING OVERNIGHT) / **SERVES.** 6

THE SWEET SPOT

Where to start with how simple and how delicious this pie is? Zesty, super fresh and with only five ingredients, it basically defies physics.

Key Lime Pie

Ingredients
9 oz (250 g) ginger snap biscuits
½ cup butter
1 x 15.5 oz (439 g) can of condensed milk
1¼ cup heavy cream
Zest and juice of 5 limes plus 1 extra for garnish

① Place the biscuits into a bowl and use a rolling pin to bash them into to a fine crumb.

② Melt the butter in the microwave in 20-second intervals (it melts quickly, so keep an eye on it). Pour over the biscuits and mix it thoroughly, then press the biscuits into the base of a 8-inch (20 cm) springform cake pan in an even layer and set aside.

③ Pour the condensed milk and cream into a mixing bowl. In a separate small bowl, mix the zest and juice of 5 limes.

④ Whisk the cream and condensed milk together for about 30 seconds to combine them well and then add the lime zest and juice and whisk for a minute. It will magically thicken.

⑤ Pour this on top of the biscuit base, smooth it out and wrap in plastic wrap. Chill in the fridge for at least 4 hours until set, or even better, overnight and enjoy the next day.

⑥ Before serving, release the sides of the loose-bottom tin and portion it up. Grate over the zest of one lime for garnish.

MAKES. 6 / **PREP TIME.** 15 MINUTES / **COOK TIME.** 20 MINUTES

THE SWEET SPOT

My take on the famous French Tarte Tatin. Inspired by my great friend Julie Davey, only five ingredients to make six delicious tarts which look as good as they taste. *Très bien*.

Apple Tarts

① Preheat your oven to 400°F (200°C).

② Cut the unrolled puff pastry into six pieces. Place your puff pastry pieces onto a baking sheet lined with baking paper (or use the paper the puff pastry came rolled in if you don't have any).

③ Using a knife, gently score a border about ½ inch (1 cm) from the edge, making sure not to cut all the way through the pastry.

④ Spread 2 tablespoons of apple sauce within each border.

⑤ Finally, thinly slice your apples and place onto the apple sauce in a neat fashion (I did two overlapping rows). Sprinkle with some cinnamon and dust most of the powdered sugar over the top.

⑥ Bake in the oven for 18–20 minutes until golden brown and the base of the tarts are cooked.

⑦ Dust with the remaining powdered sugar and serve up with some vanilla ice cream.

1 x 14 oz (396 g) package of ready-rolled puff pastry
12 tbsp apple sauce
3 dessert apples (I used Braeburn)
Sprinkle of ground cinnamon
1 tbsp powdered sugar
Vanilla ice cream, to serve

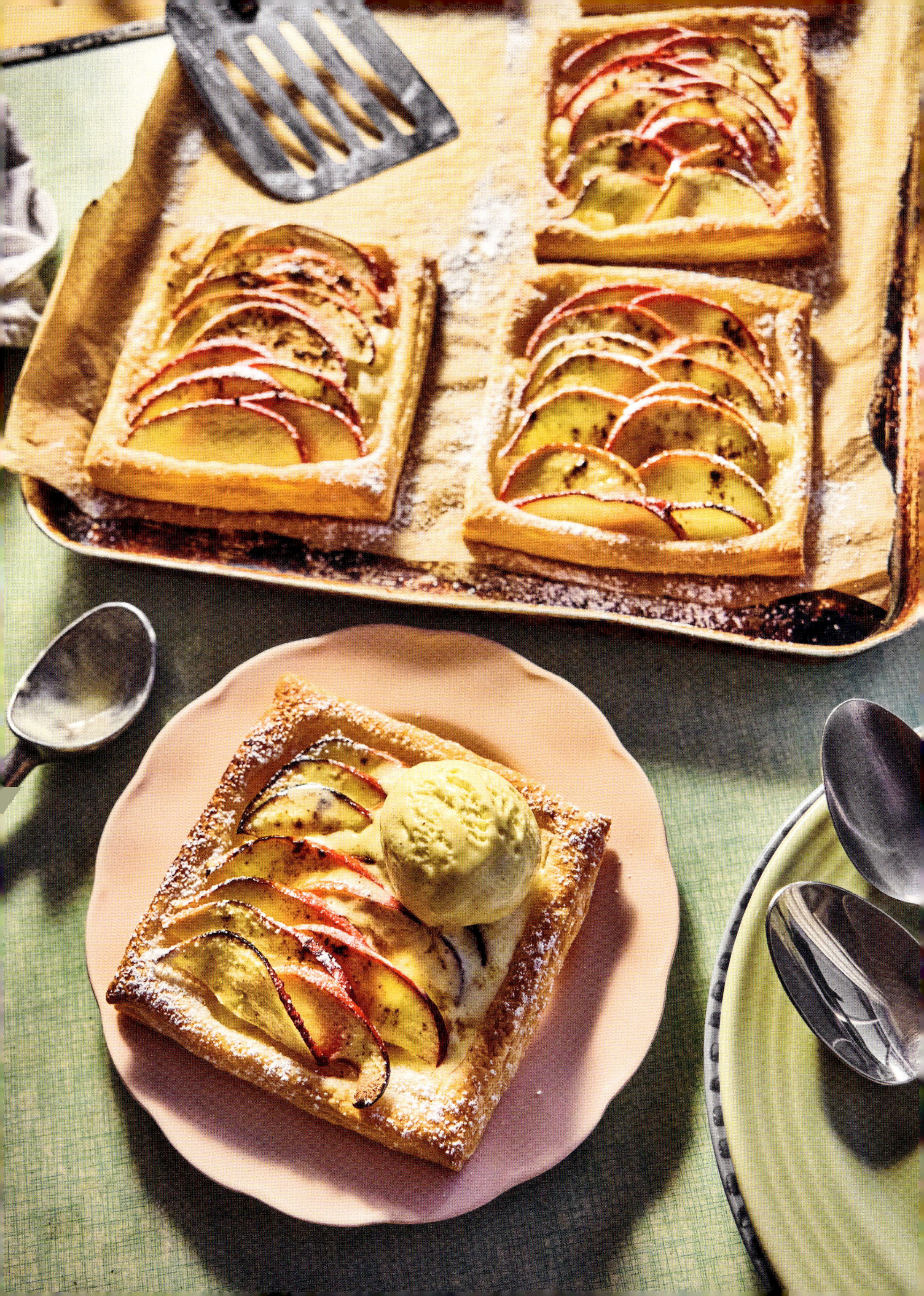

SERVES. 6 / **PREP TIME.** 15 MINUTES / **COOK TIME.** 55 MINUTES

THE SWEET SPOT

This is a wonderful Easter dessert, but now that hot cross buns are available year round, don't let the date in the diary stop you from enjoying it any time. Perfect for using up slightly stale hot cross buns (or teacakes) and a guaranteed crowd pleaser.

HOT CROSS BUN PUDDING

① Preheat your oven to 300°F (150°C).

② For the custard, crack your eggs into a bowl and add the milk, cream, sugar, cinnamon, vanilla extract and orange zest. Use a fork to whisk it all up and set aside.

③ Slice the tops off the hot cross buns (keeping the cross on top intact) and tear the remaining bread into bite-sized chunks. Add to the bowl to soak in the custard for 2–3 minutes.

④ Layer your bread into an ovenproof dish (roughly 8 x 11 inches [28 x 20 cm]), reserving the six tops of the buns. Dot the marmalade over the dish before adding the tops of the buns so the crosses are on top.

⑤ Pour over any remaining custard and sprinkle over the golden raisins. Leave the dish to stand for 5 minutes so the hot cross buns can absorb more of the custard.

⑥ Cover the top in tin foil and bake for 45 minutes. Remove the foil and drizzle over the honey, then return to the oven for a final 5–10 minutes, or until the custard is set.

⑦ Serve hot with custard and enjoy.

8 medium eggs
½ cup milk
½ cup heavy cream
½ cup superfine sugar
½ tsp ground cinnamon
Dash of vanilla extract
Zest of 1 orange
6 hot cross buns
½ cup marmalade
¼ cup golden raisins
2 tablespoons honey
Custard, to serve

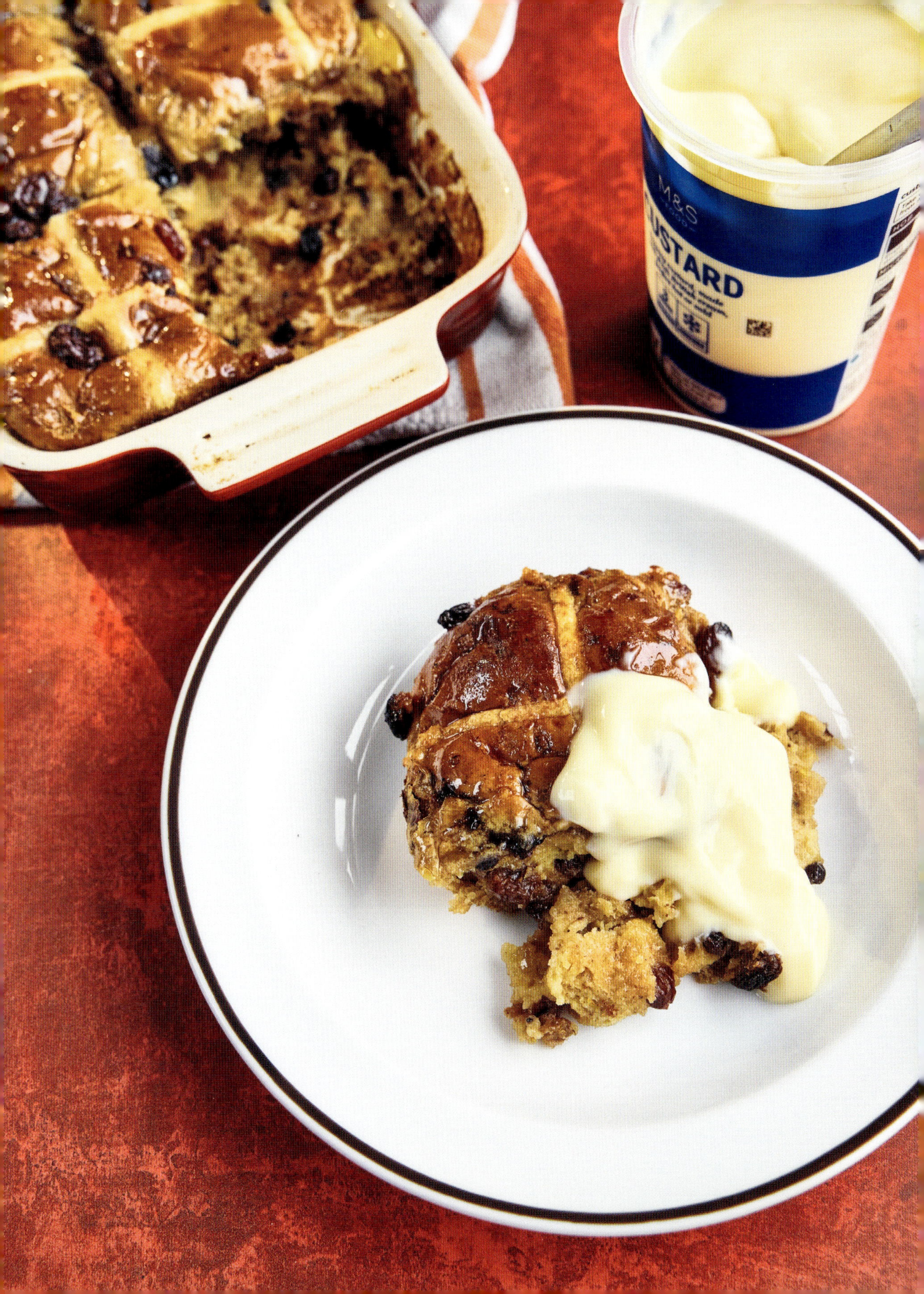
M&S

MAKES. ENOUGH FOR 4 / **PREP TIME.** 20 MINUTES (PLUS OVERNIGHT FREEZING)

FROZEN DRINKS

These boozy summer slushies are fresh, fruity and a little bit naughty. I've given you twists on some of my favorite sunny-day drinks, a sherbety strawberry daiquiri, a holiday-in-a-glass tropical fruit slushy and the ULTIMATE holiday cocktail, the pina colada. Skip the booze if you prefer and make them without, the good vibes will still be strong even if the alcohol isn't!

Pina Colada

FOR THE PINEAPPLE COCONUT ICE CUBES

1 small whole pineapple
1 x 15.5 oz (400 g) can of coconut milk
¼ cup superfine sugar

FOR 1 DRINK

10 pineapple coconut ice cubes
3 tbsp pineapple juice
1½–3 tbsp white rum
1½ tbsp Malibu

1. Use a knife to remove the top and bottom of the pineapple, then slice the outer skin off, too. Cut into quarters and remove the inner core.

2. Roughly chop the pineapple and put it in a blender with the coconut milk and sugar. Blitz until smooth, then pour through a sieve into a jug.

3. Pour into a few ice cube trays and freeze overnight.

4. To make one drink, just blitz together 10 ice cubes with pineapple juice, rum and Malibu until nice and smooth.

STRAWBERRY DAIQUIRI

MAKES. 1 / **PREP TIME.** 5 MINUTES

1 cup frozen strawberries
Juice of ¼ lime
1½–3 tbsp white rum
1 tbsp honey, plus extra to taste
2¼ tbsp water
Mint, to garnish (optional)

1. Place all the ingredients into a blender, except the mint, and blitz until smooth.
2. Add more honey to taste if you prefer it sweeter, then pour it into a glass. Garnish with the mint and voilà!

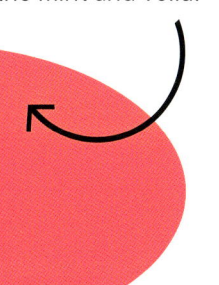

MAKES. 2 / **PREP TIME.** 5 MINUTES

TROPICAL FRUIT SLUSHY

3 passion fruits
1½ cups frozen mango
½ cup pineapple juice
3–4 tbsp white rum
Juice of ½ lime
3 tbsp water

1. Slice the passion fruits in half, remove the pulp from two of them and place into a blender.
2. Add in the frozen mango, pineapple juice, rum, lime juice and water and blitz until smooth.
3. Taste and season, then garnish with the other half of the passion fruit.

THE SWEET SPOT

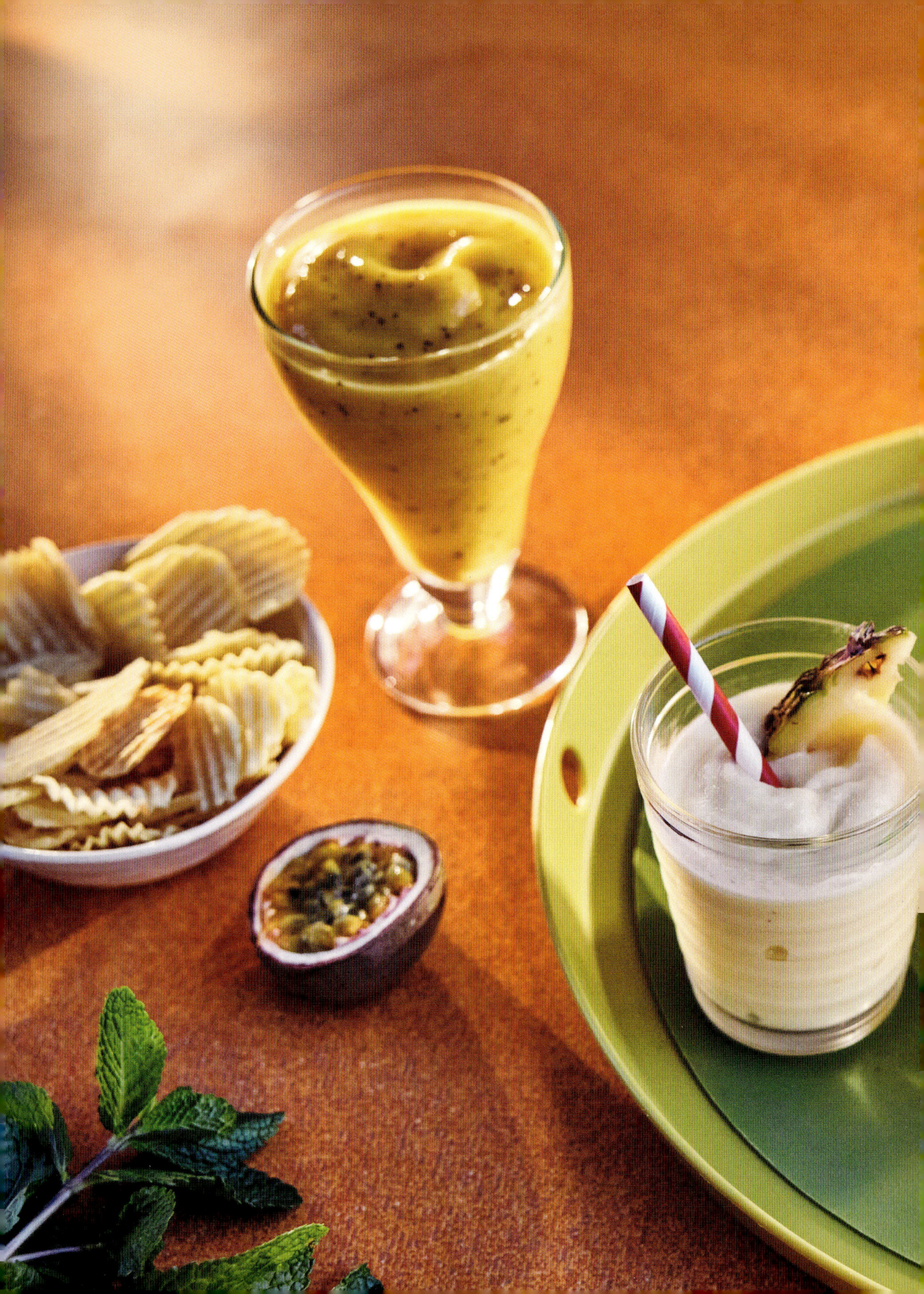

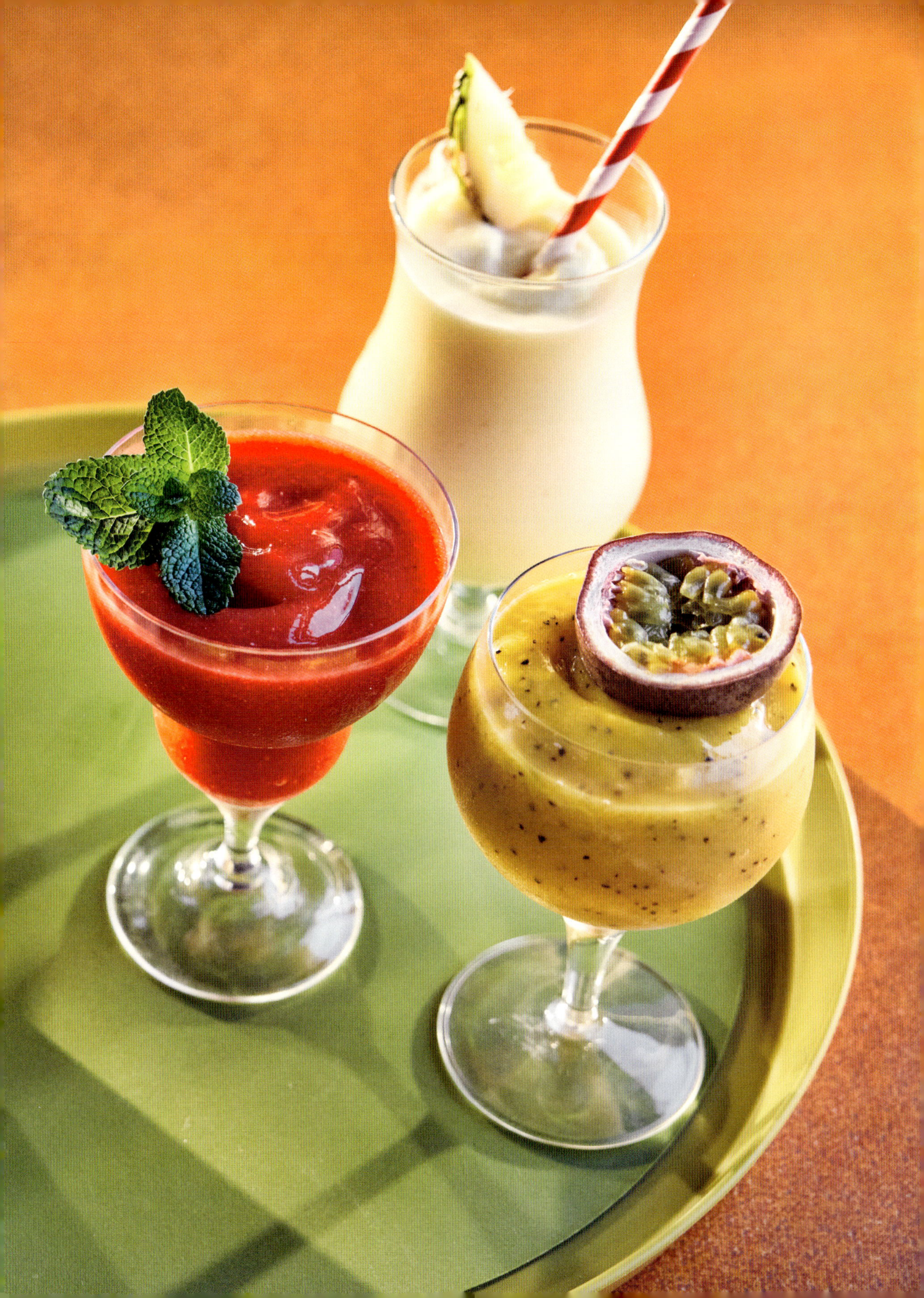

THANKS

Although I am lucky enough to have my name on the front cover, this book wasn't made by one person but by a team of hardworking, talented people, and I wanted to take this opportunity to thank them.

My partner-in-crime, Hanna Miller. Hanna was my recipe tester, food stylist and general hand-holder throughout this whole process. She has been crucial to the success of this book. This was a big labor of love and whatever success this book has, Hanna deserves to share it as well. I would also like to quickly thank: Eden, Isobel, Liv, Georgie and Libby for all their hard work during the shooting days.

To Dan and Aggie and the whole team at Michael Joseph. Thank you for giving me the opportunity of publishing my first cookbook. I have loved working with you all and am grateful for all your great advice and leadership.

My wonderful photographer, David Loftus, for bringing this book to life with your amazing pictures and for sharing a few stories along the way. A special thanks to your lovely wife, Ange, and dog, Digby, for allowing us to use your home for the photography. Hopefully the nice food made it worth your while.

Cookbooks are nothing without the vision of a very talented designer, and I have been very lucky to work with Sarah Fraser.

A big thank you to my manager, Max. It's amazing to see how far we have come in the last few years. Having this opportunity to write a book has always been a dream of mine and I'd like to thank you for helping to make it happen.

Now, none of this would have been possible without the kindness and generosity of my loving parents. From always giving me sound advice (which sometimes turns into nagging) to supporting me through culinary school, I would not be the chef I am today without your love and guidance.

To my brothers, Tom, Harry and Paddy, my amazing girlfriend, Clark, and wonderful neighbour, Julie, who have all tested recipes during the writing process and given me feedback, I am very grateful. Especially because my brothers are all rubbish in the kitchen and needed to make sure these recipes are idiot proof.

Finally, to my first cooking teacher . . . my Granny Tess. Enjoying countless delicious meals at your house growing up, it was these meals that whetted my appetite to start cooking. You have seen my whole culinary journey, and I would love to dedicate my first (but hopefully not last) cookbook to you. Love you, Granny xxx

INDEX

A almonds: granola + berry compote **190**
apples: apple tarts **210**
  German apple cake **201**
  broiled mackerel + fennel & apple slaw **73**
asparagus: roasted salmon & asparagus + pesto couscous **77**
eggplants: 15-minute Thai chicken curry **81**
  eggplant parm **145**
  ratatouille orzo **82**
avocado: movie night nachos **128**
  pork & pineapple tacos **74**
  salmon poke bowl **110**

B bacon: breakfast baskets **54**
  spaghetti carbonara **116**
bacteria **17**, **18**
baked potatoes **27**
bananas: caramelized crumpets **53**
beans: chili **167**
  minestrone **150**
  pan-fried chicken breast + a zucchini & bean stew **89**
  roasted cod + a spicy sausage cassoulet **93**
  spicy sausage beans on toast **50**
  veggie quesadillas **156**
beef: big batch Bolognese **164**
  chili **167**
  roasting **32**
  smashed burgers + smashed potatoes **120–1**
  steak sandwich **101**
beer, cooling quickly **36**
beet hummus **185**
berries: caramelized crumpets **53**
  granola + berry compote **190**
best before dates **19**
big batch Bolognese **164**
birthday cake, last-minute **202**
blueberry muffins **189**
boiling: eggs **24–5**
  potatoes **27**

Bolognese, big batch **164**
bread see also tortillas: eggplant parm **145**
  breakfast baskets **54**
  granny Tess' soda bread **195**
  refreshing **36**
  speedy pizza **109**
  spiced lamb kebab + sweet potato wedges **115**
  spicy sausage beans on toast **50**
  steak sandwich **101**
  stuffed zucchini + homemade garlic bread **140**
  sun-dried tomato & pesto-stuffed flatbreads **160**
breakfast baskets **54**
breakfast burritos **42**
broccoli: 15-minute Thai chicken curry **81**
  basic cooking method **34**
  jerk chicken tray bake + a broccoli & corn salad **90**
  pumpkin massaman curry **146**
brownies, twin baker **198**
budgeting **10**
burgers: piri piri chicken burger + homemade oven chips **127**
  smashed burgers + smashed potatoes **120–1**
  veggie burgers **138**
butter chicken **123**
buttermilk: granny Tess' soda bread **195**
butternut squash: pumpkin massaman curry **146**
  roasted butternut squash salad + quinoa & feta / leftover salad / superfood salad **137**

C Cajun chicken + spicy rice **112**
cakes and bakes: chocolate and orange cookies **205**
  German apple cake **201**
  granny Tess' Irish fruit loaf **193**
  last-minute birthday cake **202**
  twin baker brownies **198**
candied peel: granny Tess' Irish fruit loaf **193**
carrots: big batch Bolognese **164**
  chicken katsu curry **130–1**
  chicken pie filling **178–9**
  chicken satay salad **69**
  curried carrot soup **172**
  feel-better chicken noodle soup **171**

  last-minute birthday cake **202**
  minestrone **150**
  pan-fried **34**
  salmon poke bowl **110**
  special fried rice **119**
cauliflower: cauliflower cheese **34**
  roasted cauliflower traybake **134**
celery: big batch Bolognese **164**
  feel-better chicken noodle soup **171**
  minestrone **150**
cheese: eggplant parm **145**
  breakfast baskets **54**
  breakfast burritos **42**
  cauliflower cheese **34**
  cheese on toast **30**
  cheese sauce **26**
  zucchini and pea orzo **155**
  croque madame croissants **58**
  five-a-day veggie frittata **62**
  garlic butter flatbreads **161**
  Mediterranean filo pie **159**
  movie night nachos **128**
  one-pot mac 'n' cheese **66**
  one-pot sausage & leek gnocchi **86**
  one-tray veggie pasta **142**
  ratatouille orzo **82**
  roasted butternut squash salad + quinoa & feta / leftover salad / superfood salad **137**
  sausage & egg muffins **57**
  shakshuka **49**
  smashed burgers + smashed potatoes **120–1**
  spaghetti carbonara **116**
  speedy fish pie **98**
  speedy pizza **109**
  spinach & mushroom tart **94**
  stuffed zucchini + homemade garlic bread **140**
  sun-dried tomato & pesto-stuffed flatbreads **160**
  tomato & mascarpone rigatoni **85**
  veggie quesadillas **156**
chicken: 15-minute Thai chicken curry **81**
  butter chicken **123**
  Cajun chicken + spicy rice **112**
  chicken & chorizo paella **97**
  chicken bakes **179**
  chicken katsu curry **130–1**
  chicken pie filling **178–9**
  chicken satay salad **69**

INDEX

coronation chicken **175**
feel-better chicken noodle soup **171**
food hygiene **19**
jerk chicken tray bake + a broccoli & corn salad **90**
Middle-Eastern chicken couscous boxes **168**
pan-fried chicken breast + a zucchini & bean stew **89**
piri piri chicken burger + homemade oven chips **127**
roasting **33**
sesame soy chicken **102**
special fried rice **119**
yaki udon **124**
chickpeas: beet hummus **185**
bog-standard hummus **185**
roasted cauliflower traybake **134**
roasted red pepper hummus **184**
veggie burgers **138**
chili **167**
chocolate: chocolate and orange cookies **205**
rocky road **206**
twin baker brownies **198**
chopping boards **18**
chorizo: chicken & chorizo paella **97**
roasted cod + a spicy sausage cassoulet **93**
spicy sausage beans on toast **50**
coconut milk: 15-minute Thai chicken curry **81**
chicken satay salad **69**
curried carrot soup **172**
pina colada **212**
pumpkin massaman curry **146**
cod: roasted cod + a spicy sausage cassoulet **93**
condensed milk: key lime pie **209**
cookies, chocolate and orange **205**
cooking terminology **17**
coronation chicken **175**
zucchinis: zucchini and pea orzo **155**
pan-fried chicken breast + a zucchini & bean stew **89**
ratatouille orzo **82**
stuffed zucchini + homemade garlic bread **140**
couscous: Middle-Eastern chicken couscous boxes **168**
roasted salmon & asparagus + pesto couscous **77**
cream: butter chicken **123**
chicken pie filling **178–9**

hot cross bun pudding **216**
key lime pie **209**
one-pot sausage & leek gnocchi **86**
potato and leek soup **149**
cream cheese: last-minute birthday cake **202**
pea & mint sauce **184**
crème fraîche: jerk chicken tray bake + a broccoli & corn salad **90**
Mediterranean filo pie **159**
potato latkes + smoked salmon and horseradish cream **45**
crepes **46**
croque madame croissants **58**
cross-contamination **17, 18**
crumpets, caramelized **53**
cucumber: chicken satay salad **69**
Middle-Eastern chicken couscous boxes **168**
roasted butternut squash salad + quinoa & feta / leftover salad / superfood salad **137**
salmon poke bowl **110**
tzatziki **185**
currants: granny Tess' Irish fruit loaf **193**
curried carrot soup **172**
curries: 15-minute Thai chicken curry **81**
butter chicken **123**
chicken katsu curry **130–1**
pumpkin massaman curry **146**
saag aloo dhal **152**

D digestive biscuits: rocky road **206**
dips: beet hummus **185**
bog-standard hummus **185**
guacamole **128**
pea & mint sauce **184**
roasted red pepper hummus **184**
tomato salsa **128**
tzatziki **185**
drinks: pina colada **212**
strawberry daiquiri **213**
tropical fruit slushy **213**

E eggs: breakfast baskets **54**
cooking basics **24**
five-a-day veggie frittata **62**
sausage & egg muffins **57**
shakshuka **49**
spaghetti carbonara **116**
special fried rice **119**
yaki udon **124**
equipment **12–13**

F fennel: broiled mackerel + fennel & apple slaw **73**
feta: Mediterranean filo pie **159**
roasted butternut squash salad + quinoa & feta / leftover salad / superfood salad **137**
shakshuka **49**
stuffed zucchini + homemade garlic bread **140**
fish: food hygiene **19**
broiled mackerel + fennel & apple slaw **73**
potato latkes + smoked salmon and horseradish cream **45**
roasted cod + a spicy sausage cassoulet **93**
roasted salmon & asparagus + pesto couscous **77**
salmon poke bowl **110**
speedy fish pie **98**
Thai tuna & sweetcorn fishcakes **105**
five-a-day veggie frittata **62**
food hygiene **18–19**
food storage **19, 20, 36**
fridges: correct storage **20**
food hygiene **19**
fried eggs **24**
frozen drinks: pina colada **210**
strawberry daiquiri **213**
tropical fruit slushy **213**

G garlic butter flatbreads **161**
German apple cake **201**
gherkins: smashed burgers + smashed potatoes **120–1**
ginger: peeling **36**
ginger snap biscuits: key lime pie **209**
gnocchi: one-pot sausage & leek gnocchi **86**
granny Tess' Irish fruit loaf **193**
granny Tess' soda bread **195**
granola + berry compote **190**
gravy **34**
broilers: safety **19**
guacamole: breakfast burritos **42**
chili **167**
veggie quesadillas **156**

H hacks **36**
ham: croque madame croissants **58**
speedy pizza **109**
harissa paste: Cajun chicken + spicy rice **112**

INDEX

Middle-Eastern chicken couscous boxes **168**
roasted red pepper hummus **184**
shakshuka **49**
speedy seafood spaghetti **78**
herbs: storage **36**
honey: caramelized crumpets **53**
    chicken satay salad **69**
    honey mustard dressing **180**
    hot cross bun pudding **216**
    roasted butternut squash salad + quinoa & feta / leftover salad / superfood salad **137**
    salmon poke bowl **110**
    soy and sesame dressing **180**
    strawberry daiquiri **213**
horseradish sauce: potato latkes + smoked salmon and horseradish cream **45**
    steak sandwich **101**
hot cross bun pudding **216**
hummus: beet hummus **185**
    bog-standard hummus **185**
    roasted red pepper hummus **184**
hygiene **18–19**

I
ingredients: store cupboard essentials **15**
Irish fruit loaf, granny Tess' **193**

J
jalapeños: movie night nachos **128**
jerk chicken tray bake + a broccoli & corn salad **90**

K
kale: minestrone **150**
ketchup: cheese on toast **30**
    Sam's drunken noodles **70**
    sesame soy chicken **102**
    smashed burgers + smashed potatoes **120**
key lime pie **209**
kitchen equipment **12–13**
kitchen hacks **36**
knife skills **38–9**

L
lamb: roasting **33**
    spiced lamb kebab + sweet potato wedges **115**
latkes + smoked salmon and horseradish cream **45**
leeks: chicken pie filling **178–9**
    one-pot sausage & leek gnocchi **86**
    potato and leek soup **149**

speedy fish pie **98**
leftovers: storage **19**
lemons: beet hummus **185**
    bog-standard hummus **185**
    Cajun chicken + spicy rice **112**
    chicken & chorizo paella **97**
    zucchini and pea orzo **155**
    broiled mackerel + fennel & apple slaw **73**
    honey mustard dressing **180**
    jerk chicken tray bake + a broccoli & corn salad **90**
    limes **180**
    Mediterranean filo pie **159**
    Middle-Eastern chicken couscous boxes **168**
    pan-fried chicken breast + a zucchini & bean stew **89**
    pea & mint sauce **184**
    piri piri chicken burger + homemade oven chips **127**
    potato latkes + smoked salmon and horseradish cream **45**
    roasted cauliflower traybake **134**
    roasted red pepper hummus **184**
    roasted salmon & asparagus + pesto couscous **77**
    speedy seafood spaghetti **78**
    stuffed zucchini + homemade garlic bread **140**
lentils: saag aloo dhal **152**
lettuce: chicken satay salad **69**
    piri piri chicken burger + homemade oven chips **127**
    spiced lamb kebab + sweet potato wedges **115**
    veggie burgers **138**
limes: 15-minute Thai chicken curry **81**
    chicken satay salad **69**
    chili **167**
    key lime pie **209**
    movie night nachos **128**
    pork & pineapple tacos **74**
    pumpkin massaman curry **146**
    strawberry daiquiri **213**
    Thai tuna & sweetcorn fishcakes **105**
    tropical fruit slushy **213**

M
mac 'n' cheese, one-pot **66**
mackerel: broiled mackerel + fennel & apple slaw **73**
Malibu: pina colada **212**
mango: salmon poke bowl **110**

tropical fruit slushy **213**
maple syrup: granola + berry compote **190**
marshmallows: rocky road **206**
mascarpone: tomato & mascarpone rigatoni **85**
mashed potatoes **27**
mayonnaise: coronation chicken **175**
    broiled mackerel + fennel & apple slaw **73**
    salmon poke bowl **110**
    smashed burgers + smashed potatoes **120–1**
    spiced lamb kebab + sweet potato wedges **115**
meal planning **10**
meat: food hygiene **18–19**
Mediterranean filo pie **159**
microwaves: jacket potatoes **27**
    safety **19**
Middle-Eastern chicken couscous boxes **168**
milk: cheese sauce **26**
    crepes **46**
    hot cross bun pudding **216**
    one-pot mac 'n' cheese **66**
    safety **19**
    white sauce **26**
minestrone **150**
mint: pea & mint sauce **184**
    strawberry daiquiri **213**
    tzatziki **185**
mold **19**
movie night nachos **128**
muffins: blueberry muffins **189**
    sausage & egg muffins **57**
mushrooms: chicken pie filling **178–9**
    five-a-day veggie frittata **62**
    one-pot sausage & leek gnocchi **86**
    speedy pizza **109**
    spinach & mushroom tart **94**
    yaki udon **124**
mussels: speedy seafood spaghetti **78**
mustard: honey mustard dressing **180**
    one-pot mac 'n' cheese **66**
    sausage rolls **186**
    smashed burgers + smashed potatoes **120–1**

N
nachos, movie night **128**
noodles: feel-better chicken noodle soup **171**
    Sam's drunken noodles **70**

INDEX

yaki udon 124
Nutella twists 61

O
oat bran: granny Tess' soda bread 195
oats: granola + berry compote 190
olives: Mediterranean filo pie 159
    speedy pizza 109
omelettes 24
onion chutney: coronation chicken 175
    garlic butter flatbreads 161
    sausage rolls 186
    steak sandwich 101
oranges: chocolate and orange cookies 205
    hot cross bun pudding 216
orzo: zucchini and pea orzo 155
    ratatouille orzo 82
oven chips 29

P
paella, chicken & chorizo 97
pancakes: crepes 46
parsnips: pan-fried 34
passion fruits: tropical fruit slushy 213
pasta: cooking basics 23
    zucchini and pea orzo 155
    minestrone 150
    one-pot mac 'n' cheese 66
    one-tray veggie pasta 142
    ratatouille orzo 82
    spaghetti carbonara 116
    speedy seafood spaghetti 78
    tomato & mascarpone rigatoni 85
pasta water 23
peanut butter: caramelized crumpets 53
    chicken satay salad 69
    pumpkin massaman curry 146
peas: basic cooking method 34
    Cajun chicken + spicy rice 112
    chicken & chorizo paella 97
    zucchini and pea orzo 155
    pea & mint sauce 184
    special fried rice 119
pecans: granny Tess' Irish fruit loaf 193
    granola + berry compote 190
pepperoni: speedy pizza 109
peppers: Cajun chicken + spicy rice 112
    chicken & chorizo paella 97
    chopping 40
    five-a-day veggie frittata 62
    Mediterranean filo pie 159

minestrone 150
one-tray veggie pasta 142
piri piri chicken burger + homemade oven chips 127
pumpkin massaman curry 146
ratatouille orzo 82
roasted butternut squash salad + quinoa & feta / leftover salad / superfood salad 137
roasted cod + a spicy sausage c assoulet 93
roasted red pepper hummus 184
Sam's drunken noodles 70
sesame soy chicken 102
shakshuka 49
speedy pizza 109
spicy sausage beans on toast 50
veggie quesadillas 156
yaki udon 124
pesto: roasted salmon & asparagus + pesto couscous 77
    sun-dried tomato & pesto-stuffed flatbreads 160
pies: chicken bakes 179
    chicken pie filling 178–9
    key lime pie 209
    Mediterranean filo pie 159
    speedy fish pie 98
pina colada 212
pineapple: pina colada 212
    pork & pineapple tacos 74
    Sam's drunken noodles 70
    speedy pizza 109
pineapple juice: pina colada 212
    Sam's drunken noodles 70
    tropical fruit slushy 213
piri piri chicken burger + homemade oven chips 127
pizza, speedy 109
poaching 24
pork: pork & pineapple tacos 74
    roasting 33
    Sam's drunken noodles 70
potatoes: cooking basics 27
    oven chips 29
    piri piri chicken burger + homemade oven chips 127
    potato and leek soup 149
    potato latkes + smoked salmon and horseradish cream 45
    saag aloo dhal 152
safety 19
smashed burgers + smashed

potatoes 120–1
speedy fish pie 98
Thai tuna & sweetcorn fishcakes 105
prawns: special fried rice 119
    speedy seafood spaghetti 78
puddings: hot cross bun pudding 216
pumpkin massaman curry 146
pumpkin seeds: granola + berry compote 190
    stuffed zucchini + homemade garlic bread 140

Q
quinoa: roasted butternut squash salad + quinoa & feta / leftover salad / superfood salad 137

R
raisins: granny Tess' Irish fruit loaf 193
ratatouille orzo 82
recipes, how to follow 16
rice: Cajun chicken + spicy rice 112
    chicken & chorizo paella 97
    chili 167
    cooking basics 22
    risotto basics 22
    salmon poke bowl 110
    special fried rice 119
    storage 19
roast dinner meat cooking times 32–3
roast potatoes 27
rocky road 206
rum: strawberry daiquiri 213
    tropical fruit slushy 213

S
saag aloo dhal 152
salad dressings: basic method 30
    French vinaigrette 180
    honey mustard dressing 180
    soy and sesame dressing 180
salads: chicken satay salad 69
    roasted butternut squash salad + quinoa & feta / leftover salad / superfood salad 137
salami: speedy pizza 109
salmon: potato latkes + smoked salmon and horseradish cream 45
    roasted salmon & asparagus + pesto couscous 77
    salmon poke bowl 110
Sam's drunken noodles 70
sauces: burger sauce 120–1
    cheese sauce 26
    gravy 34

INDEX

pasta water 23
pea & mint sauce 184
tomato sauce 26
white sauce 26
sausages: breakfast baskets 54
    breakfast burritos 42
    one-pot sausage & leek gnocchi 86
    roasted cod + a spicy sausage cassoulet 93
    sausage & egg muffins 57
    sausage rolls 186
    spicy sausage beans on toast 50
scrambled eggs 24
seafood: special fried rice 119
    speedy seafood spaghetti 78
sesame soy chicken 102
shakshuka 49
shopping on a budget 10
slaws: broiled mackerel + fennel & apple slaw 73
smashed burgers + smashed potatoes 120–1
soda bread, granny Tess' 195
soups: curried carrot soup 172
    feel-better chicken noodle soup 171
    minestrone 150
    potato and leek soup 149
sour cream: breakfast burritos 42
    chili 167
    movie night nachos 128
    pork & pineapple tacos 74
    veggie quesadillas 156
spaghetti carbonara 116
special fried rice 119
spices: store cupboard essentials 15
spinach: five-a-day veggie frittata 62
    Mediterranean filo pie 159
    saag aloo dhal 152
    spinach & mushroom tart 94
spring onions: jerk chicken tray bake + a broccoli & corn salad 90
    salmon poke bowl 110
    Sam's drunken noodles 70
    sesame soy chicken 102
    special fried rice 119
    yaki udon 124
sriracha sauce: breakfast burritos 42
    salmon poke bowl 110
steak sandwich 101
store cupboard ingredients 15
storing food 19, 20, 36
strawberry daiquiri 213

sugar snap peas: yaki udon 124
golden raisins: coronation chicken 175
    German apple cake 201
    granny Tess' Irish fruit loaf 193
    granola + berry compote 190
    hot cross bun pudding 216
    rocky road 206
Sunday lunch crib sheet 32–4
sunflower seeds: granola + berry compote 190
    stuffed zucchini + homemade garlic bread 140
sweet potatoes: spiced lamb kebab + sweet potato wedges 115
sweetcorn: jerk chicken tray bake + a broccoli & corn salad 90
    Thai tuna & sweetcorn fishcakes 105
    veggie quesadillas 156

T
tacos, pork & pineapple 74
tahini: beet hummus 185
    bog-standard hummus 185
    roasted red pepper hummus 184
tarts: apple tarts 210
    key lime pie 209
    spinach & mushroom tart 94
terminology 17
Thai tuna & sweetcorn fishcakes 105
toasters: safety 19
tomato passata: eggplant parm 145
    shakshuka 49
    speedy pizza 109
tomatoes: big batch Bolognese 164
    breakfast baskets 54
    butter chicken 123
    chicken satay salad 69
    chopping 40
    five-a-day veggie frittata 62
    Middle-Eastern chicken couscous boxes 168
    minestrone 150
    movie night nachos 128
    one-tray veggie pasta 142
    piri piri chicken burger + homemade oven chips 127
    pork & pineapple tacos 74
    ratatouille orzo 82
    roasted butternut squash salad + quinoa & feta / leftover salad / superfood salad 137
    roasted cod + a spicy sausage cassoulet 93
    roasted salmon & asparagus +

pesto couscous 77
saag aloo dhal 152
shakshuka 49
speedy seafood spaghetti 78
spiced lamb kebab + sweet potato wedges 115
spicy sausage beans on toast 50
sun-dried tomato & pesto-stuffed flatbreads 160
tomato & mascarpone rigatoni 85
tomato sauce 26
veggie burgers 138
tortilla chips: movie night nachos 128
tortillas: breakfast burritos 42
    pork & pineapple tacos 74
    veggie quesadillas 156
tropical fruit slushy 213
tuna: Thai tuna & sweetcorn fishcakes 105
turkey: roasting 33
twin baker brownies 198
tzatziki 185

U
use by dates 19

V
vegetables see also specific vegetables: budgeting 10
    five-a-day veggie frittata 62
    one-tray veggie pasta 142
    veggie burgers 138
    veggie quesadillas 156

W
walnuts: last-minute birthday cake 202
wheat bran: granny Tess' soda bread 195
white sauce: basic recipe 26
    croque madame croissants 58
    speedy fish pie 98
    spinach & mushroom tart 94

Y
yaki udon 124
yogurt: caramelized crumpets 53
    coronation chicken 175
    garlic butter flatbreads 161
    granola + berry compote 190
    roasted cauliflower traybake 134
    speedy pizza 109
    sun-dried tomato & pesto-stuffed flatbreads 160
    tzatziki 185

Z
zest 17

DK | Penguin Random House

First published as *Sam Holland's Kitchen Kickstart* in 2025 by Michael Joseph. Michael Joseph is part of the Penguin Random House group of companies.

First American Edition, 2025
Published in the United States by DK Publishing
1745 Broadway, 20th Floor, New York, NY 10019

The authorized representative in the EEA is Dorling Kindersley Verlag GmbH. Arnulfstr. 124, 80636 Munich, Germany

Text copyright © Sam Holland, 2025
Photography copyright © David Loftus, 2025
Illustration on page 20 © V.studio/Shutterstock
DK, a Division of Penguin Random House LLC
25 26 27 28 29 10 9 8 7 6 5 4 3 2 1
001-350966-AUG2025

All rights reserved. Without limiting the rights under the copyright reserved above, no part of this publication may be reproduced, stored in or introduced into a retrieval system, or transmitted, in any form, or by any means (electronic, mechanical, photocopying, recording, or otherwise), without the prior written permission of the copyright owner.

No part of this publication may be used or reproduced in any manner for the purpose of training artificial intelligence technologies or systems. In accordance with Article 4⃞ of the DSM Directive 2019/790, DK expressly reserves this work from the text and data mining exception.

A catalog record for this book
is available from the Library of Congress.
ISBN 978-0-59397-148-2

DK books are available at special discounts when purchased in bulk for sales promotions, premiums, fund-raising, or educational use. For details, contact SpecialSales@dk.com

Printed and bound in Slovakia

www.dk.com

MIX
Paper | Supporting responsible forestry
FSC™ C018179

This book was made with Forest Stewardship Council™ certified paper – one small step in DK's commitment to a sustainable future. Learn more at
www.dk.com/uk/information/sustainability